Appalachian Passage

Appalachian
Passage

Helen B. Hiscoe

Foreword by Barbara Ellen Smith

The University of Georgia Press
ATHENS & LONDON

© 1991 by the University of Georgia Press
Athens, Georgia 30602
All rights reserved

Designed by Kathi L. Dailey
Set in Stemple Garamond with Powell Old Style by
    Tseng Information Systems, Inc.
Printed and bound by Maple-Vail Book
    Manufacturing Group

The paper in this book meets the guidelines for
permanence and durability of the Committee on
Production Guidelines for Book Longevity of the
Council on Library Resources.

Printed in the United States of America

95 94 93 92 91 C 5 4 3 2 1

Library of Congress Cataloging in Publication Data

Hiscoe, Helen B.
    Appalachian passage / Helen B. Hiscoe.
      p.   cm.
    ISBN 0-8203-1354-8 (alk. paper)
      1. Appalachian Region, Southern—Social life and customs.
      2. Appalachian Region, Southern—Social conditions.
      3. Hiscoe, Helen B.—Diaries.   I. Title.
F217.A65H57   1991
975.4—dc20   90-22168
                                                          CIP

British Library Cataloging in Publication Data available

Photograph on title page is of Road Branch, the creek bed that
provided the primary access to one of the mountain communities
under Bonta Hiscoe's medical care.

Contents

Foreword

ﻬﻴ This remarkable book recounts one woman's sojourn with her young family in a small, isolated coal camp in the mountains of southern West Virginia. The year is 1949. The war is over, her marriage is in the blush of its first years, a daughter has just been born. Her husband is embarking on his career as a physician, determined to "bring the miners and their families the best medical care [he knows] how to provide." She, trained as a zoologist, is to be his assistant. Together they greet this adventure with confidence, enthusiasm, excitement. Their ebullience not only reflects their youthful situation, but also—like so much of what is recounted in the book—typifies the historical era.

Little do they foresee what awaits them. As relatively privileged outsiders, they are part of a long succession of people who for more than a century have come to help or to exploit—often both at the same time—the mountaineers. As company doctor in the solidly unionized coalfields of southern West Virginia, Bonta Hiscoe is caught in a complex tangle of class relationships that are not of his making or knowledge, but that profoundly affect his medical practice. The treatment the Hiscoes receive, which often baffles, amuses, or irritates the author, is in many cases understandable only by reference to this prior history and larger social context.

Beginning not long after the Civil War, the rich natural resources of central Appalachia began to attract investors who sought to buy timber, mineral rights, and land from the local population. Within the space of three decades, the most valuable land in the region was transferred to outside control, and the timber and especially mineral wealth of the mountains began to leave daily, visibly, on railroad cars bound for urban markets and ports. The accompanying wage economy brought the irresistible lure of cash, prosperity, and "store-bought" goods, which rapidly transformed the subsistence farm population into a rural working class. This entire metamorphosis was carried out under the banner of modernization and salvation: the "benighted" ways of the mountaineers justified the wholesale transfer of their land and culture into more educated and capable hands. Among the most obvious and persistent cultural consequences of this history for coal-mining families are tendencies toward suspicion of the intentions of outsiders and acute sensitivity to outside perceptions (judgments) of the region.

The company doctor system was an additional by-product of the intensive industrialization of this nonetheless rural area. The companies that began to open mines in the 1870s in southern West Virginia also built towns from the ground up. They financed the construction of houses, stores, schools, and churches. They paid their workers in scrip, a nonlegal tender accepted for trade only at the company store, and thereby shored up their profit margins and reduced miners' propensity to move. The company doctor, symbol and provider of medical care, was yet another necessity that was secured and controlled by the company.

Coupled with discontent over wages and working conditions, the paternalistic and undemocratic features of the company town were the stimuli for miners' repeated attempts to unionize during the early twentieth century. Desperate to maintain their competitive advantage in relationship to northern mines, the southern coal operators resisted unionization with a ferocity and violence that was matched only by miners and their families' determination to prevail. The murderous class conflict that resulted in such places as Matewan and Blair Mountain is now the stuff of legend. It lives on, however, in the vivid if embellished memories of old-timers, fervent dedication to the United Mine Workers union, and a persistent class perspective that emphasizes the irreconcilability of operators and miners.

Through unionization during the 1930s, miners developed the power base with which to eliminate the most objectionable features of the company town and workplace. The company doctor system remained in place, however, until the 1950s, when the union-controlled Welfare and Retirement Fund assumed financial responsibility for the medical care of coal miners and their families. Hired by and accountable to the company, the doctor was paid through a checkoff from miners' wages. Unionization brought contracts negotiated locally between miners' representatives and the doctor, as Hiscoe describes, but hiring and therefore ultimate control remained with the company. Complaints about breaches of confidentiality and the quality of patient care surfaced periodically, indeed, were built into the system's financing and accountability structure. The validity of these complaints was borne out by an investigation of medical conditions in the bituminous coalfields conducted in 1946 by five teams of field researchers headed by Rear Admiral Joel T. Boone of the U.S. Navy. The so-called "Boone report" deplored the meager equipment, inattention to industrial medicine and, in a few cases, insanitary offices that the researchers found in their survey of health care delivery at 260 mines. They noted that a few companies even turned a small profit from medical care by pocketing five to ten percent of the checkoff from miners' wages. Thus, quite apart from their own philosophical commitments and academic qualifications, the Hiscoes entered a situation in which, from the perspective of many miners and their families, they were irretrievably on the "other side."

It is a great testimony to Helen Hiscoe's humanity and insight that she bears honest witness to this divide of class and culture, yet at the same time transcends it. Through her clear and humorous eyes, we are able to enjoy a rich panoply of characters who raise chickens, gossip, work in the mines, give birth, cook meals, and create places for themselves in this remote, rural coal town. Equally important, she faithfully recounts her own emotional response—however unflattering—to the many new situations that challenge her in this unfamiliar terrain. In so doing, she allows us to participate in her own life at a depth and level of detail that only the memoirs of forthright and perceptive people can provide.

The vignettes of medical practice are among the most compelling stories in the book. We follow Bonta Hiscoe as he confronts the contrast between the sterile technique of hospital medicine and the sweltering, fly-infested houses where many women deliver their babies. We join his struggle with the classic physician's dilemma of trying to provide conscientious, scientific medical care to patients who often desire reassurance more than science. We learn with him as he is humbled by the insignificance of his own interventions and the stubborn ability of people to endure, even prevail, despite the apparent wretchedness of their physical surroundings.

Even as Helen Hiscoe recorded the details of daily experience in Coal Mountain, however, the way of life that she described was becoming a relic of the past. No longer do rural physicians, of whatever affiliation or location, routinely make house calls and assist women in home births. No longer do coal miners and their families live in company towns, though the coal camps that many call home retain vestiges of that former arrangement. Paternalistic management, the company doctor, scrip, the company store—all disappeared with the company town in the period following World War II.

Adding to the historical value of Helen Hiscoe's record is the ironic timing of her sojourn in Coal Mountain: 1949–1950, during a labor-management showdown that indirectly brought about the end of the company town as a way of life. Pitted against one another in this confrontation were John L. Lewis, entering the last decade of his forty-year reign as president of the United Mine Workers, and George Love, head of the newly formed Bituminous Coal Operators Association (BCOA). Established through a series of small meetings during 1949 and 1950, the BCOA drew together the largest operators in the coal business; it gave organizational form to a core of relatively well capitalized companies that would seek to bring stability (and their own domination) to the highly fragmented and competitive coal industry.

Against a backdrop of Lewis-ordered three-day work weeks, sporadic strikes, and eventually a Taft-Hartley injunction, during the winter of 1949–1950 representatives of the BCOA and UMWA achieved a détente based on their common interest in a healthy, stable coal industry. Through a relatively high wage rate imposed industry wide, the large operators would more easily be able to push their smaller competitors out of business. Extensive introduction of continuous mining machinery would raise productivity, hold the line on coal prices, and further squeeze the small producers. The only apparent catch was that many miners would be thrown out of work (some 300,000, as it turned out, or about seventy percent of the 1950 work force). This was a sacrifice that Lewis, a lifelong believer in a more concentrated, streamlined coal industry, was readily prepared to make.

The contract that Lewis and Love signed in March of 1950 contained no references to this underlying accord, but it did contain important departures from previous agreements. Most importantly for the operators, the 1950 contract eliminated the "able and willing" clause, which was negotiated in 1947 to circumvent the Taft-Hartley Act and in effect gave miners the right to strike. The contract also placed a cap on what had been unlimited "memorial periods," or work stoppages in commemoration of mine-accident victims. Taken together, these changes signaled Lewis's agreement to forsake strikes in favor of détente, an interpretation that is bolstered by the absence of any industry wide work stoppages for the next twenty years.

In exchange, Lewis and the mine workers gained operator agreement to full implementation of the Welfare and Retirement Fund under the union's control. First negotiated in 1946, though opposed by many operators until 1950, the fund was designed in part to displace the role that Bonta Hiscoe came to Coal Mountain to fill: the company doctor. Lewis's vision was of health care delivery organized on the opposite basis from that of the company doctor system: union control and industry financing, rather than miner financing and company control. Through a royalty assessed on each ton of mined coal, the fund would be able to finance medical care, pensions, hospitalization, and other benefits for miners and their families. Although inadequate revenues and other problems eventually compromised this original vision, the fund offered in its time an innovative, even inspired, model of health care delivery.

The impact of détente between the UMW and the BCOA reverberated through the coalfields for decades. In their drive to create an efficient, capital-intensive industry, the big coal operators gradually shed their former style of industrial relations: they sold off the company houses and stores, laid off redundant miners, no longer hired local doctors, purged their management of the old-style paternalists.

Mechanization and mine closures slashed the size of the work force. Coal camps became ghost towns as miners and their families headed north in search of employment.

Helen Hiscoe's local account of the turmoil of the winter of 1949–1950 and its eventual resolution largely reflects the perspective of Mr. Ramsey, the mine superintendent. Bewildered by the sporadic work and rumors of violence, the Hiscoes inevitably turn to Ramsey for information. Although prescient about the coming unemployment of many miners, the superintendent—like almost everyone else in the coalfields at that time—does not grasp the significance of the negotiations. Their discussions of labor relations provide little insight into miners' motives and goals, but they are wonderfully revealing about the dynamics of local labor conflicts from the perspective of an intensely paternalistic manager. Indeed, both Mr. Ramsey and his wife, with her Sunday School and women's sewing activities, reflect the best and the worst aspects of paternalism: genuine concern mixed with condescension, a desire to serve combined with the prerogative to control.

Complicating the local situation is the sudden move, soon after the 1950 national wage agreement is signed, to terminate Bonta Hiscoe's contract as the company doctor. Conflicting rumors and explanations abound, making it impossible to sort out then or now the motives behind this action by a small group of miners. Viewed in the larger historical context, it seems likely that four years of strikes and other confrontations over the scope, financing, and control of health care delivery (i.e., the Welfare and Retirement Fund) may have encouraged this action, however misguided, to assert greater union control over the company doctor.

It is no coincidence, then, that the Hiscoes and the Ramseys leave Coal Mountain almost simultaneously. At the time, their departures seem the product of personal decisions and misfortunes: ill health, acceptance into a residency training program, the conflicts with the local union. But in the longer view of history their leaving marks the beginning of the end of an era: soon both the company doctor and the paternalistic manager will be memories of the past.

The point is not that Helen Hiscoe's personal explanations of events are not "true." Rather, it is precisely the discrepancy between the individual, subjective experience that she records and the impersonal forces of history that adds another priceless dimension to this book. *Appalachian Passage* allows us to view at a local and personal level a complex of events that have gone down in history as momentous and transformative; for a few of the many participants at the time, however, what happened seemed unique, accidental, individual. Thus, even as it captures the ambience of a place and time, Helen Hiscoe's record stands as a provocative reminder of the difference between history as it is conventionally written and history as it lived.

Barbara Ellen Smith

Acknowledgments

To Bonta, my husband, I want to give my sincerest thanks for his faith in me, his invaluable suggestions throughout all the revisions of this book, and his occasional but indispensable service as mediator between the computer and me. For encouragement and constructive advice in varying measure, my thanks and appreciation also go to the following: Floyd Monaghan, Edward Barry, Benjamin Hickok, Marilyn Culpepper, Donna Paananen, Stephen D. Kirk, Christy Nichols, Milka Walls, and our daughters, Nancy, Elaine, Lenore, and Susan.

Author's Note

🌿 *Appalachian Passage* is a true story. Places have been given their real names with only one minor exception. The only other liberties with the historical record relate to the discussions of patients' problems. To protect confidentiality the circumstances surrounding medical incidents may have been altered in various ways. All names except those of the author's family have been changed. Should a character's name happen to match that of a real person, this is purely coincidental. There were three especially common surnames in the area, Hatfield (the most frequent), Davis, and Morgan; there is no consistency in the way in which these have been altered.

Appalachian Passage

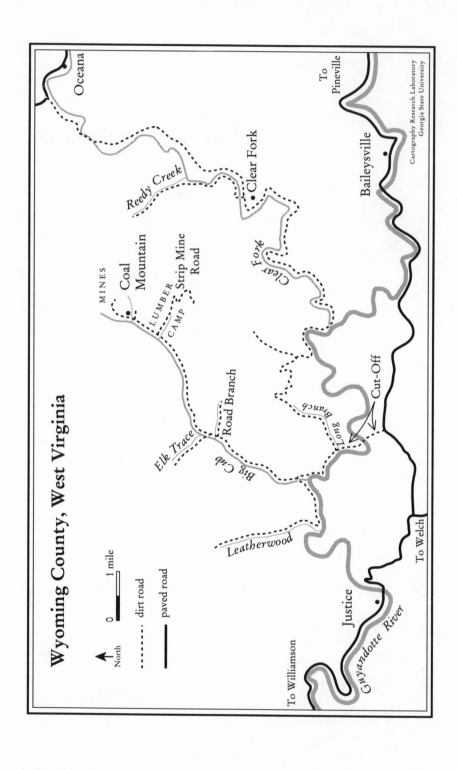

Wyoming County, West Virginia

North

0   1 mile

······· dirt road

─── paved road

Oceana

Reedy Creek

Clear Fork

To Pineville

Baileysville

Cartography Research Laboratory
Georgia State University

MINES

Coal Mountain

LUMBER

CAMP

Strip Mine Road

Clear Fork

Cut-Off

Long Branch

Elk Trace

Road Branch

Big Cub

Leatherwood

To Welch

Justice

Gwyandotte River

To Williamson

Prologue

The two years at the Great Lakes Naval Training Center which Bonta owed Uncle Sam were nearing an end. The navy's V-12 program had helped him through Columbia's College of Physicians and Surgeons in 1944–45. It was toward the end of that time that we met. Now he wanted to continue his training with a residency in surgery. A wife, a year-old daughter, and a very small savings account made that prospect bleak, since good residencies, like his internship, paid nothing but board, room, and uniforms. How could he earn and save enough to support this dream?

It was then that a fellow navy reservist, Vern Nichols, who had left Great Lakes a year earlier with the same goal, wrote suggesting that Bonta might apply to a Dr. Meade, asking to replace Vern as coal camp physician in Coal Mountain, West Virginia. It was Dr. Meade's job to see that the five mining camps belonging to the Red Jacket Coal Corporation each had a resident doctor. Bonta sent his application, and arrangements for his coming were completed by telephone and letter.

Bonta had grown up in Lowell, Massachusetts, spending the summers with his parents and sister in Duxbury, near Plymouth. His name came from his maternal grandfather, who had emigrated alone from Sicily at age fourteen, grew up thinking his surname too foreign sounding, and changed it. Later regrets led to its incorporation into his children's names.

Bonta's father taught art and history at the Lowell State Teachers College, and the academic schedule allowed him to pursue his painting during the summer at Cape Cod and at Duxbury. Bonta and his sister reveled in the country life there, riding a neighboring farmer's hay wagon, playing capture-the-flag in the fields next door, and exploring the pine woods that surrounded their modest cottage. Bonta's goal in life was to become a physician like his father's best friend, and he was overjoyed when Columbia's medical school accepted his application at the end of his third year at Tufts. The military needed doctors, and training was being accelerated during World War II.

I had grown up in the small town of Herkimer in upstate New York, with my parents and two younger sisters. My father was an attorney, and my mother had taught school; education was a top priority in the family. I was fortunate enough to go to Vassar with scholarship help, and Vassar itself helped me through graduate study in zoology. A master's degree from Brown University and a Ph.D. from UCLA prepared me to accept the offer of an instructorship at my alma mater. After two satisfying years there, I spent part of the following summer vacation as a nurse's aide at Presbyterian Hospital in New York City, responding to an appeal for help during the war.

Our group of volunteers was given board and room at the medical students' dormitory, and it was there that Bonta and I met. Before the month was out, we decided we should be married when he graduated the following March. All went as planned, and in one week Bonta gained a wife, an M.D. degree, and a commission as Lt. (jg) in the United States Naval Reserve.

He left immediately to start his internship at Michael Reese Hospital in Chicago, and I followed at the end of Vassar's winter term. I had obtained a job at the University of Chicago as a research associate under Dr. Paul Weiss, a famous experimental embryologist who was then studying nerve regeneration. Until it was time for our daughter Susan to be born, my days were spent counting nerve fibers and operating on rats.

After Bonta completed his fifteen-month internship, the navy assigned him to the Great Lakes Naval Hospital. We moved near the base, and for a year and a half I enjoyed the luxury of full-time motherhood.

The prospect of living in a coal camp in West Virginia filled us with excitement. We felt it would be a real adventure. Certainly it would give us an opportunity to work together; we wanted to bring the miners and their families the best medical care Bonta knew how to provide. We were naive, idealistic, enthusiastic, and unaware of labor-management tensions in the coalfields. We foresaw no problems at all, so long as we were together.

The only small cloud on the horizon was that no housing was immediately available in Coal Mountain, and Bonta would have to begin by living alone in the company boardinghouse. We were told, however, that a place would be ready for us in a few days. In the meantime Susan and I would enjoy our first flight ever, back to my home, where we would wait with my parents for word to join him. Letters became all important.

Settling In

Bonta opening his office for the first patients of the day. Parents often sent a child down with a note requesting medicine or asking that the child be checked for some problem or ailment.

1. Living on Letters

Helen Darling,

I've wanted to write sooner, but you just can't imagine how hectic things have been. Besides, there's so damned much to write about that I can hardly figure out where to begin.

Hope I never live through another ride like that one from Williamson to the coal camp. I met Dr. Meade as planned and settled arrangements about pay and getting drugs and stuff. Then he offered to show me the way here and introduce me to the superintendent, a Mr. Ramsey, so of course he drove his own car, and I followed him in the Chevy. Well, he might as well have had a propeller on his Buick. I just tried to ignore the squeals when I whipped around curves trying to keep up. This went on for all of fifty miles, till I began to think maybe this was a hoax and there wasn't really any camp at all. But just then he turned off onto a dirt road that was more holes than road, and we bounced and jounced over fifteen miles of that. I was feeling real queasy, wondering what I'd let us in for, when all of a sudden there was the camp.

Actually Coal Mountain itself was something of a pleasant surprise. There really is such a place after all, and it's new enough so it hasn't turned the dirty gray color of most of the towns I'd driven through earlier. You'll find it fairly attractive, at least the main part, which is called the white camp, because all the clapboard houses are painted white. We'll have one of these houses (I hope), with a bathroom and a couple of bedrooms. There are about thirty-five houses in this part of the camp. The mine itself was opened only seven years ago so all the houses are fairly new—something on the order of your folks' summer cottage—not very solid, but nice enough. Up the hollow (everything down here is a hollow) is the green camp, where they have no indoor conveniences, and the only running water comes from a spigot on the back porch. There are about twenty of those houses, too, and they are good compared to some of the outlying places, believe me.

These white and green houses were built by the company and are rented to the miners who have families. Single men stay in the boardinghouse. Of course the majority of the miners live in their own houses outside the camp, down the road or up one of the many hollows.

I found Vern and Julie, of course. They wanted me to say "Hi" to you, and asked how things were back at the naval base at Great Lakes, but we didn't spend much time reminiscing. His residency was due to start in less than a week, and they could hardly wait to leave. They were sure fed up with the place. Julie's apparently been really lonely down here. She never helped Vern in the office, but if things work out the way we plan, you ought to have more contact with people than she did. Vern grudgingly spared three hours from packing the car to indoctrinate me about the place and the job. I asked questions as fast as he could answer! Never before ran up against so much to learn and so little time to learn it in.

The medical situation down here is so primitive I can't believe it. Almost no sterile technique possible for anything, including OB. I get an ulcer thinking about it. I had to buy a bottle of Lysol to use as an antiseptic for the present and salve my conscience a little. I haven't had a delivery yet, but there's one woman who should have crashed through ten days ago, so I expect a call from her any minute. My stomach churns whenever I think of it, and I toss for hours at night trying to figure out how to do a delivery here safely.

That afternoon, when Vern and Julie and Dr. Meade all pulled out, I almost went, too. I damned near panicked. I didn't know what was in the office, who any of the people were, or anything about their medical problems. Vern had given me a quick tour of the office, what there is of it. He just waved his hand airily toward the shelves of drugs in the little lab—all proprietary names that meant not a thing to me after using the USP* terms for the stuff at Great Lakes. It seems the doctor here runs a regular drug store and is supposed to dispense all medications except vitamins and what comes out of a needle without charging anything extra. Vern said he was sorry there wasn't any ergotrate† on hand, but I could probably get hold of some soon if I sent an order out right away. This with a delivery due any minute, and the hospital and a blood transfusion forty-five miles away if she should begin to bleed, and me with no ergotrate! Wow! He didn't have much in the line of patient records—a few cards in a box. I asked him about sterilizing equipment, and he said he bought all his bandages sterile, and not to bother with anything except boiling up needles and syringes in the little electric sterilizer. For deliveries I should just use the cleanest gloves in the OB bag and things would work out all right!

Would you ask your mother if we can borrow her big canning pressure cooker? Then we could work out a system of sterilizing three by three bandages and gloves. You could make up some muslin glove packs. You'll have to help me get this place organized. I can't practice this kind of medicine for very long and stand myself.

Oh yes, I had to buy all those intimidating drugs, not knowing whether they're anything I really want, or how to use them. I had to take Vern's word for what they were worth and forked over three hundred dollars. But that's not all. Wait till you see our pitiful bank balance. He wanted to sell me his old Plymouth, too, that he'd used for house calls. It looked pretty beat up, but I sure don't want to wreck our own new car on these roads. I didn't have any time to think about it or even try the damned thing out, but I bought it anyway—for four hundred dollars. That's pretty steep, but I didn't feel like arguing. I'm just not used to throwing money around like that, and having to make so many decisions so fast almost made me sick.

It was wonderful to find your letter in yesterday's mail, and I'm so glad you got a kick out of the plane trip—also that Susan was so well behaved. It's nice that your sister Barbara's home, too, so you can all

*United States Pharmacopeia, generic

† Drug to control uterine bleeding by constriction of smooth muscle in uterus and arteries

have a good visit. I hope it won't have to be a very long one though. I want you down here. Give my love to everybody. I sure miss you.

Love and kisses,

Bonta

I read the letter twice, lingering over the last sentence. If only he knew how much I missed him already. I shut my eyes and pretended for a minute that when I opened them he would be standing there. I pictured him, probably wearing his khaki fatigues, his dark hair parted on one side with that suggestion of a wave on the other and his hazel eyes that could see right through you. It was only a few days before that he had put Susan and me on the plane in Chicago.

I tried to picture the camp as he had described it. I remembered Vern's response to one of Bonta's letters in which he'd written, "So it's rural—no problem. My summers at Duxbury sold me on the rural life."

Vern had answered, "You misunderstand. This place is rural like you never even imagined!"

He'd added that the isolation was the hardest thing to get used to. We'd smiled at each other as we read and agreed it wouldn't bother us since we'd have each other.

And now we were separated.

Bonta's letter, moreover, was disquieting. It was clear that I ought to be down there with him. This was his first solo medical practice, and he was in the midst of strangers in a situation totally unlike anything he'd ever run into, with nobody to turn to. Well, he seemed to feel it wouldn't be long before we'd be together again, and I had no choice but to be patient.

At least the delay was a good opportunity for my parents to become acquainted with their only granddaughter. And my sister Barbara's being home after her graduation from Oberlin was a bonus.

Coal Mountain, W. Va.

June 18, 1949

Dearest,

I had to go to Williamson yesterday to pick up some medical supplies, especially narcotics and that ergotrate from Dr. Meade, and of course that meant a sixty-mile drive each way. I got the stuff OK, but I sure felt discouraged and deserted on the way back. Still uptight. When you're an intern or in the navy, there's always somebody next step up you can ask—and pass the buck to if it's a nasty case. Around here, I'm the only M.D. for miles. You know how many deliveries I did in the navy dispensary—none—and even at Michael Reese I never delivered a baby at home. Here it's all up to me, unless of course they call on my competition, a couple of midwives down Long Branch way.

Anyway, to finish it all off, I got stuck in the muck on the way back into camp. They just blasted a new cut through the mountains this spring which eliminates about fifteen miles of dirt road into camp. Well, the red clay there is slick as grease, and I'd gone just too near the edge. With one mountain in front and another one behind, I actually decided to keep going in whichever direction I could make it. As luck would have it, I got over the one that took me back to Coal Mountain. You'd never recognize our beautiful new car now. That shine we gave it a couple of weeks ago is all hidden under a layer of mud. I used it for the long trip out because I don't trust Vern's Plymouth yet. But it almost hurts to punish it on these horrible roads.

Now I've got my OB and medical bags stocked and usable, and I'm in the process of learning the rest of the setup. The people want to be helpful, I guess, but there's nothing anybody else can really do. It's all up to me.

I haven't done much studying for my State Boards and don't see when I ever will. Did I write you before that I have to go up to Charleston for three days sometime in July and take a whole battery of exams before I can get my permanent West Virginia license? I have to clean this office up, rearrange patients' files, and order more drugs. And I don't know where to begin on any of them.

Actually, I feel better than I did when Vern and Julie left. And when you get here, it sure will make loads of difference. I've had some real pylorospasm,* couldn't keep a thing down, but it's gradually quieting down, though not all gone yet. At least I can eat a little something now without losing it.

Learning about the mining industry I find very interesting. I can't

---

*Spasm, with obstruction of stomach outlet, that can cause nausea and vomiting

A section of the new cut-off between the hardtop and the original dirt road into Coal Mountain. Although the cut-off significantly reduced the driving time between Coal Mountain and the nearest town, it was also treacherous and intimidating.

wait to show it all to you. There certainly is money to be earned here, but I am learning in a big hurry that money isn't the most important thing in life. Well, Vern and Julie said it's not quite so bad when you get used to it, which helps some. And I'm sure we can manage it together somehow. Meantime life at the boardinghouse is tolerable.

    All my love,
    Bonta

    I put the letter down and realized Bonta had said nothing about the house we were to have. Surely it ought to become vacant soon. I could hardly visualize him so shaken that he couldn't even keep food down. I had never thought of him as that vulnerable. I wished with all my heart that I could go down alone. I could share his room at the boardinghouse and find some way to help. Susan was the problem. If only my parents could take care of her, but there was no chance of that. Responsibility for a one-and-a-half-year-old would be a real burden for them, especially since Mother hadn't been feeling very well lately. Chasing after a busy toddler was really beyond her. Though she never said it, I had the impression that she felt she'd raised her own children and that was quite enough.

    I was glad Barbara was home. I made myself feel useful by helping her write for jobs and graduate fellowships. A fresh A.B. in psychology wasn't proving all that easy to peddle. Her problems took my mind off my own and made the waiting for Bonta's letters a little easier.

Coal Mountain, W.Va.
June 22, 1949

Dearest Helen,

    Had some excitement in the office yesterday. There was a big row up the line between a man and his wife and her sister. He got a big gash over one eye that I had to sew up. He was drunk and the women were hysterical. What a mess. While I was sewing him up, his own brother and sister came streaking in with fire in their eyes. "Who done it, Tom?" They were spoiling for a big fight. When they asked me how Tom's wife was, I started to give a sort of sympathetic description. They wheeled on me with one voice, "Are you taking sides?" I hadn't gone too far luckily, so I said I was just answering their question and clammed up. Tom was sensible enough to tell them this was his problem and they should stay out of it. Luckily they simmered down. But I can see how a feud can get under way in a hurry! You never saw such a neutral guy as I became—and will remain.

They've been holding a revival here this past week, and last night I drove down and for a few minutes sat in the car in the dark across the creek from the tent. Most of the people sit and watch, but there are a few up front who wave and weave and make enough racket so you'd think the whole meeting was in an uproar. Some say they'll handle snakes later, but if the camp authorities catch them, they'll swear out a warrant and kick them out. It all seems very strange to me. They have a loudspeaker. "Praise the Lord!" "I done felt the Lord come into my soul!" "Hallelujah!" And hymns all evening long. Most of the camp doesn't look with complete favor on these goings-on.

Incidentally, you might ask Barbara if she'd be interested in spending a couple of weeks with us down here. She could probably be a real help, either in the office, or taking care of Susan so you could help me there. Tell her if she wants to see a delivery in the raw I'll take her along on one as my nurse. Better brief her on some terms so it'll sound convincing!

All my love,
Bonta

Two things struck me. First, it was a little scary to realize he could get on the wrong side of people so innocently, and I did hope he'd be cautious in the future. And second, it was a great idea to include Barbara in the project. But if someone was to go along on a delivery, I surely hoped I'd be the one.

I had little doubt about what Barbara's response would be when I asked her whether she'd be interested in going to Coal Mountain with Susan and me. She'd never yet turned down a chance for an adventure.

Sure enough, her gray-green eyes lit up, and she looked up from the stool in the kitchen where she was peeling potatoes for dinner, all ready to take off. "Boy, would that be neat! How soon?"

"Would that I could tell you," I said with feeling. "Well, we'll have to see what Mother and Dad think about it. But I'd sure love to have you come down with us."

Coal Mountain, W. Va.
June 25, 1949

Dearest Helen,

Well, the awful moment came, and thank goodness I'm still around to write about it. Night before last I was just drifting off to sleep after a dreadful day in the office when I heard heavy footsteps clomping up the steps to the porch just outside my room. As usual I held my breath hoping they'd go on by, but this time they stopped in front of my door. Then a loud knock (sometimes they don't bother to knock— just barge in).

"Hey, Doc!" It was Isaac Harper all right. Sure enough, in a sort of offhand way, he delivered the message I'd been dreading, "Guess the old lady's coming down, Doc."

Nothing for it but to throw on my clothes, grab my OB bag and the Kelly's pad (in case you don't know, that's a big rubber pad with a rim around it and a sort of funnel that can carry any fluid or blood down into a bucket). I followed Isaac's truck in my car for a couple miles. As soon as we got there, he disappeared, but luckily a neighbor lady was there to help. Four kids were asleep in one bed in the single bedroom, with Mrs. Harper in labor in the other bed.

I'd worked my plan out carefully during these many sleepless nights, and I started to put it into effect by asking the neighbor lady to boil lots of water. Just the way they do in the movies.

I got out a razor to shave the pubic hair, but she threw up her hands at that. "Lord have mercy! None of that. It itches too much when it grows back in!"

So I had to settle for scrubbing her perineum* with soap until it fairly shone.

When the water finally boiled, I set up two big pans with sterile water near my chair, poured Lysol into one, and put my instruments in that one to soak. The idea was to put my gloves on, soak my hands

*Genital area

in the Lysol solution, then rinse gloves and instruments in the other pan of plain sterile water, and then go to work.

Well, Mrs. Harper was getting ready to deliver, so on went the gloves, and into the Lysol. You must understand this was a hot summer night. The windows were wide open, no screens, and flies all over the place. (I learned afterward that the privy wasn't far away.) Anyway, I'm sitting there sterilizing my gloves, when I look over at my patient, and I see with horror that several flies have become trapped in the pubic hair. No help for it, so I concentrate on my gloves.

About then a fly hovers over my pan, and the steam and Lysol fumes get to him, and down he plunges into the pan. So I spend the next few minutes flicking flies out of the Lysol with my "sterile" gloves. This is bad enough, but the same thing is happening to the other pan I was going to rinse things in.

Too late to worry about it. Mrs. Harper is pushing hard, so I just go ahead and "catch the baby" as they say hereabouts. Nice healthy baby. Luckily she'd had four already, so no need for an episiotomy and sewing her up. I cut the cord, and it didn't take long for the placenta to come.

The children hadn't even stirred. Pretty efficient performance on Mrs. Harper's part, I must say!

And very humbling to find out how little difference I made.

Anyway, I got out my little notebook to record the information I'd need for the birth certificate, and she told me that the baby's name would be John L. Harper. You must realize that John L. Lewis, head of the UMW, currently fighting for a more favorable contract for his men, is second only to God around here.

Still no sign of the missing husband, so the neighbor lady and I cleaned up things, and I left. I feel kind of crummy about asking for the thirty-three dollars I'm supposed to get for a delivery, considering the flies and how little I really did. But I guess nobody could have done anything much different under the circumstances.

When I went to check on her yesterday, I found one of the children had a runny nose and a temp, so, to protect the new baby, I suggested maybe they'd better send the kid to a neighbor. But she said, "Oh, he must be feeling pretty good. He's been hugging and kissing the baby all day." So much for that idea. It's survival of the fittest, I guess.

You can see why my stomach's been in knots. Thank God I've gotten past that hurdle. And it could have been worse.

'Nough for now. I'm so tired it'll take more than those ominous footsteps to wake me up tonight. Need at least a few hours' sleep. Take care. I love you.

   Bonta

It was hard to believe that scenario! What a gutsy gal! Thinking of the contrast between Bonta's description and the kind of procedures he was used to, I could see why he was working on an ulcer. My own experience with deliveries was strictly limited, but Mrs. Harper's had little in common with the one I witnessed during Bonta's internship.

One of the OB men had agreed I could step into the delivery room after the patient had been put to sleep. Bonta said it was time I saw the real thing after teaching embryology for three years at Vassar.

Secretly nervous though I was over the thought that my weak stomach might disgrace him and me, too, I walked in nonchalantly enough. All I could see was white everywhere: white uniforms, white caps, white drapes. Then the baby's head crowned, and blood began to stain the white drapes. To my horror the room began to spin. I was so embarrassed. They'd made me promise I'd leave if I felt faint, so I dutifully went out and lay down on a cart in the hall, mortified. Everybody laughed as I left, and the obstetrician called out kiddingly, so I could hear, "That ought to teach her a lesson. Ph.D's just can't take it!" and he laughed again.

I didn't remember much about my own delivery, since, like most other women in 1947, I was alone during labor and put to sleep at the end. Things were certainly different in Coal Mountain!

I had never known Bonta to be so tense. Even when things were rough at the hospital, he had managed to be philosophical about it all. He would say, "Well, that's just the price of the ticket. Everybody else's paid it, so I can't complain." But of course there he was surrounded by experts and other house staff going through the same ordeal, and on the rare weekends when he was off, he was ready to forget it all and relax.

I thought back to the little room where we had lived in Chicago. It was on the third floor of an old brownstone at Fifty-third and Dorchester, a mile from the university, where I worked. It had once been the living room of an apartment that occupied the whole floor. The individual rooms were rented out, so we shared the single bathroom with the five other tenants. It was, nevertheless, our first home, and Bonta had searched long to find it, since housing for an intern without any income was nearly nonexistent in Chicago in 1946, right after the war. We were immensely happy and inordinately fond of it.

The years at the base had finally given Bonta a little time to indulge himself, and he enjoyed being with the other young physicians there. He had found a chess partner, and ongoing games filled spare moments with pleasure. He was so people oriented that I could see why being all alone down in West Virginia was so stressful.

Coal Mountain, W. Va.
June 28, 1949

Dearest,

That car I bought from Vern darned near did me in last night, and I don't dare drive it again till it's fixed. I took it down to Dave Kennedy to see if he can do anything with it. He's supposedly a mechanic. Operates out of an old army tent down the line.

Somebody told me I was needed over by Leatherwood. Had to ford the creek to get there. That was bad enough, but there's no way to tell you how bad the road is from there on—barely wide enough for a single car, with a sheer drop down to the big Guyandotte River on one side and a jagged rock wall on the other. Well, I was heading up this road when all of a sudden I found a rockslide in front of me. Not a real big one, but there was no way around it. Also no way to turn around. When I started to back down, I discovered the foot brake had failed. So I had to coast backward down that narrow winding road in the dark—no light but the taillight—relying on the hand brake till I reached a wide enough place to turn around. Used up a lot of adrenaline on that one.

From now on I'm driving our own black Chevy.

Today is supposed to be reserved for prenatal checkups. Don't know if it will work out that way, but I've hired a girl to come in and help for the day just in case. She's the only one in camp who finished high school last year. Tells me she stuck it out (twenty-six miles of dirt

road on the school bus each way) because she liked being a cheer-
leader at the basketball games. More power to her! She seems very
intelligent. Really cute, too. Eloise's her name. She was supposed to
be here at eight-thirty; it's now a little after that, and the waiting room
is filling up.

All for now. Swamped!

Love,

Bonta

I was glad he had finally found some help. This Eloise sounded
pretty enterprising, and I wondered if she might be willing to take
care of Susan sometimes, too, so that I could help Bonta in the office.
I tried to imagine being so devoted to cheerleading as to endure that
kind of trip every day. Of course, I hadn't seen the roads yet, but
Bonta's descriptions were graphic. Was cheerleading such fun, or did
it bring so much prestige? I looked forward to meeting her soon and
finding out more about her—and everything else in Coal Mountain.

Coal Mountain, W. Va.

July 6, 1949

Hi, Honey,

Just a note to say I love you and would give a lot to have you here
with me. This is the first time I have had the office door open without
half a dozen people outside in the waiting room, and I don't know
how long it will last. Once it starts, it doesn't seem to let up. I haven't
had a chance to sweep out lately at all, and it's a mess in here. They're
used to dropping things wherever it's convenient—candy wrappers,
coke bottles, paper bags—and I guess it was a real jolt to them when
they first saw me sweeping the place out. Some old lady muttered
more to herself than me, "Well, if it don't beat everything. Never seen
no doctor do that before!" Some of them still don't realize why I put
those big tin cans in the waiting room, but I'm trying.

I had patients till nine o'clock last night and then spent an hour like
a madman alone in the office, stalking flies. Must have killed a hundred
in one room. You could stand still and hear their steady hum. Today
there are just as many new ones. The superintendent said they'd fix
the screens, but like all other things, that will be later.

Probably much later because no one is working this week. The UMW has put the men on a three-day workweek, a slowdown tactic to put pressure on the company while they're negotiating a new contract. The old one expired June 30. Mr. Ramsey says Lewis wants to cut down the current surplus of coal to weaken the companies' bargaining position.

But this week the local union decided to take even those three days off as a "vacation period." You see the company is responsible for whatever kind of work is done in camp, and if the men aren't working at the mine, they're not working at anything else either, except for the few people who run the company store and some of the supervisory personnel in the company office. There's almost no free enterprise here at all. That car mechanic, and one fellow who runs a little beer joint outside the camp aways, but that's about it. As a matter of fact, this unofficial strike is actually making it a little easier for me, since things are pretty quiet in camp. When the men don't go through the "center of town" and past my office on their way to the mine, they don't have as much opportunity to call on the doctor, so I can catch up a bit on my paperwork.

Didn't have to get up last night at all but kept waking up and hearing footsteps and was sure someone was coming for me. It can really wreck a night's sleep.

I hate having to go all through the day till four-thirty before I can get the mail. I sure do look for your letters and appreciate your writing every day. No news about the house I'm hoping Mr. Ramsey will let us have, but I keep pestering. The people in it are supposed to be leaving the coalfields for greener pastures, but they just don't do things in a hurry around here. It's a lot like the navy. If you want something, you wait, except in the navy there is a lot more you can wait for.

This evening I hope to get off to the big city to take my licensure exams. Haven't done much studying for them, as you know, but they'll just have to take me as I am. That biochem book you sent helped a lot, and I ran over some anatomy. Have just had too many other things on my mind. Wish me luck.

    Your ever lovin' boy,

    Bonta

More than two weeks had passed, and I was getting discouraged. It seemed as though we'd never get that house if things moved so slowly down there. I did miss him so. This was the first time we'd been separated since we were married, and it was doubly hard, knowing that he not only missed me but needed me.

And so the days passed much too slowly.

Only one thing really captured my interest. Since Bonta mentioned the UMW contract negotiations, I wanted to learn what I could about them. Our local paper merely mentioned the problems in the coalfields, but one of our neighbors subscribed to the *New York Times*. From its pages I learned much more. To reduce the stockpile of coal, Lewis called for the three-day workweek rather than a stoppage. A walkout might have induced the government to invoke the antistrike measures in the Taft-Hartley Law. The men had already been idle for a two-week memorial period back in March, anticipating the need to strengthen the union's hand, though ostensibly to honor the men who had died or were injured in the mines. A ten-day vacation period in June, "a stabilizing period of inaction," had just come to an end. After the expiration of their contract on June 30, the men were surprised to be ordered back to work, even if for only three days a week, since their longtime slogan had been "No contract, no work."

The mine owners were distressed by the slowdown because their costs were based on the expectation of full production; many fixed expenses could not be reduced to match the loss of income. They predicted a significant rise in the cost of coal. In the meantime, negotiations had been called off until July 19.

Coal Mountain, W. Va.
July 11, 1949

Dearest Wif,

Back at the old business again and am pretty rushed. But three cheers. I saw Mr. Ramsey and we will get the house I have been hoping for. All we have to do is wait till it's vacated and gets fixed up. I'd like to use dynamite around this place once in a while, but it's no use. Mr. Ramsey only moves so fast himself, and he has a lot to do. Since the men are still only working three days a week, those are the only days when they can work on the house. Looks as though it may be three weeks before it'll be ready.

Maybe I'll have to bring you into the boardinghouse and squeeze them into speeding things up. Don't want to, but it can be done. They like to keep those best front rooms open for visiting company big shots, and I'm blocking one of them already. Anyway, keep the weekend of the twenty-third and twenty-fourth open just in case. When you come down, if I can't get to the airport in Charleston, you can take a taxi to the tourist home where I stayed while I took the exams. Mrs. Stokes was really nice to me and promised to take good care of you if necessary. She is anxious to see our baby. So am I!

Incidentally this Mr. Ramsey is a remarkable guy. As you've gathered, he's the superintendent, with complete responsibility for running everything in Coal Mountain. He represents Red Jacket, and Red Jacket owns everything here—the mine, the store, and all the houses. Everybody who works in the camp or the mine was hired by Mr. Ramsey, and he handles all negotiations with the union. He's had only six grades of formal education, but he's astonishingly urbane, a steady sort of character not easily rattled, not likely to jump to conclusions without considering first. Very reassuring to have him to talk to when things get rough.

My arm is still sore from writing those exams for two and a half days. I was so sick of it I almost walked out in the middle. Wrote almost two whole pads of yellow legal paper on one side—ten exams, two hours each, and I'll bet my handwriting is worse than ever now. Don't know how I did yet, of course, but I trust they'll be generous when they grade them. Actually, the questions didn't seem too bad, though a session like that reminds me how long it's been since I was in med school and geared to such stuff.

Have to quit if this is to get out in the mail today. Somebody just came to the door—big gash in his leg. Guess he'll be more careful next time he uses an ax.

Love,
Bonta

Three more weeks! I wondered whether he'd have everything figured out by the time I got there and I wouldn't really be part of it.

Coal Mountain, W. Va.
July 12, 1949

Sweetheart,

If I get four lines down, I'll be lucky. I've been going like mad since yesterday morning. Got through at ten o'clock last night and started again early this morning. I have so much to do and can't even start for all the interruptions. These are the times I wish you could help. But don't get jumpy. If you should try to come to the boardinghouse with Susan, you'd be no help at all. Did you ask Barbara about coming down, maybe even alone, since you don't feel you can leave the baby? Of course, it's you I really need, because you know more about procedures. It's terribly frustrating having you tied down up there. Kids can sure gum up the works sometimes.

But don't worry and do anything rash like coming down now alone at this late date. I'm getting a bit caught up today by keeping the door to the office locked and looking as though I'm not here. Mostly this is stupid frustration at all the dillydally that goes on that I can't do anything about.

I answered a frantic knock on my door last night at twelve-thirty. One of the miners who lives here at the clubhouse stood there, almost breathless. "Hey, Doc, you got to come quick! There's been a shooting down by Elk Trace and somebody's hurt real bad."

I didn't waste any time getting there. Found two men lying near the railroad track across the creek from the road, about fifteen feet from each other. Such gore you've never seen! The first one had been hit by two bullets. One had lodged in his left lung near the heart and the other in his face. The second had a shotgun blast in the left groin. The first one was almost dead, so we put him in the ambulance the union recently acquired, and I was afraid he'd die before getting to the hospital. (He did.) Meantime I hurriedly splinted the other man, gave him a shot of morphine, and sent him off in the same ambulance. He lived as far as the hospital, but has only a fifty-fifty chance of making it.

It all happened because Azel Ritter, the man who died, is a born-again Christian and felt it his duty to go to the defense of a young woman who was being beaten up by her husband out in the field. She was about six months pregnant. Azel apparently picked up Jimmy

Babcock, the husband, by the collar—Jimmy's pretty small—and said, "That ain't a very nice thing to do!"

Jimmy wasn't just fooling when he said, "How dare you butt into our business? I'm going to get my brother and we're going to kill you." Azel believed him, too. Went to the tent where he lived and got his gun, walked over by the railroad tracks to wait for them so his family wouldn't get involved. Pretty soon Jimmy and his brother came along, and I guess the brother fired a shot to scare Azel. Don't know which one drew blood first, but there sure was plenty of it when I arrived. The only one who came off unscathed was little Jimmy who started the whole mess in the first place by beating up his wife.

Oh yes, Liddie, his wife, was there afterward, too, and what do you suppose she had to say about it? "Well, it sure serves him right—not minding his own damn business!"

This morning everyone up and down the hollow is talking about it. The ambulance driver says Azel forgave Jimmy's brother before he died. They say such violence is a bit unusual, even for these parts, but apparently it can happen.

Lots to get used to around here! At least it's not boring.

Love,

Bonta

I shook my head in disbelief. Such melodrama belonged in a grade B Western, not real life as we'd known it. And it didn't make me any happier about Bonta's being down there, either. I thought back to the angry accusation that he was taking sides in that one family fracas.

Even worse than that, the tone of this letter made me feel he was getting pretty desperate. Not only was he feeling terribly alone and just wanted me with him, but there were things I should be doing to help him with the job. And the remark about Barbara's coming down if I didn't feel I could leave the baby was distressing. I certainly didn't want Barbara to take my place.

My enthusiasm about being home again had long since worn thin. All the family news had been discussed, all the old friends visited, and all the letters of application for Barbara written. Once you leave the nest it's never quite the same when you return, and I felt that my parents wouldn't be altogether sorry to have their own privacy back either.

This should have been our adventure. We'd always tackled problems together, and here he was facing the biggest one of all without me. It upset me to think that he had only Mr. Ramsey and Eloise to turn to.

Coal Mountain, W. Va.
July 18, 1949

Dearest Helen,

Well, both the men who were shot have died, and Jimmy has confessed to shooting Azel after Azel and Jimmy's brother had exchanged the first shots. What a tragedy! It's the first shooting like this in several years, I hear, so don't get worried.

Nothing has happened yet about "our house." If this keeps up too long I'm going to go nuts. The Grays haven't even moved out yet. This week the men aren't working at all, so we couldn't get the place fixed up anyway. No news of our things that the navy is supposed to be shipping here either, not that there'd be any place to put the stuff if it did arrive. Keep your chin up, and I'll let you know as soon as I see a break. I did make a down payment on a stove and refrigerator at Sears Saturday when I left the hollow for a trip to Williamson. What sort of washing machine would you like? I figure if you'll be putting up with all you'll have to put up with down here, at least I want you to have a few luxuries.

As I said, the miners decided not to work again today. I'm not sure why, but Bert, who lives here in the clubhouse, said he thought it had to do with a dispute over the mine inspection. Mr. Ramsey has been too busy to talk, so I haven't been able to find out what the problem really is. I think this is a strictly local affair. They didn't work yesterday either. "Unwilling and unable," I was told by someone quoting a clause in the union contract they say permits a strike. Tomorrow they are going to hold a memorial for the two fellows in the gun fight.

For whatever reasons, there go the three work days for this week. They all need every nickel they can lay their hands on against the big strike that will presumably be called in the not too distant future. John L. isn't getting all he wants from the companies. It baffles me, but I swear there's a real undercurrent of excitement around—almost anticipation! I don't think they realize how much a big strike could hurt them in the long run.

I'm awake today, but barely. Last night at ten o'clock Jake Arnold came to say his wife was in labor. A friend had driven him into camp. She was in false labor, as it turned out, but I didn't dare leave their place because he had no car to come and get me with if she started up again. I left my equipment set up and slept in the front seat of the car from midnight to about 5:00 A.M. Sort of cramped. She was still having pains but not making progress an hour later, so I came back to the clubhouse, had breakfast, and went to bed for an hour.

Called again, this time to see a little eight-year-old boy suffering an epileptic seizure up in the green camp. Luckily he didn't hurt himself and had come out of it by the time I got there.

So that delivery is still hanging fire. Now I'm about to open the office on this nice sunny day. Lots of people will probably decide to go on an outing to the doctor's office.

Oh yes, one bright spot yesterday. Red Jacket's assistant manager came over with his son for a short while yesterday. This young fellow had just finished his internship, and it was real fun to talk with him. I never realized before how important it is just to have somebody around who speaks the same language. There's nobody here at all. Mr. Ramsey is the only one who comes close.

I sure wish I could see you and Susan for a while. It would make things less bleak by about a hundred percent.

All my love,
Bonta

It was probably foolish to dwell with such intensity on every word Bonta wrote, but I did. What else did I have to go on? I slept every night with his latest letter under my pillow, but it was a poor substitute at best.

Coal Mountain, W.Va.
July 28, 1949

Darling,

Hallelujah! Our house will be empty tomorrow! It will still take a couple of weeks to fix it up at best, but you better figure on coming down next weekend and staying in the boardinghouse. I hope Barbara is still willing to come along as you wrote she might do. It would sure be nice if she could take care of Susan so you could help me. I'll be calling you with details, maybe even before you get this letter.

I just might not be able to meet you at the airport in Charleston because Bart Toler and Sam Mitchell came in yesterday and told me their wives are due any time now, and I don't want to leave the camp till they crash through. If I'm not there, take a taxi to that tourist home (Mrs. Albert Stokes, 3214 West Oak Drive) and wait there for word as to what's happening.

It's been hot as blazes the past few days, and that takes the starch out of me, but at least I'm keeping afloat. People are waiting outside the office. A couple of trucks are pulled up there across the creek, so I'd better get on over. Be seeing you soon!

I love you.

Bonta

2. My Turn

The less said about the flight down the better. It was fun until the long wait to change planes in New York. As things dragged on, Susan got fussier and dirtier, trotting about exploring and eventually poking her hands into a messy ashtray. To distract her Barbara and I went up to the observation deck to watch planes taking off. Whenever we moved, we had to count: Barbara's purse, my purse, diaper bag, toy bag, her carry-on bag, my carry-on bag—and Susan. The logistics seemed daunting in the heat.

Once aboard the plane to Charleston, we settled back to enjoy the trip. It was a small plane, and the lack of effective ventilation began to make me a little airsick. At the first of the two stops en route, the heat worsened, magnifying my queasiness. By the time we touched down in Washington, I was grateful for the little bag on the back of the seat in front of me. Without Barbara to take care of Susan, I don't know how we would have coped. Even the most miserable things finally come to an end, however, and the plane eventually did land.

Just as Barbara and I had feared, there was no sign of Bonta at the gate, nor anywhere else in the airport. Though still pretty wobbly, I located a phone and put in a call for him at Coal Mountain. The operator told me he didn't have a phone. Who ever heard of a doctor being without a telephone? I soon discovered that there was only one phone in camp, the one in the coal company office, closed by then. Luckily the operator got hold of Mr. Ramsey, who had an extension in his home. He sounded very sympathetic but told me, "Far as I know, he left early this morning, and he should have been there a while ago. You just be patient, though. I'm sure he'll be along soon."

This report was hardly calculated to make me feel any better. Barbara and I decided to take a taxi to the tourist home and wait, as Bonta had said. On the way we saw a truck towing a black Fleetline Chevrolet that had been totaled. Ours? No license plate was visible. How would we ever know if anything had happened to Bonta? Who would know how to reach us? In fact, who would know that we should be reached? Even Barbara was shaken. We managed to feed Susan, but neither of us could face the thought of food, and as it got later and later, the knot in my stomach got tighter and tighter.

At nine-thirty the phone rang, and Mrs. Stokes handed the receiver to me. It was Bonta.

"Of course I'm OK, but dammit, I'm still at camp! I've just run out on Mrs. Toler—one of the women I wrote you were due any minute. Told her I just had to phone you from Mr. Ramsey's house. I tried to sneak out of camp early this morning, all dressed in my city clothes, when along came Bart Toler. 'Hey, Doc, my wife's coming down; reckon you'd better stick around a while.'

"So nothing for it but I had to change back into my old navy fatigues and go down the road to see how she was doing. I've been kidding her along, telling her to hurry up—push hard—because my wife and baby are waiting for me in Charleston. She's a good sport. She smiles between contractions and says, 'Doc, I'd sure like to be out of this shape myself, but wishing ain't doing no good!'

"I'll either come on up as soon as the baby's born, or I'll ask one of the men at the clubhouse to come for you. You ought to go on to bed, because Mrs. Toler might not even deliver till tomorrow."

But happy sound! At 3:00 A.M. the doorbell rang, and there was Bonta, looking bleary-eyed but wonderful. I burst into tears as I flung my arms around him and buried my face on his shoulder. It had been such a long wait!

Barbara brought Susan from the bedroom, still half asleep and very suspicious of this strange man. I wanted him to see how much she'd grown and how cute she looked in her pink pj's. I couldn't wait for us to become once again the close threesome we'd been, and I looked hopefully to see how he greeted her. His face was leaner and shadowed by the stubble of his beard, but I found the warmth I needed in his blue-gray eyes and his appreciative grin. As he picked her up, he said to me, "You certainly haven't been starving her! She's a bigger armful than I remember!"

There was too much to be said at such an hour, and we just contented ourselves with looking at each other while we engaged in small talk about the trip down and our fright at seeing the wrecked car. It was actually difficult to say anything very significant after such a long absence. There was too much to cover.

We set out for Coal Mountain right after we ate the lunch Mrs. Stokes fixed for us. She was a motherly soul, happy with her cooking and crocheting. She even invited us to come back just for a visit "when things get too much for you down there, dearie." The thought of a friendly haven was reassuring. I guess she sensed some of my uncertainty about how I'd find this new life, or perhaps she had a better idea of what I faced than I did.

Bonta had learned to drive like a native by this time and squealed the tires on every curve, glancing at me now and then to see my reaction. I must have looked appropriately alarmed. Actually, the roller coaster effect and the hairpin turns brought back a little of my motion sickness, and I felt a bit wan.

That didn't keep me from paying attention to the passing scene, however. Weatherworn cabins occupied precarious perches near the base of the steep cliffs edging the road; many appeared ready to collapse in the next high wind. Such poverty was a revelation to me. And I marveled at the isolation of the drab little mining camps we passed. Most of the small houses in them had given up whatever color they might originally have possessed in favor of uniform coal dust gray. I was curious, too, about the clusters of people gathered by some of the little streams. Bonta explained that they must be holding religious services, probably conducting baptisms, since this was Sunday afternoon. The most important features in the few little towns we went through were the rail yards with their mountains of coal and the big black tipples. These tall, ungainly structures reminded me of some prehistoric monsters. Bonta explained that the coal was brought to them from the mine for washing to separate it from the slate if necessary, and for sorting it by the size of the lumps. In the portion of the tipple which extended over the coal cars below were screens with openings of different sizes. As the coal passed over these screens, the pieces that could pass through successively larger meshes fell into the appropriate waiting car below. As soon as a car was filled, it was sent on its way while an empty one moved into position.

My idea of civilization stretched thinner and thinner the farther we drove, and I began to feel more and more a stranger. Would I ever fit into this territory, so different from any I'd known? At least I now understood the strange comment in one of Bonta's letters, that most of these settlements were pretty useless. From the traveler's perspective, it seemed almost true; they had no stores except perhaps a little mom-and-pop grocery with a gas pump in front, no movie houses, no place to stay, and no place to eat.

But all of this paled by comparison with the Appalachians themselves. They were magnificent, their steep green slopes looming above and around us. Each curve—and the road was nothing but curves—rewarded us with a new reason for exclamation.

After about a hundred miles of this, Bonta suddenly turned left onto a rather broad but bumpy dirt road and announced, "This is the new cutoff you remember I wrote you about." He clearly identified with the place, sounding almost proprietary about the engineering feat that had cut off fifteen miles of dirt road by creating a new access to the hardtop closer to Coal Mountain. I was too astonished by the craters in the road to appreciate the information properly. What I did pick up from his tone was the pride of belonging, and I quaked as the thought flitted across my mind that he might even think of me as an intruder!

Suddenly up ahead loomed a truly overwhelming mountain of rock, through which a deep cleft had been gouged. The scar was still raw with shaggy roots of upended trees groping for a foothold. The rock face showed dynamite drill holes on either side of the road, and it looked as though boulders might come crashing down at any minute. Where the crushed rock covering thinned, the red clay had deep ruts in it. Bonta explained that this was where he had been stuck that day when he would have been glad to leave in either direction.

On the other side of the cut, my spirits soared as a breathtaking panorama spread out away below on the left. The mountain dropped sheer down to the riverbed, hundreds of feet below, and the blue waters of the Guyandotte sparkled in the late afternoon sun. A tenuous thread of railroad track ran along beside it, until it disappeared into the tunnel below us.

We drove on at what seemed to Barbara and me a breakneck rate of speed, jouncing over holes in the road in spite of Bonta's knowledge of every bad place and his skill at avoiding the worst. As the road paralleled the course of Cub Creek, a small tributary of the Guyandotte, Bonta animatedly pointed out all sorts of landmarks.

First the place where he had made his first house call. I stared at the log cabin, the spaces between the rough-hewn square logs chinked with mud. It was on the other side of the little creek, and the visitor reached the cabin by a bridge made of a single log. Someone had nailed a flat plank to the top of this log, and there was even a suggestion of a handrail on one side, with a spindly upright at either end. Bonta assured us that this was one of the more substantial bridges he used. Worse was the sight of the garbage strewn along the bank of the creek in front of the house. Chickens were scratching around among tin cans and old shoes. Up the sides of the cabin clambered trumpet vines in full bloom, their orange blossoms competing with the most luxuriant climbing red roses I had ever seen. Nature seemed to be doing her best to compensate for some of the mess that people had made.

I glanced at Bonta to see what he thought about this amazing study in contrasts. His matter-of-factness showed me that he had established a relationship with the people who lived there, and this was of special interest to him only for its possible effect on me. He belonged. His role in the community gave him an entrée I would not have, and I only hoped I could make a place for myself here, too. I simply could not imagine having much in common with people who called that cabin home, who cooked dinner there, slept there, raised their children there. If only we had arrived together, I would have reveled in our common adventure; now it was a catch-up game.

But looking again at the roses cheered me up. They reinforced the feeling so much of the trip had already given me. If one could only ignore what was underfoot—pitted roads, dust and grime, even garbage—this country was surpassingly lovely.

Farther on we passed the house where Bonta had faced his first delivery. This was by no means as primitive as the log cabin, but I tried to imagine what it must have been like for that woman to give birth in such a place, and my heart went out to her. The open windows had no screens; pigs were rooting near the front porch. No wonder Bonta had had nightmares about planning for deliveries in places like this after being trained in sterile hospital suites.

Half a mile beyond and next to a cornfield was the theater, a cement block building that looked like a garage but was identified by a small sign that declared, "Theater."

Bonta explained, "This theater is new, but it's not paying too well in spite of heavy patronage. You see, one of the co-owners is Nick Morgan, and he lets all the Morgans come in free. That takes in a good chunk of the local population. I've got thirty-six Morgan families in my files."

"It seems as though we've been going down this road forever. Each time we come to some buildings I think we've arrived. Isn't the theater part of the camp?" I asked.

"Oh, no. We've quite a ways to go yet. I suppose the Morgans just had some land out here and decided to put their theater on it," Bonta answered.

A bit farther on he pointed out the tent where the local garage mechanic ran his business. There was a new frame "churchhouse" just beyond and, a little down the road, a tiny sawmill run by another of the Morgan clan. Next we passed the schoolhouse—the only substantial building I'd seen all afternoon. It was brick, modern, and well built; Bonta said the company and the county had shared the cost of erecting it. Barbara asked him about a high school.

"Oh, that's a long way off in another community on the other side of Coal Mountain. Most of the young people don't figure it's worth the trouble to attend. The guys can get good paying jobs in the mine, and the girls can get married, so why bother? That's what makes Eloise such an exception."

Before I could ask him how Eloise was getting along in the office, he called our attention to the way the creek at one point looked like two streams flowing in one bed—one yellowish and the other dark gray. The one half came from the lumber camp, all full of mud, and took a long time to mix with the other half, that dirty gray water that came down from the tipple where the coal was washed. He asked, incidentally, whether we had noticed that all the paths of transportation followed the watercourses.

We had a quick glimpse of the lumber camp, as we passed the mouth of that hollow, and I wondered how Coal Mountain would compare with this camp. Bonta reminded me that he took care of the people here as well as those in the coal camp. This was a crude affair, with unfinished wooden cabins marching up the rutted road that paralleled the little yellowish creek. And doing sentry duty on the rise just behind each cabin perched a small outhouse. The most striking thing about the lumber camp was a smoldering volcano of sawdust and scrap lumber, continuously fed by the waste wood chips and broken boards dropped off the conveyer belt leading from the sawmill to the top of the heap. The breeze brought a faint whiff of the pungent fragrance of burning wood. Bonta told us we should see it at night if we wanted to see something really eerie.

A bit farther on and across the creek the valley widened to provide the only flat open area I'd seen on the drive in. Bonta said it was there the Holinesses had pitched the tent for the revival meeting. I tried to imagine the scene he had described in his letter but without much success.

Around a curve in the road the camp itself suddenly appeared. After some of the places we had passed on the way in, it came as a distinctly pleasant shock to find the clapboard houses here neat, clean, and white, each surrounded by its own tiny fenced yard. The camp filled what little level space the mountains allowed it. The main road continued along the creek through the center of the small community, with a few side roads branching off to the right as far as the mountains permitted, most only far enough for two or three houses, until we came to the last branch, which followed a tiny rivulet up a smaller hollow. The white houses followed this streamlet as far as I could see, but Bonta pointed out that beyond them was the green camp he had written about. There the houses were painted green and lacked indoor plumbing. He explained that only Red Jacket employees could live in the camp itself.

Bonta pulled the car up in front of a big rectangular building, with a narrow porch extending the length of one side and across the end that faced the main road. This was the clubhouse where we'd stay.

Bonta leaving a home in the lumber camp where he had previously delivered twins.

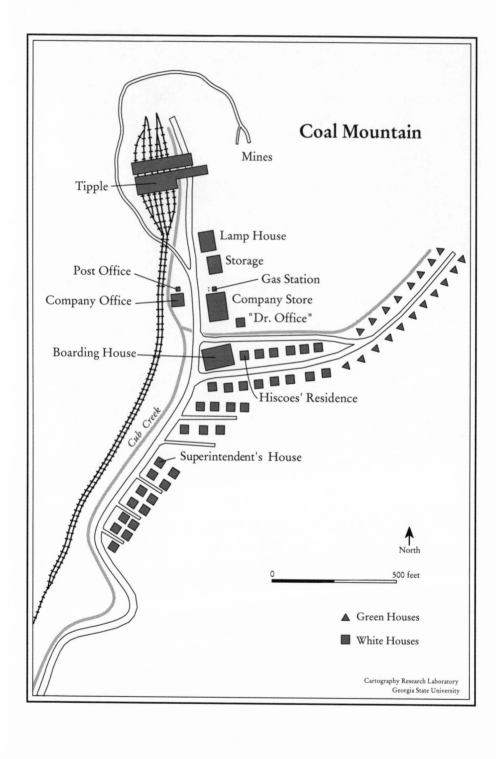

Coal Mountain

Mines

Tipple

Lamp House

Storage

Post Office

Gas Station

Company Office

Company Store

"Dr. Office"

Boarding House

Hiscoes' Residence

Cub Creek

Superintendent's House

North

0   500 feet

▲ Green Houses

■ White Houses

Cartography Research Laboratory
Georgia State University

"It's a boardinghouse for the miners who don't have any family. There's a sort of dormitory upstairs for them, with just a few rooms downstairs. Pretty spartan but adequate."

A couple of men in boots and work clothes stood on the steps talking but also clearly evaluating the doctor's passengers. Barbara and I would have to get used to being stared at.

Bonta pointed out the house that would eventually be ours, behind the clubhouse and up a little side hollow. I looked at it appreciatively. It was like all the others, square, with corner windows and a tiny back porch with a railing. Its small yard was enclosed by a fence made of rough crisscrossed boards, stained dark green.

When I asked him why they went to the trouble of fencing all the yards, he said, "Got to keep out the cows—there are a few in camp—and the occasional horse that wanders up from the lumber camp. There are a couple of mules that make themselves at home, too. You'll meet Ho-Gin and Daisy one of these days."

The little structure by the back fence turned out to be the coal shed. I pictured myself wielding shovel and coal scuttle.

Just across the tiny branch of Cub that ran behind "our" house was a small frame building with a little sign that said "Dr. Office." Bonta pointed it out with a deprecatory smile, but there was no disguising the pride in his voice as he promised to take us through it shortly. It was obvious why he wanted that particular house for us. From either of the two back windows one could keep track of who went in and out of the office, and it was only a few steps across the dirt road and the little plank bridge over the streamlet to its front door. Behind the office a wooded hill rose steeply. In front of its overgrown patch of yard—also fenced in—was the large bare parking area next to the company store.

This store was much the largest building in camp and seemed to be a gathering place even on a Sunday evening. Several men squatted on the bare earth beside the steps, deep in conversation. Bonta waved his hand toward the remaining buildings: the company office, the post office, the lamphouse, and the gas pump. The huge black tipple farther up the road toward the mine entrance brooded over everything.

Bonta said matter-of-factly, "You realize the road dead-ends up at the entrance to the mine."

View of Coal Mountain from above: Our house, typical of the homes in the white camp, is in the center; Bonta's office is directly behind it. The two-story structure on the left is the boarding house, the large building to the left of Bonta's office is the company store, the building in the rear is the lamp house.

I certainly had not realized it, and I wondered for a moment about the possible symbolism in his phrase, "dead-ends." So this was Coal Mountain, my new home, a compact little universe, set apart from everything familiar.

At the clubhouse Barbara and Susan were given one of the two end bedrooms facing the main road, while across the hall Bonta and I now shared the other one. He assured us that these were the very best rooms, available to us as a special favor. We even had a private bathroom. No wonder Bonta's sleep was interrupted every time a miner came or went, since everybody had to enter the building by the door at the end of this hall and pass between the two bedroom doors on the way to the upstairs dormitory.

Barbara and I felt self-conscious as we made our way shortly into the dining room. It was large enough to accommodate three tables, each seating perhaps six people. All eyes were fastened on us. As the doctor's daughter, Susan attracted her share of attention, too. She was a friendly little character, bubbling with good ideas she had not learned to express. Her short blonde hair had not yet come in in front, and what there was stood up like a fine halo around her head. Her chubby cheeks made her look deceptively cherubic; she could wangle her own way in a most uncherubic fashion.

A slender, auburn-haired, middle-aged woman brought in platters of sliced tomatoes, ripe ears of corn, ham, fried potatoes, cole slaw, and baked beans. She smiled a welcome as she set them on the table. The array was overwhelming. Susan dove into her dinner as though she hadn't seen food for a week, while Bonta introduced Barbara and me to Mrs. Jennings. She seemed somehow too fragile to be running a boardinghouse for a crew of miners all by herself. In a self-effacing manner she introduced us in turn to her daughter Vonnie, who was on vacation from boarding school and waited tables. Vonnie tossed her curls and murmured an acknowledgment with a South Carolina accent that sounded like a recent acquisition. They struck me as a rather incongruous pair. How did a hardworking woman in such an inelegant spot come to send her daughter to a finishing school for young ladies? Somehow neither of them seemed to fit my preconceived ideas of the people I would find in a mining camp.

After supper Bonta introduced us to Barney Glendon, who had just finished eating at the next table. He was a dark-haired, squarely built young fellow, one of a group of miners rather recently come to the coalfields from other jobs. His jaunty air and lack of self-consciousness were very appealing. Bonta told us that Barney was originally from Pikeville, Kentucky, and had started out near there as a miner but left to work in Detroit at Ford. If it was the city that turned him off, he had certainly found the perfect antithesis here in Coal Mountain. Being single, he lived at the boardinghouse, though he was keeping company with a young woman who worked in the store. His job at the coal-washing shed required more than average skill, and he throve on the responsibility.

When he invited us for a ride up to the portal of the mine, we gladly accepted, since Mrs. Jennings offered to keep an ear cocked for Susan, once we got her safely into bed. Barney drove us in his car, which must have been at least ten years old. I was relieved it wasn't ours, since it threatened to pitch over the edge of the narrow twisting road at every turn. Barbara and I exchanged horrified glances, and our stifled gasps induced our host to become even more expansive than before. He clearly relished showing a couple of greenhorns how matter-of-factly he took the hazards of life in Coal Mountain.

"Shucks! You ought to come up here when it's slick after a rain. This ain't nothing. Oh yes," he added with studied casualness, "right here we come across a big rattler last evening. Forty-three inches he were and madder than a mess of hornets when we picked him up!"

I quickly discovered that this mine was reached by going up the mountain—a new idea to me—since the coal was to be found in two horizontal strata at quite an elevation. The one seam was about five to six feet thick, the other only about forty inches, so there were really two distinct mines. Barney took considerable pride in explaining that the latter seam was so high-grade that it was used almost entirely for coal-tar derivatives. Coal from the thicker seam had to be washed before it could be sorted at the tipple and loaded into the waiting coal cars. To prove to Barbara that this was truly soft coal, he dared her to lift a big chunk from the exposed surface of the vein. She expected a struggle and nearly fell backward when she pulled it away effortlessly.

Bonta and Barney discussed the current three-day workweek and the vote due the next day on whether the men should quit altogether.

Barney gave an appreciative chuckle as he commented, "Hey, Doc, you better figure on a lot of deliveries in about nine months if they do!"

Noticing my inquiring look at the chalked message on the large slate bulletin board at the mouth of the mine, Barney explained that this meant the safety check for that shift had been made by the foreman and all was well inside. "This here is not a gassy mine anyway, not much danger of any explosions or anything, but sometimes it gets pretty damp along the main haulage, and wet spots like that weaken them big timbers. They prop up the mountain while the coal is being dug out, and then when the seam from one part is all cleaned out, the men come back out, blasting them timbers as they go, so the whole darned mountain settles down that much shorter than it was before. Kind of tricky business."

Barbara asked him how high the tunnels were, and Barney said this depended on which of the two mines you were talking about. "You can always stand up in the main haulage, but off to the sides and in the rooms in this one you can't do no more than kneel up—this seam's pretty thin. Sure does cramp you up a bit before the shift's over. Now in the other mine the rooms on the sides are big enough so you can stand up in them OK."

To Barbara's hopeful suggestion that maybe she could go through the mine before she had to leave, Barney shook his head. "Shucks, no, ma'am! That'd be just plumb bad luck, letting a woman in the mine. The men wouldn't hear to none of that, no more than the navy'd let you come aboard a battle wagon. Sorry, ma'am, but I can't fix that up any different." He turned to Bonta. "Doc here now, that'd be OK, and I'd be proud to show you round one of these days when things get back on regular schedule."

That was disappointing. It seemed a shame to live in a mining camp and never have a chance to explore the most important thing there.

Back at the clubhouse we found nobody had missed us, but just as we were about to turn out the light and let Bonta catch up on some of the sleep he had missed, what with the delivery and the trip to get us the night before, along came an unwelcome knock. A sick youngster needed attention; luckily he lived nearby in the white camp.

After Bonta left, I crept out onto the porch by our room to see what the night was like. It was darker than any I could ever remember: no moon, no street lights, and only an infrequent lighted window in the camp. The community retired early. But just across the road and Cub Creek ran the railroad track, carved into the steep face of the mountain. At intervals a coal car creaked and groaned, easing its way from the tipple down the carefully planned grade till it lurched into the car already in position ahead of it. Running alongside the cars or walking on them were the men of the Hoot Owl shift, coupling them securely when they slammed together and standing ready to operate the brakes if need be. The shafts of light from their miners' caps wove vivid geometric patterns in the blackness. The only other sounds were those of crickets and katydids adding their friendly chirping to the warm summer night.

3. First Impressions

On Monday morning, as soon as Bonta left for the office Barbara and I set about organizing our new living quarters. While Susan amused herself by dragging her kitty blanket up and down the hallway, Barbara and I rushed around. Our morale rose as we unpacked and brought order out of confusion. Then, while I wrote a quick note to our parents, she settled Susan for her morning nap and checked with Mrs. Jennings to make sure it would still be all right for us to leave for a little while.

In high spirits we left for the office. The small waiting room with its two benches was occupied by two barefoot youngsters, one with sores oozing pus on one leg, a pale woman in a faded cotton dress nursing her baby, and one stooped old man staring at the floor. It was still littered with candy wrappers from the Saturday before, and the cans Bonta had put out for wastepaper stood neglected in the corner. As we walked in the door, the waiting group suddenly came to attention; their air of indifference vanished as four heads turned to stare at us. Did we pass inspection? Were we too cheerful looking? Did we acknowledge them adequately? Were we guilty of too much familiarity as we smiled a bit uncertainly at them? Did their lack of response mean that they simply withheld any opinion or that they resented our walking in ahead of them, or were they just too reserved to show any friendliness? Perhaps we were not dressed just right. A dozen doubts assailed us as we walked the short distance to the door that led into the consultation room.

This was a small area scarcely deserving such a term. It was large enough for Bonta's desk and the chair in which he was sitting, plus a straight-backed kitchen chair at one side for his patient and a small table for minor supplies. On this stood two eight-ounce mayonnaise jars full of alcohol. Thermometers were stuck through holes in their covers for sterilization. A box of facial tissues, a jam jar full of cotton balls, and a tin can full of tongue depressors completed the array. Behind the desk hung a clipboard, which proved to be Bonta's OB calendar. Here he kept track of who was due when and other bits of information, such as whether a prenatal serology had been sent to the health department,* whether this was a first pregnancy, or what number along the way. As for the desk itself, it might have seen long service in a one-room schoolhouse; it was thoroughly utilitarian and much marred. I made a mental note to be careful of my nylons around it. To Bonta's left a door led into a small examining room next to the little lab; to his right was the main treatment room.

Bonta was talking in a friendly fashion with a rather thin little girl who was sitting beside his desk. I judged her to be about eleven. Just behind her stood a big broad-shouldered fellow, who seemed slightly ill at ease. His occasional glances toward the girl suggested some emotional involvement, but what their relationship might be I could only guess.

Bonta was speaking reassuringly to the girl. "Now Pearlie, it wasn't too bad, was it? I told you it would only hurt a minute. After all, you've got to act like a big girl now, haven't you?" Bonta's bantering tone frequently won cooperation when a more formal approach might have failed. I was impressed by the friendly interest he was showing in Pearlie, since I recalled the impersonality of the mass inspections he'd described at Great Lakes.

It was a moment or two before he looked up at Barbara and me. Short as it was, this interval struck me like a written notification that here in his office he took his own good time to pay any attention to me, that this was his domain, his patient, and his business, and all this assumed priority over our personal relationship. I felt rebuffed, and

*The West Virginia State Health Department, like those of other states, provided selected laboratory services to physicians free of charge.

the enthusiasm that had begun to ebb under the blank appraisal in the waiting room drained rapidly to a thin trickle.

"Well, greetings and welcome to the office," Bonta said. Turning to the young pair, he explained, "Pearlie and Benjie, this is my wife and my sister-in-law, Miss Brush." Barbara and I smiled and nodded. Pearlie and Benjie stared. Bonta looked at us. "Say, anybody waiting outside to see me?"

When we nodded affirmatively, he continued, "Well, Helen, while I go ahead and see them, why don't you take Benjie and Pearlie into the lab through that door and fill out these slips for me. I'll probably find a job for you in a minute, Barbara, if you'll just hang around."

As I sat down on the stool by the long counter in the lab, I tried to give the impression that this was all old stuff to me, but I was sure they weren't fooled. As I poised the pencil over the blue slips Bonta had handed me, I realized that they were forms to be sent to the state health lab with premarital blood specimens. Light dawned. Coming to one of the blank spaces, I asked Benjie their ages. "I'm eighteen and Pearlie here's thirteen." I concealed my astonishment as best as I could, filled out the slips, and sent them on their way.

I emerged from the lab slightly jarred by this experience and found Barbara in the main examining room filling an ointment tin with salve for the sores on the legs of the little girl we'd noticed in the waiting room.

Bonta tried to give us things to do, but since we didn't know where anything was to be found, or how to do even the simplest task like boiling the syringes without his showing us, we merely succeeded in slowing him down. Far from feeling useful as I had hoped, I felt not only superfluous but in the way; all his routines were an old story to him and an enigma to me. Why hadn't I somehow managed to get down there long before to help him set things up so I'd know what was going on, too! I found myself looking anxiously for the escape that lunch hour and the end of Susan's nap would provide. At least Susan still needed me.

Toward the end of the morning, Bonta became so busy that he couldn't even take time off for lunch. Barbara and I had a chance to talk things over privately and decided that it was imperative for me to take on all the office work I could so I'd be able to fit in effectively as quickly as possible. She offered to take care of Susan, and I appreciated her willingness to assume this less glamorous role.

After lunch I spent the rather quiet afternoon office hours looking over drug catalogs. No drug company representatives anxious to sell their products ever found their way to this isolated spot. The catalogs were Bonta's only source of medical supplies unless he drove the sixty miles to Williamson, and even there choices were extremely limited. Bonta told me he had a long list of things he needed urgently, since some supplies were low. The whole business of ordering took time he didn't have, so he was anxious that I assume this responsibility. Under his arrangements with the coal company and the union he had to buy all the drugs he needed and supply most of them to his patients free of charge. The exceptions were those that had to be given by hypodermic, and for these he charged the rate customary in the coalfields. This overhead expense came out of his income—$3.00 per month per miner—so he had found it worthwhile to take advantage of special offers whenever he could. I could hardly believe it when he instructed me to buy two gallons of cough syrup and 10,000 5 grain aspirin tablets, with other items in comparable quantities.

As I looked over the pile of folders, I thanked heaven for my background in biology. At least it helped a bit in the morass of unfamiliar terminology. I soon discovered that there were nearly as many names for some compounds as there were drug houses making them, and it seemed that almost every drug was available in pills of different strengths and colors. Then I found it necessary to evaluate the various financial inducements from each concern; maybe it was their general low price or their quantity discounts or their low price on particular drugs. How would I ever get this all unsnarled so I could get the order out properly and in a hurry?

Barbara came over later in the afternoon with Susan. When Bonta heard us talking in the lab, he came in, too. "Things are kind of quiet here at the moment. Why don't the three of you go on a little tour and pick up the mail at the post office? The truck usually brings it in about midafternoon, unless the weather's bad. Mrs. Morrell—she's the postmistress—usually has it sorted by now." He added facetiously, "Now don't get lost! Just follow the crowd."

We went out the rear door of the office through the deep grass and weeds in back and past the rusting metal barrel that was apparently the office incinerator. As we came out into the roadway, our feet kicked up little puffs of dust. Again we were conscious of curious stares from the others waiting for the mail. We found the post office was just a sort of covered passageway; you went in one end, passed the window where you received your mail from the postmistress, and then left by the far door. As we stepped up to the window to explain who we were and to ask for the doctor's mail, Mrs. Morrell slid the right packet under the grille to us before we could open our mouths. Well, it would be difficult for a newcomer to be inconspicuous. The day's accumulation consisted chiefly of ads from drug and supply houses, most of them still addressed to Bonta's predecessor. At least these meant more to me than they would have earlier in the day; I only dreaded finding something from a new company to add to my confusion.

We stood by the bottom step still looking over the collection when a green Ford whizzed down the road from the tipple and pulled to a jarring halt just a few feet from us. Out jumped a miner with his face and clothing black from work. The whites of his eyes were a startling contrast to the rest of his face. He was wearing his miner's cap, and the lamp that looked out from the center of it still shone, though its light was only a sickly gleam in the afternoon sunshine. A cord ran from the cap to the batteries on his hip, and as he raced toward the building opposite, he started taking off both the cap and batteries. Over one arm swung a tall, cylindrical dinner pail. We surely would have suspected some emergency as the reason for all the haste—perhaps an accident in the mine?—except that immediately behind this first car came a second and then a third. Cars and trucks of all descriptions streamed down from the mine, each raising its own cloud of dust, until the whole place became a bedlam of tooting cars, pedestrians scattering for cover, and miners shouting good-natured remarks as they raced toward this one building, rapidly forming a long line in front of it. Barbara nudged me. "Looks like the front row in a minstrel show, doesn't it?"

"Sure does," I answered, patting Susan's head reassuringly, for she had wrapped herself around my legs in alarm at the sudden confusion. "Well, at least we know now what they mean when they say the day shift is out. Wow! Glad we were over here sort of off to one side when it began happening! No doubt now which building is the lamphouse."

As the men emerged wearing hats now divested of their lamps, they joined the stream heading from the post office to the store, so we decided to follow the throng. Inside there was already a line at the checkout counter near the door, apparently because so many were signing slips rather than paying cash. The cashier was a cheerful young woman probably in her early twenties; she had short dark hair and strong features, with rather high cheekbones. We noticed that she was familiar with all her customers, kidding some, exchanging a personal word with each one. The store was filled with the noise of many conversations, the local substitute for a daily paper.

To avoid getting coal dust on our clothes, we edged our way around a group of men who hadn't showered and changed clothing since coming down from the mine. Others had obviously just finished cleaning up at the lamphouse, with faces shiny from scrubbing. Even they retained a line of black that clung like mascara outlining their eyes. Most of the men wore hard black hats, but I noticed a few with the same rounded shape and narrow beak in front, only white. Bonta explained later that those with white hats were foremen.

We found ourselves in the middle of a still bigger crowd around the candy and soda pop counter, heavily infiltrated with small fry. One mother had set her baby on the counter and was deep in conversation with the woman next to her, while the baby, about nine months old, sucked contentedly on a bottle of orange pop fitted with a nipple.

The grocery section included a small meat counter, shelves of canned goods, some fresh vegetables and fruits—most of the essentials but small quantities of each. To the left were several racks of clothing, a table loaded with fabrics, a notions counter, and even a small shoe department. The price tags on some children's socks caught my eye; the figure was several cents above what I usually paid for Susan's socks. A check of several other items confirmed my impression that things were pretty expensive, but then I remembered the problems involved in getting them all here—also the fact that the company had a monopoly in the camp.

We worked our way through the crowd toward the back of the store. Here were the hardware and home furnishings sections, where one could pick up anything from a nail to an electric stove. As long as

A group of miners at the company store, where everything from food to building supplies could be purchased on credit.

we were there, we took a look at the rolls of linoleum leaning against one wall. We hadn't yet been in our house and didn't know a thing about it except that Bonta had said the kitchen floor would have to have new linoleum. This corner was a bit more peaceful than the front part of the store, and as we were comparing ideas about the color and amount we might need, we were startled when the young clerk sidled up to us and chimed in with, "Well now, this here piece ought to be about the right size. Your kitchen is probably ten by eleven like everybody else's, and this color'd go pretty good with most anything you'd want." He seemed to know more about "our house" than we did.

After dinner Bonta suggested that I go along with him to check on Mrs. Toler and the new baby, whose arrival had kept him from meeting our plane. This was especially exciting because I'd discovered I'd be meeting my namesake. He told me that when he asked for the baby's name on the birth certificate Mrs. Toler said she'd already decided it should be Helen. All evening she'd been told, "Let's get on with it, Helen's waiting!" And she guessed if the doctor thought Helen was so great, it would be a good thing to name the baby after her. So Helen Toler it was. Imagine having a baby named after you when you and the family had never even met!

The Tolers lived about a mile down the road from the camp in a weathered cabin. The wood was dark, and one corner of the house sagged a little; cracks between the vertical boards must have provided considerable ventilation. The roof was covered with four or five rows of long, narrow wooden shingles. The bottom row projected over the doorstep and gave the appearance of having been permanently ruffled by the last windstorm. The bare earth had been beaten into a hard, brown area in front of the two wooden steps that led up to the front door. Along one wall stakes supported a row of tall plants. Whether these were fruitful or ornamental I couldn't tell. Around the corner of the house was a small vegetable garden; a few rows of corn were tassled out, and some cabbages were heading up. Nearby was a well covered by a rough rectangular shelter that supported a wooden windlass. A frail old woman was just hauling a battered scrub pail above the rim of the well. She looked up as our car stopped. Leaving the pail resting on the frame, she laboriously made her way toward us.

We left Susan in the car—we'd taken her with us so Barbara could write a letter at the boardinghouse in peace—and crossed Cub Creek on the single plank laid across rocks; it bent under our weight till it was just awash. As we neared the house I was astonished to see chickens climbing in the shrubbery, then scattering noisily before us. We reached the front of the house just about the same time the woman did. She was thin and stooped; her gray hair was drawn straight back to a knot; her dress was dark and plain, and she had a light gray shawl drawn around her shoulders. Something about her expression was very strange. A closer look revealed that she had only one eye; the other lid closed over the sunken socket. This was the matriarch of the Davis clan. She had seven sons and one daughter, Bonta's patient; all of her children still lived up and down Cub Creek, and many had grown children of their own. How many grandchildren and even great-grandchildren must she have (especially if many of them married at Pearlie's age)? She stayed with her various children, but Bonta had concluded that she preferred the Toler household for its plain living. He had already been called a number of times to see her because of her heart condition, but she refused to give in to increasing frailty.

As we met, Bonta chided her gently, "Now, Sarah, I told you to take it easy and let the kids draw the water! Whatever am I going to do with you?"

She laughed on a high-pitched cackling note, "Well, Doc, just got to keep going. With Marthy down, there's so much to do."

Bonta introduced me, and she led us inside. Her daughter lay in a double bed in the main room of the cabin under a worn coverlet, fondling her new little girl. She was a quiet, gentle-looking woman and seemed to appreciate Bonta's help during her delivery. Old Sarah added with emphasis, "Why Doc here, he does the best doctoring we ever had around here."

They proudly showed me the baby, who looked more like a pink china doll than flesh and blood. I'd forgotten how tiny newborn babies are. She had more hair already than Susan had managed to grow, and she wrapped her little fingers ever so tightly around my big one.

I was enchanted by the two little girls, Lulu Ann and Opal, who sat on one of the three double beds in the room, staring soberly at me with big brown eyes. They were so well behaved and so pretty with their fair wavy hair and the fresh complexions all healthy children share.

Except for their soiled dresses, they looked as though they had just stepped out of a lovely daguerreotype. Every now and then when our eyes met they gave me a shy smile.

Bonta sat down on the straight chair beside Mrs. Toler's bed to examine her. As he and the two women chatted a bit, my eyes wandered discreetly around the cabin. The paper on the ceiling was torn and hung down in several places; the whole room was dingy, and I noticed some broken crackers and watermelon seeds on the floor. Flies were so thick I kept flicking them off my hand as unobtrusively as possible. The walls were decorated with several pictures cut from magazines: one of a farmyard full of cows and chickens, one of mountains and a waterfall, and another of a mother surrounded by her small children. Over the door hung a miner's cap and a rifle. Through one door the cluttered kitchen was visible, with a table piled high with clean laundry. In all, three rooms housed the whole family—five children including the new baby, plus the parents and the grandmother.

Both women seemed oblivious of the flies, the crowding, and the lack of comforts I took for granted. I wondered about the source of their serenity; perhaps it was their innate sense of dignity or a spirit of fatalism. Whatever it was, they provided a lesson in accepting reality and making the best of it.

As we turned to leave, Mrs. Toler spoke up in her drawling way, "Doctor, you sure got yourself a pretty woman!" No compliment had ever pleased me more. I was glad she didn't seem to regret naming the baby after me and determined to give her no cause to change her mind.

Bonta suggested that we stop briefly at the Ramseys' house on our way back, so I could meet the superintendent and his wife. I looked forward to this because Bonta held Mr. Ramsey in such high regard, and I was grateful to him in advance for having kept Bonta's spirits up during some of the rough adjustments.

The Ramseys lived in one of the standard white houses. The entrance was flanked by two clumps of small orchid chrysanthemums, and as we went up the front steps, we heard someone playing "Rock of Ages" on a piano. Mr. Ramsey answered our knock. He was a solidly built man with a ruddy complexion, a bit shorter than Bonta; his gray hair was thinning above his temples, and I judged him to be in his mid-fifties. He wore working clothes, khaki pants, and heavy shoes; his short-sleeved white shirt was open at the neck. He called to his wife, "Alma, come see who's here—the doctor and his wife and baby!"

The piano playing stopped in the middle of a chord, and Mrs. Ramsey appeared. Her figure threatened to overflow her low-cut white peasant blouse. Once blonde, her short wavy hair was now irregularly darkened and brushed back casually. Bonta had told me she'd grown up in a small mining town in Kentucky. Camp gossip was that this was her first, but rather late, marriage; it was Mr. Ramsey's second. Supposedly he had a grown son somewhere, and it was whispered that this young man had once been in some kind of trouble.

As she invited us inside, a welcoming smile lit up her broad face. The men lingered on the porch to chat. Mr. Ramsey leaned against the post at the top of the steps and now and then spat a squirt of tobacco juice over the railing.

While the house was a vast improvement over the one we had just visited, it was still not what I had expected as the home of the superintendent of the whole camp. It was similar to the one we expected to have, only slightly larger. The furnishings reflected an unsophisticated taste. The heavy overstuffed chairs and davenport were slipcovered in a bright print of pink and white peonies, carefully protected by transparent plastic covers. I decided Mrs. Ramsey must be a very meticulous housekeeper; everything was spotless and in its proper place. Lacy net curtains were flanked by draperies in a dark green and brown plaid. Against the far wall stood the upright piano on which Mrs. Ramsey had been playing; a couple of hymn books lay open on its rack. Crepe paper flowers and several small china dogs graced the piano; other inexpensive knickknacks cluttered the window sills and the table next to the davenport. A coal stove with a conspicuous black pipe stood against another wall.

The one feature that really set this house apart from all others in the community was the perfectly ordinary black telephone that rested on a stand near the front door. This was the extension of the one in the company office, from which Bonta had called me that night. I looked at it with the respect due the only phone in camp.

Mrs. Ramsey took charge. "You just come along into the kitchen while I take these molasses cookies out of the oven. They smell like they're done. And you can pour us some coke. Here's the glasses, and there's the bottle opener."

As I did her bidding, I looked around the kitchen. Her stove was an impressive modern model with more push buttons than I could count. I was startled by the contrast between the range and the primitive water heater. The tank was heated by a little black potbellied coal stove sporting a lid lifter with a coiled wire handle. I hadn't seen one of those since I was a youngster visiting my grandmother. Mrs. Ramsey fixed a plate of cookies, and we all went back to the front room to visit a while, Susan happily clutching a cookie in each hand. The men were already settled there.

Mr. Ramsey asked, "Well, what do you think of Coal Mountain so far? I wouldn't be surprised if it takes a little while getting used to things."

I was grateful that he realized this was all pretty strange to me.

"I hope you'll like it. Dr. Nichols's wife had kind of a hard time at first, I remember, but things worked out by and by. Doc tells me you may be going to help in the office some."

"I'd like to, if only we can find somebody to take care of the baby. Bonta and I like to work together."

"Might be a mighty good idea." Mr. Ramsey nodded thoughtfully. "You'd get to know folks sooner that way. And folks might even like having the doctor's wife in the office better than somebody they know. Might figure it was a little more privatelike."

That did make sense, and I was pleased to think I might contribute something special to Bonta's practice.

As we visited over cookies and cokes, Mrs. Ramsey had a comment to make about every name that came up, some friendly, some critical. When Bonta mentioned the possibility of having Eloise help in the office on a regular basis, Mrs. Ramsey said, "She's a bright girl, and if she's anything like her sister Eva—she's the cashier at the store—she'd work real hard. I'm sure glad she quit going with that Jake Harper. He's just too wild. The way he'd drive up and down this road was something to behold. It's a miracle he ain't smashed up that car his father give him—or killed somebody. Guess she only went out with him a couple times, when you come down to it; she's got a fair bit of sense. Besides, Joe—that's her father—he's mighty strict with those girls of his."

When Bonta and Mr. Ramsey started talking politics, Mrs. Ramsey bowed herself out with the remark, "That's where I quit—never could keep track of all them arguments the way John does. Seems to me it don't make much difference whether I do or not. They keep right on scrapping, so I just don't worry about it."

Luck was with us that night, for not a single person knocked on our door. I quickly learned what Bonta meant when he wrote about dreaming that people were looking for him. I started hearing imaginary footsteps myself.

Barbara and I spent most of the next morning at the office, scrubbing shelves and windowsills and taking the worst of the dirt off the walls and doorjambs. Thank goodness Mrs. Jennings offered to check on Susan now and then while she napped at the clubhouse. At least we felt useful, and the improvements pleased Bonta. He had tried to tidy things up, but it was almost hopeless. Ads had accumulated in piles that overran the desk and shelves in the lab. Behind the waiting room benches were little drifts of sand from boots and bare feet.

Bonta interrupted our housecleaning once to ask me to help a patient, a Mrs. Bill James, onto the examining table so he could check her abdomen; she'd recently had a miscarriage.

She was a relatively young woman, but she looked worn out, thin and pale, with stringy light brown hair hanging to her shoulders and a dress so loose I figured it must have been her maternity outfit. She was the least self-conscious person I'd encountered in the office so far and chatted matter-of-factly about her children.

"Lost this baby and things ain't been easy lately. I been having to live with the in-laws, and you know how hard that can be, specially with five young ones, and the oldest only seven. Makes it kind of crowded." She brightened as she added, "Sure would like to see the doctor's young one."

As we compared notes on toddlers, I was grateful for her easy acceptance of me, because I still felt awkward in my new role as office assistant as well as doctor's wife. Between us, we bared her abdomen and draped a sheet over her, then called Bonta.

I jotted notes on her record as he dictated them. Her belly was all soft and wobbly, just about like yeast dough ready for kneading, and all covered by white stretch marks. I made a mental note that if having five children automatically did that I would settle for fewer. I knew I shouldn't feel that way, especially when I wanted so badly to be helpful. I just had a long way to go before I could deal comfortably with strangers' bodies. And any injury, even a little cut, made my stomach twist into knots—it still does. But I was resolved to become an effective assistant.

After supper Barbara and I decided that it would be only fair if she went on the first delivery that came along, since she would be here for so short a time, and she did want to be involved as much as possible. After all, I would have chances later. Our conversation was interrupted by a loud knocking on the door. I opened it to find a tall blonde man standing there.

"Where's the doc?" He peered behind me. "The wife's bleeding right smart. Sadie Hatfield's taking care of her, but I guess things ain't going just right, cause she sent me to fetch the doc. So I've come to get him."

I recognized Sadie Hatfield's name as one of the two midwives who were kept busy in the outlying areas, especially down Long Branch way. In spite of this worrisome report, the man continued to wear a disconcertingly vacuous grin. We sent him to find Bonta, who had sneaked off to see if the owner of the gas station would cut his hair; barbering was his spare time business. Barbara eagerly took out the bobbie pins she'd just put in her hair so that she'd be ready to go. Bonta drove up shortly and told us it was probably much too late already if the midwife was in trouble with a breech. But he and Barbara set out to see if anything could be done.

I had no sooner settled down to write a letter than a frantic knock made me jump. A distraught father stood there with a little boy about two years old in his arms. The child was wailing loudly. I started to ask what the trouble was when part of the answer became all too apparent; the youngster started to vomit all over the floor, the door, the wall, and my white robe! The father appeared not to notice what was happening. He was obviously terribly upset about the boy, so I told him I wished I could help, but the doctor was out on a delivery about eighteen miles down the road and I couldn't do a thing myself. Without a word in reply, nor any acknowledgment from either of us about the child's vomiting, the man abruptly turned on his heel and disappeared.

It occurred to me that I ought to know Bonta's whereabouts for my own good.

I spent the next half hour trying to repair the damage and fuming to myself. It was bad enough to have to clean up after Susan once in a while, but to have to do this for a strange child who might have heaven knew what disease, and for such a thoroughly inconsiderate man, was almost more than I could bear!

Since I had nothing to clean up with, I hunted in the clubhouse kitchen for rags, trying not to disturb Mrs. Jennings. I happened to intrude on an intimate moment that Vonnie was sharing with her current passion, a young chap named Mark who worked in the general store. I was more flustered than they were and backed out of the scene with a stammered apology. I finally found a rag in the broom closet, muttering to myself that they'd better enjoy their romantic notions now because these could lead to babies and some very unromantic moments.

Not long after, the father returned, even more worried than before, begging to know whose baby the doctor was delivering so that he could go see him there. The little guy was worse. I really felt sorry for them both, but since I'd neglected to get the name of the OB patient in the rush of seeing Bonta and Barbara off, I couldn't even help him with that.

I decided this was one oversight I should never permit myself again, as much for my own sake as for an emergency like this one. I could just imagine how I'd feel if it were Susan who was so sick and I couldn't reach Bonta. Being married to a doctor had spoiled me, for I'd let him do all the worrying about the health of the family if any needed to be done; the trouble with this arrangement was that without him I was worse than helpless. I did find out this man's name and promised I would tell the doctor about his problem the minute he came in.

I didn't exactly lose myself in sleep that night. I kept listening for the car, and if I drifted off, the least sound would bring me back with a jolt, and I'd start listening all over again. It seemed as though hours must have passed when I finally heard the car doors slam. As they came in, Barbara's sober expression told me things had not gone well.

Bonta set his bag on the floor by the door and said, "Well, it was just as I figured—the baby was dead when we got there. Must have died even before Jimmy got here to call me. Those midwives simply don't know how to cope with a breech. She wasn't dilated enough when Sadie had to jump in and try to rush things with a shot of quinine. So the body was delivered, but the head couldn't make it. The poor thing strangled." He shook his head at the recollection.

"It took her quite a while to finish the job, baby dead or not," Barbara added, still recovering from the shock of seeing her first birth, and one with such a tragic outcome. "Poor woman, going through all that for nothing but to get unpregnant!" She shuddered, thinking about the woman's pain and grief. As an afterthought she said, "At least it wasn't her first."

"Yes, things certainly can get rough sometimes." Bonta's tone, though sympathetic, was philosophical. It wasn't the first time he'd bumped into a situation beyond help. Thinking of Sadie's efforts, he mused, "And a little knowledge can really be a dangerous thing." He started to unbutton his shirt when he thought better of it. "Anything happen here while we were away?"

"Oh good heavens yes! You're not through yet tonight. I almost forgot. You have a call to make on a sick little boy up in the green camp. His father is frantic, and I guess I can see why. His name is Mark Hatfield, and he says he lives next to the Denlows. He says you've been there, so you should be able to find his place. But oh boy, you should have seen the horrrible mess I had to clean up after this little boy threw up all over the place. And do you suppose Mr. Hatfield offered to help? He didn't even notice! I wouldn't have let him help if he had offered, with a sick youngster on his hands, but he just might have said he was sorry—or have acted just a little embarrassed about it or something—but he didn't even seem to see."

Bonta looked sharply at me, and a frown flickered over his face. I could see this report riled him a bit, and suddenly I wished I had never said a word about it. Just suppose he said something to Mark Hatfield. I didn't want to be responsible for getting someone down on him. And now that the affair was over and done and I'd had the satisfaction of unburdening myself to someone else about it, it seemed very trivial and very understandable. I was ashamed of myself.

When Bonta reached the Hatfields' house, he found the little boy sleeping peacefully. Apparently it was one of those children's upsets that go almost as fast as they come.

☙ Next morning, while Bonta and Barbara slept late, I took Susan with me to the office. Since nobody was waiting, I looked over drug catalogs some more, while she played with the white stool in the treatment room till she accidentally twisted the top off. This scared her half to death but did no other harm, and we decided to wander back and see if "Da" and "Bi" were awake yet. They were already enjoying the coffee Mrs. Jennings had offered. The aroma persuaded me to share a cup, too.

Since things were quiet, Bonta suggested that we all take a few minutes and look over our house-to-be. Mr. Ramsey had given him a key at the company office the day before when he went to turn in the extra charge slips for that pay period. When a patient required some service for which Bonta's contract specified an extra charge, he wrote out a slip for the patient to sign, authorizing the company to deduct the charge from his next paycheck. He had the same arrangement with the lumber company for its employees.

We discovered that it had rained briefly while we lingered over coffee and were greeted by the evocative smell of fresh rain on dry earth. The powdery dust of the road that went up the hollow had been pockmarked by the raindrops. The pattern of tiny volcanic craters was marred by two sets of prints, where four bare feet had flattened them on their way down the road. It seemed a shame to spoil the effect with our own prosaic shoes.

We opened the back gate to the small yard; one of the hinges was loose and the gate swung in at a drunken angle. I peered into the partly open door of the coal shed as we went by. It was more than half full of the oddest assortment of coal lumps. Some of them were as big as a football, but a lot of the coal looked like nothing much more than shiny black sand. The coal house was right on the fence between our house and the next one up the hollow and was really double, with a partition down the middle to separate our coal from theirs. It was only a few steps to the back porch, on which stood an imposing water heater. None of the houses farther up the road was blessed with such a convenience. Bonta answered my comment about this.

"Well, that's a big concession to the camp doctor from Mr. Ramsey. All the rest of the camp uses tanks heated by a coal stove in the kitchen."

"Yes, even Mrs. Ramsey herself," I thought to myself, with a special feeling of gratitude to Mr. Ramsey.

"Too bad we can't move in till they fix the kitchen floor. And you know how long that can take," Bonta said as he unlocked the back door. It opened into the medium-sized kitchen, empty but for the sink with its white wooden cupboard base. As Bonta had said, it surely did need new linoleum. Mentally placing a refrigerator, stove, and dinette set in it, I decided it would be a tight squeeze to get a washing machine in too, but it would all have to fit somehow. Beyond the kitchen were the living room, two small but adequate bedrooms, and a little bathroom. Regretfully I noticed there was no shower over the tub, but then I remembered we were lucky to have a bathroom at all. This was all of it: no basement, no attic, not even any closets. While it was still summer—so it didn't matter—it was clear there was no provision for heating the house.

"We'll have to buy a coal stove for the living room, but I guess there's not too much hurry about it. Can't do everything at once," Bonta reflected.

The thought of a dirty old coal stove in the middle of the living room appalled me.

"Don't worry. They aren't all made of black cast iron any more. Of course, we'll have a time teaching Susan to leave it and the coal scuttle alone, and I'll have to get used to taking ashes out." Suddenly he burst out laughing. "Say, aren't you sorry we didn't get those two red quilted satin fireside chairs we looked at so long at King's Furniture before we left the Lakes? I think they'd look charming drawn up on either side of our coal stove!"

I laughed, too, remembering how those exquisite chairs had somehow symbolized the nice home we hoped to have some day. And we had thought then that maybe Coal Mountain would be the place where we could start. "Oh my, how I did want them. And that lipstick red was such a beautiful color!"

Bonta missed dinner for two house calls. He seemed very matter-of-fact about these interruptions. It was only when they interfered with his sleep that they appeared to bother him. Otherwise one might imagine he had just been waiting for the call for help. Those that came at dinnertime made me more anxious than ever to get into our own house where I could feed him whenever he came home. It was too much to be asking Mrs. Jennings for meals at odd hours; in fact, this time he settled for a piece of pie and a glass of milk when he returned late in the evening.

4. As a Stranger

It was about 2:00 A.M. on Thursday, August 11, when a commotion at the door woke us up with a start. Someone was trying to get in, banging on the door and rattling the doorknob back and forth. Thank heaven Bonta always took the precaution of locking the door. It was a young man, with the greeting that was becoming all too familiar, "Hey, Doc, my wife needs you. She's down all right."

I snuggled out of sight under the sheet listening.

"How long has she been having pains? How far apart are they?" Bonta asked.

"Well, Doc, it's her first, and she's bleeding right smart. You just follow me, 'cause we live a far piece, down to Bailey Corners beyond Long Branch." His boyish face and slight build made him seem much too young to be a father. He was clearly worried.

"But I need to know a little more. Do you work for Red Jacket?"

The fellow shook his head but hastened to add, "But my Pa does."

"I see. Well, have I seen your wife in the office? And what's your name, by the way?"

"My name's Ernest Cline, and no, you ain't."

"OK, Ernest, now what do you mean, 'she's bleeding right smart'? How much is 'right smart'?"

"Oh, she's bleeding right smart, all right, and you just got to come." His impatience was obvious.

Bonta gave up trying and asked him to wait outside, promising to be out as soon as he could dress. He told him he would be bringing along a girl who helped him on deliveries and asked me to wake Barbara and tell her they were off.

At least this time as I watched them drive off, I knew they were heading for Ernest Cline's house at Bailey Corners beyond Long Branch, but where that really was or when they would be back I had not the faintest idea. Neither did they. I only wished I could be the one to go along this time instead of Barbara.

I thought they'd surely be back by breakfast time, but there was no sign of them. I spent a rather aimless morning expecting them momentarily. Shortly after the office should have opened, I went over to let several people waiting on the step know that the doctor was out on a call. As I posted a little sign on the door for the benefit of any who might come later and were able to read it, I was surprised when one of the men thanked me for the information as he turned away. My limited experience had been that most people seemed to accept whatever came along, good or bad, without much comment.

They still hadn't returned by six o'clock, and I began to conjure up dreadful things that might have happened—a moment's inattention as they rounded one of those unguarded curves—they were all unguarded—where the road narrowed and the mountain fell away sheer to the river below. Or maybe Bonta had had some trouble with the family, though I didn't see how that could be; still that young man hadn't sounded altogether reasonable in the middle of the night. Maybe in the clouds of dust that every car stirred up he had crashed into an oncoming car while trying to pass. I probably would have had word of a collision because someone would have been driving along and seen the car, but a car could drop over the edge and just disappear without anyone's ever being the wiser. And no matter what trouble there might be, there was no telephone anywhere to send word of it. Perhaps the worst thing of all was having no one to talk to. Suddenly I understood Bonta's feelings of abandonment those weeks when he was all alone.

Mrs. Jennings was friendly enough, but I didn't want to let her know how worried I was; I was the doctor's wife and had to act grown up and sensible. Susan was some small comfort but no help. I wished I had a car; then I'd go to Bailey Corners myself, wherever it was, and find the Cline house and see what was keeping them so long. After all, how long did it take to have a baby? I knew it could drag on, of course, but apparently she had been well on her way when they left, and more than sixteen hours had gone by. Besides, I couldn't help being envious of Barbara's chance to be in on this prolonged affair, however it was going. Here I'd been back with Bonta for less than a week, and now someone else was filling the role I longed to fill. It really didn't seem fair.

Seven o'clock came and still no word. Not many more hours before it would be dark. I thought of the cliffs and the curves again. I began to feel panicky. Suddenly I had an inspiration. I could go talk to the Ramseys. Bonta had gone to Mr. Ramsey when he was concerned about things, and I would too.

When I had told him my story, Mr. Ramsey smiled in a fatherly way and said, "Well, I'm sure there's nothing to worry about really. She's probably just taking her own good time about having that baby. But I can see it's been kind of a hard day for you, not knowing what's happening. Would it help any if Mrs. Ramsey and I drove you down there so you could find out for yourself?"

I could have kissed him in gratitude, but I just blinked hard and nodded emphatically.

Little did I know just how generous he was being! Bailey Corners proved to be twenty-one miles away over mountain roads bumpier and ruttier than anything I could possibly have imagined. We finally arrived, however, and my worst fears were immediately allayed by the sight of our car pulled partially off the road, listing toward the ditch. As relief flooded over me, I began to feel a little foolish. But it was too late for remorse, and it was a blessing to wipe away the vision of the car smashed on the riverbank.

Mr. Ramsey pointed out the Clines' house to me, a well-built frame house at the top of the hill and beyond a bit of rough open terrain. The Ramseys kept Susan in the car with them while I made my way to the house. It was a warm evening, and when I finally knocked on the door, I was puffing a bit, partly from exertion and partly from nervousness. Perhaps Bonta would be annoyed that I'd pursued him way down here and bothered the Ramseys to boot.

A middle-aged man opened the door, and when I told him who I was, he motioned me into the bedroom without a word. The room was stifling; all the windows were shut. On the bed was a young girl who couldn't have been more than seventeen years old. She was tossing about and moaning continuously, apparently in great pain. My sympathy went out to her; she was much too young to be going through this. But when I took a good look at Barbara and Bonta, I felt at least as sorry for them. They both looked desperately tired and hot, and Bonta looked worried. His face was stubbled with a day's growth of beard, adding to his haggard appearance. Barbara was sitting cross-legged at the top of the bed, her limp skirt bunched between her knees, giving the girl a whiff of anesthetic when she needed it most.

Bonta looked up as I walked in with a startled, "Well, how on earth did you get here!"

I told him I had been pretty worried since they had been away so long and that the Ramseys had kindly offered to bring me.

"Well, you can see we're still working away at it," he said grimly.

He took me out on the porch to get beyond earshot of the several people in the room and said in a low voice, "What a rough one this has turned out to be! Barb and I've had just about five minutes' worth of sleep since we left last night. The family hasn't offered us a thing to eat or drink all day. They started out friendly enough. In fact, they were real nice—gave us coffee and a roll shortly after we arrived— asked about our family and all. I found out that Ernest works at the little sawmill down the road run by his father-in-law, but he's thinking of going into the mine because the pay is better. His father works in Number Twelve mine.

"But they're a real spastic bunch, and as things dragged on and they got stewing over Vernetta and nothing much happened, they cooled off more and more, and now they're hardly speaking to us. I think they thought I ought to send her to the hospital, but it's too late to move her all that long way over these bumpy roads. Vernetta's just a kid, and it's her first. She has had a pretty rough time of it, but she's not exactly stoic, and that's not helped any.

"Barb and I snuck out a couple times to prowl for something our-selves and located a little country store—just a hole in the wall, down the road aways—where at least we got a coke and a couple of dough-nuts."

I thought back to the fact that he'd had only a piece of pie and some milk for dinner the night before and wished I'd thought to bring them something.

"Vernetta isn't making much headway even yet. The baby seems to be hung up fairly far down, and I just may have to use forceps to get things over with before she wears herself out. Worst problem is the family. Every time she moans a little, they carry on so badly I figure I'd better keep her snowed with Demerol, but every time I quiet her down with that, she just quits having pains altogether. Got to figure my way out of this somehow."

I couldn't think of a single helpful comment.

"Trouble is I'm plain scared to bring out those hooks from my bag, because if her family sees them and they figure I'm going to have to use them on her, they could really go berserk. They'll think for sure she's going to die or that I'm going to kill the baby or who knows what! They're the jumpiest bunch, and I gather this is the first grandchild. I just can't seem to get to them. All they do is stand around and look horrified. Besides if I have to put the hooks on, it'll mean Barbara'll have to put her down to fairly deep anesthesia. This is sort of tricky, because I'll be busy worrying about my own job and can't keep track of the anesthesia. Barb never went near a chloroform bottle before today. Bad enough to use chloroform in the first place, but it's all I've got!"

Seeing him so tired and worried, I felt so frustrated by the whole situation that I almost burst into tears. No doubt a share of my reaction was purely selfish. I wanted more than anything to be the one helping him through this tight spot. Barbara looked pretty miserable herself, with sweat beaded on her forehead, her hair all damp and straggly, sitting in that awkward position, cramped up on the rumpled, hot-looking bed. When I offered to relieve her, she naturally refused, saying she wanted to finish what she'd begun. I certainly couldn't blame her. They both said there was nothing I could do.

So, mindful that the Ramseys were waiting for me, I turned to hide the tears that were ready to spill over and walked out. If only there'd been something I could have said to the Clines to ease the situation. But all I could do was get out of the way. My feeling of uselessness was complete. I'd have been better off if I'd stayed home and not barged into the middle of all the tension.

I didn't want the Ramseys to know how upset I was, though I'm sure Mr. Ramsey understood. He told me he didn't know much about Ernest, but Ernest's father had worked in the mine ever since it was opened, and Vernetta's father became involved with the sawmill after he hurt his leg in the mine. The accident persuaded him to stay above ground. I told him Bonta would surely be interested to know.

I struggled to chat brightly of this and that all the way back, while I kept thinking of how unreasonable it was to expect Bonta to do so much all by himself, without any cooperation or understanding; of the fact that I knew he had another delivery due any moment (this one had been unexpected, of course), so I didn't see when he would ever get a chance to rest. I busied myself resenting everything and everybody that came between us. I hated the way people seemed to treat him as though he were some commodity like a chunk of cheese they were collecting because they'd paid for it. If they needed a doctor, they just came and demanded him. It also hurt a little to realize that basically he seemed to accept this without much complaint. He had agreed to take care of them, so this was his obligation, regardless of their manners, his state of exhaustion, or any plans we might have made together. I knew I'd been spoiled by Bonta's regular hours at Great Lakes and realized I was being unreasonable, but somehow I couldn't help it.

What I didn't realize was that this was only the start of my indoctrination as wife of a doctor in private practice.

By the time we reached camp and I had thanked the Ramseys for their most generous assistance, it was dark and way past Susan's bedtime. I tucked her in and tried to work out some of my frustrations by scrubbing an accumulation of dirty clothes. It didn't help much. However hard I tried to reason with myself that nobody meant to leave me out of this, that I'd gaily sent Barbara off myself, that they'd both rather have been comfortably home where I was, that Barbara was generously helping us both and that she and I had agreed that it was fair to let her go on the big calls while she was down here, none of these arguments seemed to lessen my grudge against the world in general and even both of them for sharing this crisis without me. I dreaded facing them when they did get back, feeling as sorry for myself as I did, when I knew very well it was they who deserved all the sympathy. I was thoroughly ashamed of myself, but there it was.

Shortly after 11:00 P.M. Bonta's car pulled up outside the club-house, and he and Barbara dragged themselves up the steps. They came in silently, too tired to say anything. "Well?" I asked, trying to sound sympathetic and interested, hiding my own aggrieved feelings.

"Oh, I was right about the family. You'd have thought using forceps was something figured out by the devil himself. The worst of the lot was her mother, who ought to have known better. She's had a bunch of her own. I had to send every one of them out of the room except her husband and her father. Needed them to hold her legs. Poor Ernest was so hot and scared the sweat just poured off his brow onto his pants. Barb snowed her with chloroform—did it like a veteran—and kept track of things pretty well." He gave her an approving glance, which she had certainly earned.

"Actually things went very smoothly once we faced up to it. I could have delivered the baby right then, but since they felt so vehemently that this was all abnormal and wrong, I took the hooks off just short of finishing the job and let her push the baby the rest of the way. It didn't take long then. Soon as it was all over and everybody knew the baby was OK and breathing, they took her and Vernetta right over, ignored us completely, and left Barb and me to clean up our things as best as we could. Don't know that anyone even saw us to the door. We just left."

Luckily Barbara was too tired to notice any constraint on my part and left for bed immediately. I couldn't hide anything from Bonta, however; he could always read my mind, sometimes better than I could myself. A few attempts at irrelevant conversation confirmed his suspicion that something was wrong.

"All right, honey, what's the trouble? Out with it." He drew me down beside him on the bed where I sat stiffly.

At first I could hardly say anything. Since I would have to admit to so many unflattering feelings, I fought down the impulse to spill it all and find some relief. Besides, I knew I'd end up crying, which I de-spised doing. It was just that I choked up when it came to sharing my feelings, and tears were the only way to get the words flowing. In spite of everything, I knew I had to talk this out with him, even though I also knew he was dead tired and needed sleep more than anything else. But once begun, the story flooded out: how lonesome I'd been, how

worried over him, and how envious of Barbara for being with him.
And how unhappy I was that he still didn't seem to understand why I
hadn't been able to come down to Coal Mountain earlier. Most of all,
how unhappy I was that it looked as though he'd never have time for
Susan and me, because he seemed to belong to everybody else.

He put his hand on my knee and turned my head so I had to face
him. "Yes, there are some things to straighten out and some new things
to learn. True enough, I was very unhappy about your staying with
Susan when I needed you so badly. But I've tried to understand your
reasons. You'd only have been another problem if you'd come down
with her before we had a house, and I have to believe you when you
say there just wasn't any way to leave her up there. Anyway, that's
all behind us. You're here now and that's what matters. We're going
to work on being partners in this job." He continued encouragingly.
"You'll see, it will work out. But you have to give it some time. Of
course you feel like an outsider right now, because it's true that I've
run the show all these weeks, and it is all mine. I didn't have any
alternative."

As for my resentment about the attitude of the people in camp, he
listened thoughtfully and then said, "Well, honey, I know it's kind of
rough sometimes, but you've already got your own problem pretty
well figured out, and that's half the battle. This is just your first expo-
sure to medical practice where there aren't hours on duty and hours
off duty the way there were in the navy! And down here especially,
they don't even think of the doctor as a person at all. They're just
concentrating on the help he can give them when they need it most.
People in trouble are like children. They get scared and don't think of
anybody but themselves. After all, I agreed to take care of them, and
that's simply a responsibility I've got to carry out. I know it's kind
of hard for you, used to a career where the spotlight was on you, settling now for a supporting role. But you've got a big job, too, honest.
You're important to me first of all because I love you. But besides that
I need your help. You've already lightened my load by getting those
drug orders out. And you're important in your role as my wife. You
can make a real difference in the way people here accept us both. It'll
take time, but you'll come to see it that way eventually. Believe me."

As he switched off the light on the bedside table, he put his arms around me and said in a tone that must have been accompanied by a grin, "I may be dead tired, but I could still try to convince you we're in this together."

As I clung to him, this reassurance banished all the anxieties of the past few days, and the tears he kissed away were tears of relief and happiness.

Life certainly looked better the next morning, and Barbara and I straightened things out between us with no problem. She knew I was feeling left out and admitted she'd have felt the same if things had been reversed.

As Bonta left to see two patients before going to the office, he said, "Today's Friday—prenatal day. Remember I told you I'd hired a young girl to be on hand when I examine these pregnant women? Well, Eloise'll be in this morning, and you'll have a chance to meet her."

The added help proved to be a good thing. By midmorning when Bonta had finished with the two house calls and we both got to the office, Eloise had already opened the place up, and the waiting room was full, all piled up from yesterday. Bonta introduced us to each other. Eloise had a freshly scrubbed look about her, her slender frame accented by her starched and belted dress. She had a clear olive complexion, and I envied her her wavy black hair. Her wide-set gray eyes and high cheekbones gave her a somewhat exotic appearance.

She had obviously studied me. I caught her furtively checking my beige dress and brown penny-loafers as we walked in, and I hoped I passed the inspection. All she said was, "Hello," with a little half smile and then looked quickly away.

We had time for no more than a smile and a hello anyway, as she took the first of the women into the examining room to ready her for her checkup, and I started getting out her record. We had barely begun, however, when a loud tramping and urgent shouts indicated that something really serious had happened. We opened the door of the examining room to a procession led by two men staggering under the awkward weight of a young fellow who was apparently unconscious. Eloise helped the other patient out as quickly as possible, and the men hoisted the boy onto the examining table. He was a big stocky kid, probably about fifteen or sixteen. No sooner was he stretched out

Bonta, Eloise, and a patient. The mayonnaise jars on the right, in which thermometers are being sterilized, indicate the level of sophistication afforded Bonta in his practice at Coal Mountain.

on his back than he began to spout vomitus like a fountain. This was so unexpected that everything was a dreadful mess before I could get a basin anywhere near him. Bonta was, of course, much more concerned about his aspirating than about the mess.

Perhaps six other men had followed into the room, all loudly discussing the accident and arguing about how it had happened.

"Well, goddamn it, he ought to have looked where he was going on that there bike. He come up over that hill right out in the middle of the road. I seen it myself."

"Yeah, you can't help hitting him when you can't even see him before you're right on top of him!"

"By God, Joe, you could've been driving more careful. That's my boy, and if you've killed him . . ."

"I didn't mean to hit him, and I'm sure sorry he's got hurt, but he should've knowed better than to ride right out in the middle. With all the dust you can't see a damned thing. It wasn't my fault."

"He's only a kid, and if you hadn't been tearing along paying no attention to anything it wouldn't have happened. God damn you!"

"Now don't you start cussing at me!"

The tempers were about to erupt into blows when Bonta looked up from his patient. "That's enough." His tone left no doubt about who was in charge. "Everybody out of here except for his parents, and you," nodding to Eloise and me. "Just clear out. You're not helping a bit with all this hullabaloo."

The men left rather sheepishly, still passing half-whispered remarks over their shoulders as they filed out. The boy's mother emerged from the background to step nearer the table where her son lay. She stood, clasping and unclasping her hands. The father stood grimly by, anger still dominating his expression. Once peace had been restored, Bonta finished checking his patient's reflexes and looked at the pupils of his eyes. He turned to Eloise and said quietly, "Find somebody to go for the ambulance right away. He's got to get to the hospital as fast as they can get him there."

The ambulance driver and two miners he'd enlisted to help appeared with a stretcher in an unbelievably short time. As soon as they lifted the boy into the ambulance, it roared down the road. As the dust billowed behind it, Bonta remarked to me, "Looks pretty bad—could be a brain injury." I was still shocked by the sudden drama and most impressed by Bonta's calm handling of the whole situation.

Eloise and I were left to cope with the soiled sheets and towels. She looked pretty green and indicated that she was going to be sick herself any minute. The awful smell left me feeling none too rugged myself, but I figured I'd better be big enough to do the unavoidable dirty job. So I sent her in to help Bonta with the women, while I gathered up the wretched pile to work on it all in our own backyard. I could at least have plenty of fresh air while dousing the sheets in the scrub pail I had found in the back closet. And there was an abundance of clean water I could carry up from the creek, until the sheets were rinsed enough for hot water and soap. When they were at last flapping on the line behind the clubhouse, I was relieved to return to the office. Bonta asked me to run some urine tests; he had already shown me how during a quiet moment, when I had discovered that an alcohol lamp was an adequate substitute for a Bunsen burner. After all, gas was a no-no in a coal camp.

Things eventually quieted down, and Eloise and I sat in the lab where we visited over the cokes I'd brought from the clubhouse. "I hear you were a big help, Eloise, when the doctor was here all alone. Now I can see for myself." I was encouraged by her answering smile. "I think I've seen your sister at the store. Do you have any other brothers or sisters?"

"Oh yes, there's seven of us kids. Eva, she's the cashier. She's older than me. She's twenty-one!" As if twenty-one were ancient beyond belief. "Then there's me. I'm nineteen." She seemed pleased to talk about her family. "Next there's Jimmy. He's sixteen. He's just finished a year of high school, and he's talking about quitting and going into the mine. That kind of talk makes Daddy real mad. I just know he'll whup him real good if he don't go back to school. Daddy sets a mighty big store by learning, he does." Her satisfaction at having finished school herself came through loud and clear. "Then there's Nan. She's fifteen, and she's finished a year of high school, just like Jimmy. She's sweet on one of the boys, and she's talking about getting married." Did I detect a wistful note at the thought? "Betty's only twelve, and she's a big old nuisance sometimes. She thinks she's so big, but she don't know hardly nothing."

Apparently once she decided to talk, the words just flowed. "Now Johnny, he's ten. He's kind of cute. But Daddy caught him smoking the other day behind the outhouse, and did he ever get it!" Eloise obviously thought justice had been rendered. "Oh, and then there's Pete. He's the baby. He's only eight, and he's in third grade."

I found later that there was no mistaking any of the Horvath children. They all shared Eloise's coloring and those high cheekbones.

Bonta had told me the Horvaths' home in the green camp had only two bedrooms, and I was mentally trying to fit them all in.

Eloise added philosophically, "We all get called Hunks cause Mother and Daddy come from Hungary. We get teased something awful, but we just sass them back."

I was amazed to find such intolerance in camp, but I only remarked, "Your mother sure has her hands full with a crew like that."

Her expression clouded. "Mother ain't been feeling so good lately. Her stomach hurts her so bad, and she has to rest a lot, so me and Eva take care of a lot of things."

I knew that her mother was suffering from an abdominal cancer. Shortly after Bonta arrived, he had to send her to the hospital in Welch, where the doctors did exploratory surgery, only to find there was nothing that could be done for her but palliation. Trying to keep her as comfortable as possible was the only treatment available. This was not information to be shared with Eloise just then, nor transmitted by me.

"Mother can't eat much, and she's been losing a lot of weight. Oh sure, she's still pretty heavy." She paused before completing the roster. "Course there's Daddy. He don't say much, except when he gets mad at something. He works in Number Nine."

That was the low coal mine, and I thought to myself the poor man couldn't even stand up, digging away at the mountain day after day.

When I asked her how she liked living in Coal Mountain, she said, "It's kind of boring. Oh, the new the-ater helps some. I went there some with Jake, but him and me had a falling-out a while back. Ain't nothing to do now except go to church. I used to sing in a quartet at the Methodist church, but that broke up a while ago."

I wondered where that church was; I hadn't heard about it before.

Since the screens were still in need of repair, our conversation had been punctuated now and then by sharp whacks from the flyswatter I kept at the ready.

"I don't go for the way them Holinesses carry on. You know their churchhouse is right next door to our house. I sure wish it was somewheres else. You think all that noise is going to quit, and they all go outside to get in their cars and go home. And then somebody else'll get the spirit and have to be saved, and they leave the motor running while they run back in the churchhouse again and holler and yell some more. And this'll go on two or three times till you're just ready to die. You're so mad at them for keeping you awake!"

I tried to visualize the scene; at least I could empathize with her distress over the noise. She chattered on, expressing her disapproval of two girls from outside the camp who had shown up at the company store in shorts "where all the men could stare at them." I was thankful I hadn't been tempted by the warm weather to put on my own! And apparently the pop counter boy at the store "liked" Barbara and asked Eloise to arrange a date with her for him.

By the end of the afternoon, I felt I had learned at least something about the community and quite a bit about the Horvaths. As we locked the door behind us at six o'clock, I decided that helping in the office was already becoming much more comfortable. And I thought happily of our plans for the next day—a trip to the big city and some needed shopping.

Barbara and I were overjoyed when Bonta was able to leave after lunch on Saturday without being delayed. I knew the trip out to the hardtop was difficult, but I had almost forgotten how tortuous even the main road was. At one steep stretch it made two hairpin turns, so that three times at three different levels we passed the same trees.

We finally reached Williamson, sixty miles away, approaching the city past enormous freight yards full of more coal cars than I had ever seen in one place. It was our local metropolis, but Bonta said the latest census counted all of eight thousand inhabitants. Before the day was over, I decided what it might lack in people it made up for in coal dust.

We piled into Sears as if we'd never seen a store before and spent most of the afternoon there, buying things as though possessed. We had to collect enough essentials to start housekeeping when our house became available, since our own things hadn't arrived yet. Susan wandered patiently around, getting sootier by the minute. I hardly wanted to admit knowing her. She and a little boy struck up an acquaintance and became absorbed in watching a transparent demonstration washing machine swish clothes around.

The thrill of the afternoon was the sound of some good old "Top Ten" songs over the loudspeaker from the record department. I just wished I could see the new musical from which those wonderful songs came—"Bali Ha'i" and "Some Enchanted Evening." As I listened, the drab surroundings seemed to fade, replaced by visions of tropical islands where lovers wandered hand in hand. I had heard nothing but hymns, quartets, and country music since I had been in camp—apparently the only music carried by the one radio station we could get.

We trudged through a couple of other stores where Susan added several more layers of coal dust. Hoping to clean up and eat before going back to Coal Mountain, we finally staggered into the hotel where Bonta had stayed his first night down there. There was no soap, but water helped a little, and food helped a lot. Then we returned to the car, glad to be on our way "home." Who would have dreamed that by the end of the day we would be overjoyed to be heading back to the coal camp?

On the way in we stopped at Bailey Corners to see Vernetta and the baby for whom Barbara and Bonta had worked so long. The two of them climbed up the hill while Susan and I waited in the car. The darkness was unrelieved except for the lighted windows of the Cline house. Nearby crickets were chirping. Far off a dog was barking, but the chief sound was that of hymn singing from the meeting house we had passed a little distance down the road. The fervent voices rose and fell in the regular rhythms I was getting used to. Already I knew most of the words to "I'm on the Heavenly High Road." Tarheel Ruby had belted it out every day that week on station WWYO, and it did kind of sing itself. I found myself humming along.

Sooner than I expected, Bonta and Barbara came back down the hill. To my surprise they wanted us to go back up with them. Bonta hoisted Susan on his shoulder and led us at a smart clip. He seemed more than usually pleased about something. When we reached the house, we were greeted most cordially and invited to the bedroom where the new baby was snuggled in fluffy pink blankets beside Vernetta, who looked little more than a child herself. It was hard to realize that she now bore the responsibilities of motherhood.

Everyone seemed especially interested in Susan as she babbled on appreciatively about the baby. We all chatted a bit, and I finally asked what they had named their little girl.

Vernetta's face brightened as she answered, "Well, we studied about it for a while. Ma wanted us to name her after her sister Josie. But then we got to thinking about how the doctor helped me out when I was having such a hard time having her. He told us you had a little girl, too, named Susan, so we figured to name her for your little girl here. So she's Susan Cline." She beamed at the baby proudly and gave our Susan a shy smile.

Susan and I had been there hardly a week and already two coal camp babies were named after us! I couldn't help wondering if there would ever be a little Bonta running around the place to make it unanimous. Now I realized that what seemed like rudeness at the time might be mostly worry.

5. Settling In

I had been helping in the office for a little more than a week when Bonta casually turned to me and said, "Helen, here's Mrs. Sharp. She needs a shot of penicillin. Would you please take care of her while I see the lady Eloise has waiting for me in the examining room?"

I had watched him give shots many times, but the thought of doing it myself turned me to jelly. Still, I could hardly demur in front of Mrs. Sharp, who looked trustingly at me. Giving Bonta a look compounded of shock, distress, and rebuke, I ushered her into the lab. I took the boiled syringe and needle from the sterilizer, fitted them together, and drew the correct amount from the ampoule of penicillin. I wiped Mrs. Sharp's arm with an alcohol sponge and was vaguely aware that she was telling me about the spoiled orange she had found in her bag of groceries the day before. Orange, I thought. That's what nurses practice giving shots to. Well, there was nothing for it but to pretend her arm was an orange and proceed. I wanted to shut my eyes and not look while it was happening, but since that was impossible, I pinched her arm and plunged the needle in. It all happened so smoothly that my patient kept right on talking. "And would you believe, he made me pay for it anyway?"

I fumbled for the slip I had to write out for her signature and found I was shaking so I could hardly write. But I had done it!

When I reported this to Bonta, he gave me an approving glance and said, "OK. Good. So now you're ready to draw a blood for us. Benjie—you remember him and Pearlie—well, Benjie needs a pre-employment blood test. He's waiting in the treatment room."

This was going too fast. I ought to be able to savor one triumph before facing an even harder test. This meant locating a vein. But whenever Bonta said, "Do this," or "Do that," it seemed impossible to argue. He believed in providing opportunities for growth for those around him—and still does. Lest this seem an unwarranted delegation of responsibility to a nonprofessional, one must remember that this was long ago and far away, and I was the only semitrained help Bonta had. At least I knew sterile technique from bacteriology courses, had drawn blood on laboratory animals, and performed many operations on rats. And the public's concern over medical malpractice was far in the future.

I took the little rubber tourniquet to bind Benjie's arm, collected the needed equipment, and proceeded as to my doom.

"Hello, Benjie," I said, forcing what I hoped was a lighthearted tone.

Benjie grunted. He was no conversationalist. He watched with interest as I tightened the tourniquet. As I sought the vein, I wished he would look away. Luckily he had a great bulging vessel one could hardly miss. With a show of courage I inserted the needle and almost gasped with relief when the dark blood welled up behind the plunger. I was busy concentrating on getting just the right amount and failed to notice Benjie's pallor. As I withdrew the needle, he suddenly slumped down on the examining table where he had been sitting. A frantic summons brought Bonta to the rescue, but he said, "Just let him lie there; he'll come to in a minute. Sometimes the bigger they are the more likely they'll pass out."

Sure enough, Benjie shortly opened his eyes, sat up, and looked cautiously around to see who had witnessed his embarrassing predicament.

Bonta reassured him. "Don't worry. Lots of people faint at the sight of blood. Feeling OK now?"

After Bonta ushered him out, he turned to me. "That may have been rough on you as well as Benjie, but you may look back on it with nostalgia some day." He laughed. "Not every patient's going to fall for you like that."

The evening went to a discussion of Barbara's future. She had received an offer of an assistantship in the psychology department at Wellesley where she could work toward a master's degree, but for some reason she wasn't quite sure that was the right course for her. Both Bonta and I believed even back then that every woman should be prepared to take care of herself, and the more credentials the better. Barbara had no firm alternatives; none of the job applications we had sent out had brought a response. By bedtime we had almost convinced her that Wellesley was the answer.

By Saturday, August 20, Nick Morgan had finished the necessary work on our house. We felt like celebrating. Sears had already delivered the stove and refrigerator, so we could move in any time. There were a few things we still needed, especially venetian blinds to give us some privacy. We also had to buy enough dishes and a pan or two to tide us over till our possessions arrived.

We set out for Welch as soon as Bonta finished caring for the last patient a little after noon. He planned to visit the hospital there while Barbara and I took Susan and shopped. He looked forward to meeting the doctors to whom he referred the patients requiring hospital care.

Barbara and I decided that all West Virginia towns must be crowded into the cracks between mountains, suffering from an oversupply of coal and an undersupply of parking space.

We ended up in an A & P we spied down one narrow street and nearly bought the place out. Both our carts overflowed, and the bill came to $40.25. We were embarrassed at being so conspicuous and holding up the woman behind us at the counter. I was also horrified by the amount we'd spent. The boy who helped us carry the bags out asked if we had sixteen children. Little did I dream that forty dollars might one day buy only a single bag of groceries.

Once again we were glad to be heading back to Coal Mountain. It had begun to feel as though we belonged there. This time the rock walls of the cutoff loomed like guardians of our homeward way.

The next day, Sunday, was hectic, but we knew we would be sleeping in our own house that night. Mrs. Jennings had lent us chairs from the clubhouse, and both the Ramseys and Tim Bailey, the electrician, had lent us cots.

Bonta had come to know Tim when he'd brought one of his youngsters to the office with whooping cough. Luckily it proved to be a fairly mild case. From the conversation he learned that Tim, like the

Horvaths, had grown up in Hungary. He'd spent three years studying engineering there before he realized his dream of coming to America. His job as company electrician meant keeping the lights on and the coal cars running in the mine and handling all electrical crises, both in the mine and in the camp. It was a source of great pride to him. When Bonta mentioned our impending move and joked about our lack of furniture, he quickly volunteered the cot.

Barbara and I did most of the lugging because Bonta's efforts were so often interrupted.

"Hey, Doc, would you look at my eye? Got something in it and can't get it out."

"Doc, the young one's got the colic, and the old woman wants something to soothe him."

"See this here cut! I was just chopping some wood, and a piece hit Willie right here in the leg. Think it needs sewing up?"

Late in the afternoon he did join us to help organize the kitchen. We were just putting the boxes of cereal on the shelf when there came a knock on the front door. Bonta muttered under his breath at the intrusion, expecting he would have to leave again. But there stood Mrs. Ramsey with something carefully held in a brown paper bag. She was all smiles.

"I knew this was the big day—your moving in and all. And I knew you couldn't be doing any baking yet, even if you do have a pretty new stove. So I popped this in the oven this evening." (I was getting used to the fact that evening meant what I called afternoon.) With a flourish she extracted her offering. "Here's an apple pie!"

Bonta's eyes lit up appreciatively; apple pie topped his list of favorites. "We'll press the new ironing board into service," he said, as he set the pie on it. Still hot, it emitted a tantalizing aroma of cinnamon.

As we were admiring the pie, we heard another knock, this time at the back door. I knew the peace was too good to last. But this time it was Mrs. Jennings. She, too, carried something in a paper bag.

"Got a little something in this sack for your first dinner in your new house. Raised it and cleaned it myself." She reached in and triumphantly pulled out a plump little chicken.

Despite the bare walls and few pieces of borrowed furniture, the house seemed overflowing with warmth and welcome.

A few days later as we were eating lunch at the dinette table, newly arrived from Sears, we noticed a train headed for the tipple. In addition to the usual solid line of coal cars, this train incorporated a box car.

Barbara joked, "There's your stuff from Great Lakes. Guess it took a whole freight car!"

We concluded it probably contained machinery for the mine or supplies for the store.

Just as I was about to leave the office in the afternoon to get the mail, Barbara burst in excitedly with Susan. "Guess what! A fellow from the store came over a few minutes ago to tell us that there are a lot of boxes on that freight car for the doc. And from the way he described them," here she gesticulated wildly, "it really has to be your things from the Lakes!"

I could hardly believe it. After all, nearly three months had elapsed since we left the base, and I had almost given up hope.

One of the men who worked at the tipple brought it all over just before dinner. I'd never seen so many crates, barrels, and boxes, all out of proportion to anything I knew we owned.

Word of their arrival spread faster than the chicken pox. The entire neighborhood's worth of kids began gathering in the road behind our yard. By the time we finished supper, an expectant gallery of twenty youngsters waited. The bigger ones perched nonchalantly on the top rail of the fence, and the younger ones crowded around the gate. None actually dared come inside the yard, but they all watched bug-eyed as we started unpacking the first box.

We'd barely begun when Bonta had to leave to see a sick baby up the hollow, and this emboldened two of the children to slide down from the fence to observe from a closer vantage point. Barbara and I made the mistake of smiling at them, and at this sign of encouragement the rest stole silently nearer, one by one. The attention riveted on each object as it emerged from its wrapping was embarrassing. Only crown jewels deserve such scrutiny. I couldn't believe the elaborate care the navy had given our modest belongings. An admiral's Spode and Chippendale couldn't have been treated better.

I squirmed inwardly at the paltriness of so many of the items. My discomfiture was complete as I unwrapped the old cake mixer Mother had passed on to me when she bought her new one, and I overheard one ten-year-old say to another in a disparaging aside, "We got one at home that looks a lot better than that old thing!"

Susan's big woolly lamb was, however, an instant hit. When I wound it up and "Mary Had a Little Lamb" tinkled forth, it seemed to make up for the cake mixer.

I noticed one child with a smudge on her upturned nose, dressed in faded pink, staring hard at a picture propped on the porch step. This was Susan's nursery print of a little girl in a blue nightie, kneeling in prayer. When she realized that I was watching her, she flashed a radiant smile, folded her hands as she stepped back, and said simply, "It's real pretty, ain't it?"

Finally one of the older boys screwed up his courage. "Hey, lady, can I have them broken barrel covers and pieces of wood off from them boxes?"

This loosed a torrent of claims for the barrels and boxes as well. I glanced beyond the fence to discover that a whole fleet of carts and wagons in assorted states of dilapidation had been gathered while Barbara and I were absorbed in our unpacking. They were apparently available to haul off whatever booty could be scavenged. When we said, "Well, all right. Take just the broken pieces lying around," a mad scramble ensued. The bigger boys won, of course, but we were too busy to referee.

When I emptied the first barrel, a little barefoot fellow with a thatch of unruly straw-colored hair and a dirty plaid shirt pushed his way over to me. He looked up with big pleading eyes and begged, "Can I have that barrel, lady?" He saw me waver and pursued his advantage. "We don't have no barrel at all at our house. All the other kids, they got barrels."

I melted. Surely the remaining barrel would be enough for our trash. Manfully he set about rolling the unwieldy thing over to his wagon, luckily getting some help from a bigger boy. He rattled off up the road with it and was back fifteen minutes later to wait quietly for another windfall.

An older kid scoffed, "Huh, that barrel you just took home weren't anything. We got one lots bigger than that!"

Ho-Gin pulling a sled for boys in Long Branch, an older and poorer settlement approximately ten miles from camp, where Bonta made house calls and performed occasional deliveries.

The little guy dug his big toe into the dirt, thought for a moment, and then defended his recent prize. "Well, anyway, I bet yours ain't any rounder!"

Meantime some of the children had discovered the excelsior that had been used for packing one or two of the crates; I was vaguely aware that a couple of them back by the fence were bombarding each other with big handfuls of it. Shyness had long since evaporated, and they were pushing each other to see better or chasing each other to capture various trophies.

At this point Bonta returned. He was really irked at the mess the children were making and the loss of all the kindling Barbara and I had given away. He just hadn't seen all those expectant little faces staring up so hopefully before the scramble began.

So I told the children rather lamely that they had to go now and couldn't take anything but what they already had their hands on. Of course, each one grabbed the nearest thing and dashed off, leaving the yard stripped of almost everything worth picking up and littered with splintered fragments of boxes and quantities of excelsior.

It was dark before we hauled the last armful inside, and we were so tired we could hardly make it up the porch steps, but Bonta insisted that we clean up the yard before quitting. Barbara held the flashlight while he hacked apart some of the few boxes left and stowed the kindling in the coal house so the little scavengers wouldn't make off with it in the morning before we were up. We had saved the other barrel and a couple of the more substantial crates to serve as storage chests in Susan's room. I could disguise them with fabric. And then we went crawling around the yard picking up excelsior and chips of wood we could feel or see by the erratic beam of the flashlight.

What a shock next morning when I glanced out the kitchen window to see if anyone was waiting by the office. The bushes by the creek were festooned with excelsior, and as far as I could see up and down the hollow, the children had draped it artistically on the lower branches of trees, tucked bits into the angles of fence rails, and just trailed shreds up the road. Barbara confirmed that it was equally bad out the front window. We apologized to Mr. Ramsey that afternoon for contributing to such a mess, and he allowed as how he'd had to assign a man to spend most of the day picking it all up! He was awfully decent about it, but he did say he hoped we weren't expecting any more boxes from the navy right away.

♟   I had no idea that another growing experience awaited me before the weekend ended. We planned to drive to Williamson as soon as Saturday office hours were over so that Barbara could take the bus to Columbus. She had agreed to pick up a new car for us there and drive it back.

Mr. Kennedy hadn't been able to fix the Plymouth, and meantime, of course, Bonta had had to drive the Chevy. We had resigned ourselves to the fact that it was being badly abused on house calls. We decided to try to sell it when we left, much as it would hurt to part with the first car we had ever owned. We had saved up for it and proudly paid cash.

One day Bonta mentioned to Randall Hatfield, manager of the company office, that he wished he could get his hands on a car he could keep for trips out of the hollow. To his surprise, Randall offered to let him use the company's discount and buy a car through their office. This was too good a chance to pass up, so we were about to become the proud owners of a new blue Chevrolet. As Bonta said, I could take it out if need be, when he was tied up in camp.

As we left the camp, the sun was shining, the road had recently been scraped so the holes were only half as deep as usual, and we felt like kids on vacation. The Guyandotte had never sparkled more brightly, and the hills smiled down at us. Susan chattered endlessly as she bounced in her car bed in the back seat, calling our attention to pigs, a school bus, and several horses along the way.

Barbara informed us that she was seriously considering the Wellesley offer. "But I'm going to talk it over with Katy in Columbus." Katy had been her best friend at Oberlin, and the chance for a visit with her made the trip to pick up the car a welcome opportunity.

We saw Barbara on her way, and by the time we picked up groceries and had dinner at a little Chinese restaurant we unexpectedly discovered up a side street, it was turning dusk. I started toward the passenger side of the car when Bonta suggested, "How about your driving home?"

"Oh, not now—it's getting dark, and I'm just not ready," I objected somewhat lamely. The truth was that I knew I would have to face this crisis sooner or later, but the prospect was unnerving.

Impossible though it may seem now that a thirty-year-old woman couldn't drive, it wasn't quite so unusual then. Somehow I had never needed to drive. I grew up in such a small town that walking took me anywhere I needed to go. Somehow the opportunity to learn never arose until six months earlier when we acquired the Chevy and Bonta taught me. Now I hadn't touched a steering wheel since those lessons back in Illinois.

Bonta was firm. "Now's as good a time as any. You know you need to get in practice for the new one."

Reluctantly I got in on the driver's side and turned the key. Though I developed a tension headache before we reached home, it actually wasn't as bad as I'd feared. It was just as well, however, that the last part of the trip was in the dark so that I couldn't see those appalling cliffs at the edge of the dirt road into camp. I certainly didn't enjoy the trip, but I felt better for having met the challenge.

☞ We hoped that eventually Eloise would work in the office mornings and in our home afternoons so that I could do the reverse. We asked her to take care of Susan while Barbara was away. Just as we were finishing breakfast Monday morning there came an uncertain knock at the door.

"Good morning, Eloise. Come on in. We're almost ready. Won't you join us for coffee?"

"Oh, no." And she disappeared into the living room where she sat silently waiting. Susan undertook to entertain her, making up in enthusiasm what she lacked in words, but we didn't hear any response.

When I explained to her what needed to be done, she listened without comment, and I felt a bit uneasy about the situation when I left.

Later in the morning when I came back from the office ostensibly to get some vaccine from the refrigerator, I was happy to find that she and Susan were getting along famously, and Eloise seemed much more relaxed. I decided she'd just been nervous about coming into our home and assuming unknown responsibilities. Now she smiled as she reported, "Susan's been reading up a storm out of her picture book, but I can't understand a word she says!"

At lunchtime Eloise insisted on going home to eat, though we told her she was more than welcome to share the vegetable soup she had made for us. She was sitting in the living room, tying Susan's shoes.

Bonta teased her. "Guess you think it'll make you sick, is that it?"

"Aw, shit," she said, looking down at the floor. She clasped her hands between her knees and twisted the palms away from her body. "Aw, shit, you're just fooling me!"

In those days that four-letter word was never heard in polite society, let alone uttered by a pretty young girl. Bonta and I exchanged amused glances over her head. This proved to be her response whenever she was embarrassed.

Barbara returned about midnight Tuesday with the new car. It was a beauty, dark blue with pale blue upholstery. Bonta couldn't wait to try it out. But we felt conspicuous, in fact, downright embarrassed, with three cars parked by the back fence. Next day Barney Glendon asked if we were opening a dealership. It was Barney who had driven us up to the portal the day Barbara and I arrived, and we had seen him quite frequently at the clubhouse before we moved into our own house. I was pleased he felt comfortable enough to make a joke at our expense.

Barbara reported that she and Katy had had a long talk, which convinced her that going to Wellesley was indeed the right thing to do, and she had wired her acceptance from Columbus. When Katy told her that she herself was about to start a new job in Connecticut, the two girls decided to drive north together. Katy thought it would be about a week before she could be ready to leave.

On Thursday we found a telegram in the packet of mail at the post office. Receiving a telegram by mail was something of a surprise. Suppose it contained something urgent? In fact, it did. It was from Katy, announcing her arrival that very day in time for dinner. Barbara scrambled to get her things together, and I set an extra place at the table.

On her arrival Katy's first words were, "I don't believe it! You're actually here. I was ready to give up half a dozen times on the way in. Never knew such a godforsaken spot existed!"

The breezy, outdoors type, she was dressed casually and looked travel-worn. After greeting us all, she turned to Barbara. "Well, are you all set to leave first thing in the morning?"

"Hardly! You realize, don't you, that we just got your telegram two hours ago?"

"You must be kidding! I sent it two days ago—almost as soon as you left, in fact—when I realized things wouldn't take as long as I'd thought. What happened?"

I explained. "You see, we don't have any telephones in camp, except for the company's business phone, so Western Union just sends telegrams along with the regular mail."

Later, while Katy helped Barbara finish packing, Bonta asked if I would like to go with him while he went up the hollow to check on Mrs. Horvath. Eloise had reported earlier that her mother was having a lot of pain.

The late summer night was soft and still; the stars hung suspended just overhead. It was a setting for romance, but unfortunately the condition of the road required all of Bonta's attention.

He explained that we had to go the back way because cars kept getting stuck in one particular rut in the front road. Every time this happened, the poor fellow who lived right there was called on to help push the car out. Eventually he complained so loudly about his aching shoulder and how he would take it "personal and unkindly" if anyone else got stuck there that everybody started going up the back way. I wondered why nobody fixed the front road instead, but that was futile speculation. Anyway, from what I saw of the back way it appeared likely it would soon be unusable, too. There was one particular place where I held my breath. Half of the dirt road had been washed out, making a sort of gully that led into the little stream a few feet away on the left. This left only a narrow strip intact for passage. This was bad enough, but right opposite the hole was an old rusted wreck of a car that encroached on the road that remained. I could see why the little trip up to the green camp was something Bonta thought about twice.

While he went in to take care of Eloise's mother, I sat in the car and watched the goings-on at the "churchhouse" next door. It was just the way Eloise had described it, but I had never experienced anything like it—loud amens, hallelujahs, wailing, even groans. I could see a number of men on their knees with raised hands and women weaving back and forth on the benches at the side. Eloise said these Holinesses were carrying on a running feud with the Baptists in the camp, and she was betting on the Holinesses to win. It gave me an odd feeling to realize these were the same people who seemed so reserved in the office.

On our return we chatted with Katy a while about what was going on in the world outside, and it was a big treat to catch up a little. Radio reception was erratic, and we rarely heard the news programs we were used to following. Needless to say, there was no daily paper to keep us current. We had lost sight of almost everything but patients and survival. Meantime an alliance of North Atlantic nations had been formed, Tito was struggling against the Cominform, and Harry Vaughn was having some difficulty explaining his deep freezers.

Barbara and Katy left Friday right after breakfast. Their departure made me feel that Coal Mountain had finally claimed us. There was no one left now to share the past. We just had each other. I was deeply thankful that Barbara had been with us for a little while. Besides the fun of having her there and the help she gave us, she would be someone to whom we could write about everyday occurrences in camp who would be able to visualize it all. No one else we knew could possibly appreciate what Coal Mountain was like. Somehow that seemed very important as we waved and waved good-bye until the car was swallowed up in its own trail of dust.

Once Barbara had gone, I felt strangely different about this place. I realized then that while she was with us I had felt like a visitor, too, sort of detached. Suddenly that tentative feeling was gone. It was as though the dress rehearsal was over and the performance itself was beginning. Actually it was good to buckle down to establishing our own pattern for the long haul.

We made the most of the Labor Day holiday. With no office hours, Bonta spent some time catching up on the medical journals that had accumulated, and I ran a load of laundry in my new washing machine. It was an automatic, round and shiny white, avant-garde in appearance, the very latest development in washers, and Sears's best. From the moment Nick Morgan had installed it for us, bolting it firmly to the floor, it had been a source of great satisfaction. It was true that it occasionally threatened to shake the house apart when it spun with an unbalanced load. That was merely the price we paid for anchoring it in place; without that it would have lurched around the kitchen with every load.

As I hung the clothes on the line outside, I recalled my embarrassment when the neighbors caught me hanging them out on the previous Sunday. They said nothing, of course, but I was acutely aware of the disapproving stares from nearby porches. I had felt like an unregenerate heathen for the rest of the day and waited till the cover of darkness before gathering them in.

Bonta was called out just as we sat down to dinner. Mrs. Clay Morgan was in labor, so he gobbled the rest of his macaroni and left. I had met Mrs. Morgan in the office on the last prenatal day. She was cheerful and friendly, middle-aged, with straight dark hair pulled back in a bun. Her light brown dress was shapeless, but what was there to flatter a woman eight and a half months pregnant?

She talked animatedly about her problems. "Keeping up with the young ones and the geese ain't easy, me in this shape!" She laughed as she added, "Don't know who looks funnier—me out to here chasing that big gander or him flapping his wings and squawking up a storm!"

She was such a genuine soul that she endeared herself to me instantly. I asked her about her family.

"Oh, I got seven young ones running round the place already. All girls, too," she added ruefully. "Course ain't nothing wrong with girls, I always say, excepting the old man, he's got his mind set on a boy. Maybe this'll be a boy for him." She looked hopefully at her protruding abdomen. "Sure do hope it's the last one. Been in this shape too many times already. Lost two babies, you know." A shadow flitted across her face, but she smiled as she said, "Guess the good Lord needed them more than I did."

I had seen their home down the road beyond the theater, and I could hardly imagine how they all fit in. Yes, this one ought to be the last. Now she had started labor a little ahead of schedule, and I just hoped all would go well for her.

Bonta unexpectedly walked in the back door a few hours later. "Well, she's not making much progress, and there's no room down there to sit and read while I'm waiting." That certainly was no surprise.

"Too many flies and not enough light anyway. Since I'll probably be up most of the night, I'm even thinking of catching a quick nap, but first. . . ." He paused and looked hopefully toward the refrigerator. "First maybe I could have the bread pudding I didn't have time to eat earlier. And some coffee."

Between mouthfuls he said, "You know, that family doesn't have anything to spare, but when Mrs. Morgan's father-in-law—he lives across the road—heard I was going to be there for a while, he offered to catch a chicken and have his wife fry it for me."

He left again after a brief nap, and I finally decided I might as well go to bed, since my staying up couldn't help him. But it was a strange night. I kept waking, imagining I heard him driving up or fumbling at the kitchen door. A couple times I actually got up to see but found nothing except a stray dog and one of the two donkeys that wandered around the camp.

It was 6:00 A.M. when Bonta finally returned. To my surprise he was more interested in conversation than sleep.

"Guess where I've been since I saw you last!"

"Well, if you weren't at the Morgans' house, I sure wouldn't have the faintest idea," I said, still a little groggy with sleep.

"I've been to Welch and back!"

That woke me up, and I realized he needed some breakfast while he told me the story.

"When she really got going, I discovered the baby was presenting face up and would have to be repositioned. Poor gal was in considerable distress, begging me to help her 'get out of this shape.' I could have done it, but I don't have any long gloves, and I didn't want to contaminate the field, going in beyond my short ones." He paused to drink some orange juice.

"So nothing for it but to get her to the hospital. I thought of just sending her in the ambulance, but she was too far along and having too much trouble to let her go alone. So I went with her.

"We got her into the delivery room, and the resident there took over. But what do you suppose?" He looked disgusted all over again. "He didn't put on long gloves, and he kept going farther and farther, and pretty soon he was in above his gloves. Talk about being disillusioned! I could have done that myself and saved both of us a lot of time." He looked thoughtful as he buttered the toast. "Well, I suppose she won't develop any infection from it, but it sure annoyed the hell out of me."

He looked up just as I was about to ask a question. "Oh yes, the baby came out just fine, a nice little girl."

I sighed. The eighth girl! But the important thing was that they were both all right. "Please don't go for that boy," I said to myself, hoping her husband would receive the telepathic message.

"On the way back," he continued, "I had a chance to talk with Harvey Burgess. He was driving the ambulance last night. You remember seeing Harvey around—the big fellow with sandy hair, lives up near the Horvaths? Well anyway, seems I didn't go over so well around here at first. The story made the rounds that I'd talked right smart to Mark Hatfield about his youngster throwing up at the clubhouse."

I cringed. I had known then that I never should have told him about it.

"Well, don't worry—that wasn't the only thing. Apparently some people thought I 'talked hateful at them' when they came to the office after hours. Luckily things are better now. But you sure do have to be mighty careful. You can put your foot in your mouth real easy."

I said, "It's partly that they just don't trust outsiders. I wonder how long it takes to belong." Then I thought back to Eloise's remarks about being called Hunks. Maybe outsiders could never belong. I recalled the shooting episode Bonta had written about with its two victims. "They can even take offense at their own pretty quickly."

Bonta went into the bedroom, pulling off his shirt as he said, "I guess I'd better rethink some other policies, too. To quote Burgess again, there are those who think I 'don't know much about taking care of young ones.'"

"Well, of all the ridiculous things!" I jumped to his defense.

"Yes, but you know what? I've just been too honest. When they bring a kid in with a sore throat, I say, 'It could be any one of several things, maybe only a cold, maybe flu, or even measles. We'll just have to wait and see how it goes. Meantime here are some aspirin to make him feel better. Just be sure to bring him back tomorrow.' You and I know that's the truth." He finished buttoning his pajamas. "But I'm going to try a new strategy. From now on I'll say the kid has pharyngitis or rhinitis or maybe laryngitis, and I'll offer them pharyngitis pills without mentioning that they're really aspirin. I guess a little hocus-pocus won't do any harm, and it might do both them and me some good."

Bonta emerged later that morning to find Dan Dubois standing by our back fence talking with another miner. Dan was a well-known figure around camp, a strong union supporter with an opinion about every local issue that he was always willing to share. Bonta had met him shortly after coming to Coal Mountain. When Dan saw Bonta, he called out, "Hey, Doc, I heared you went to Welch last night in the ambulance!"

"News sure travels fast! Yes, I thought I'd better go with her."

Bonta was interested in what Dan might have to say about it because of his importance in the local union and his apparent leadership in the community. He seemed to keep track of everything that went on in camp. He lived a couple of houses down and across the road in front of our house, and I often saw him heading for the store or the post office. There was no mistaking him, even from a distance. A slate fall had injured his back, leaving him unable to straighten up completely. He always walked with his right side leading and his right shoulder much lower than his left. His left hand he held against his lower back to relieve the strain on those muscles. His back was hunched between his shoulders, and when he talked to you, he had to twist his head a little to the side to see you better.

Mrs. Ramsey told us this accident had occurred during his first year here in the mine, and his recovery had been slow and painful. For a time it looked as though he'd never work again. He became embittered until the passage of time and involvement in the local church improved his outlook. For multiple reasons the company found it in both their best interest and his to look out for his welfare, and when his strength finally returned, they found a job for him that he could handle. He was soon in the thick of union affairs once more.

Dan liked nothing better than being involved. It was not only interesting but often useful to chat with him. He frequently offered what seemed like good advice.

This morning he peered up at Bonta. "Yes, sir. That was one of the best things you could have done around here. Shows the men you really care." He nodded emphatically. "Yes, sir, that was a good thing."

Bonta suddenly became aware of the absence of the usual noise of coal cars being loaded and noticed a cluster of miners in front of the company store and another group by the post office. "What's going on? Aren't the men working today?"

Dan suddenly seemed less anxious to talk. He answered tersely, "Nope. They walked out." Apparently union business was better not discussed with outsiders.

We had heard rumors that a walkout might take place any day, and every morning when we woke we listened and looked up toward the tipple to see if the coal cars were moving. If the men were working, there was always some bustling activity in the center of camp. When I managed to pick up Edward R. Murrow's broadcast only the night before, he had predicted a strike in the near future and more trouble in the coalfields. It was a rare treat to hear our favorite, if pessimistic, commentator when the radio waves occasionally bounced our way. Could this be the big one everyone was anticipating?

That afternoon on the way to the post office I became curious about a ring of men and boys squatting in the dust. It seemed unlikely that union matters were the attraction. Craning over their backs, I discovered that someone had brought a rattlesnake down from the mine, held captive by a string around its neck. They were prodding the poor thing with a stick to make it rattle. It looked and sounded ferocious, twisting in the dust in a futile attempt to escape. That was my first genuine West Virginia reptile. Shortly afterward we saw one of the youngsters sauntering up the road toward the green camp, a stick over his shoulder; dangling ignominiously from it was the rattler, still writhing in protest.

"Pretty tough little big shot!" Bonta commented. "Best we check the date on that antisnake venom in the refrigerator when we get home."

I wondered what his mother would say when he appeared at the door.

6. Study in Contrasts

The men were back at work the very next day. Wearing his black miner's hat, Barney Glendon whistled as he returned from the company store. He came over to chat by the back fence when he saw us coming home from the office late in the afternoon.

"What do you think about the walkout yesterday, Doc?" Barney asked as he plucked a long-stemmed grass and chewed contemplatively on the end of it.

"Well, it didn't last very long, that's for sure. What was it all about, anyway?"

"Oh, a couple of the big shots heard a rumor that everybody was going out, and they pulled out our men. Turned out there was nothing to it. We was the only mine shut down, and some of us thought it was just a mite embarrassing."

Barney leaned back against the fence, hooking his left heel over the bottom board. He didn't seem as caught up in the local union as many of the other miners, and we wondered if his experience in Detroit had made him a little more worldly than those who'd never left the area. Perhaps the shift in jobs from mine to factory and back again had left him feeling somewhat detached. Or maybe it was just his happy-go-lucky nature that kept him from taking things too seriously.

"How about it? Do you think Lewis can avoid a real strike?" Bonta asked.

"Only the good Lord knows, Doc, but if you ask me, I don't reckon he can. The companies ain't going to go along with all he's asking for. Guess right now they're fighting over them royalties."

We were aware that Lewis wanted the companies to pay more than the current twenty cents per ton of coal mined as their contribution to the UMW welfare fund. This fund paid the hospital bills for patients Bonta sent to Welch, the medical bills for disabled miners, and pensions of a hundred dollars a month for miners who reached the age of sixty or had completed twenty years working in the mines.

"And the men, they ain't about to give up their 'willing and able' clause," Barney added knowingly. "They'd walk out before that."

Barney always talked as though he were an observer, not a union member himself. He was actually a relative newcomer, and perhaps he still felt some kinship with Ford Motors back in Detroit.

The operators claimed that this "willing and able" clause in the old contract meant that individual miners need work only when willing and able. They said the union abused it by interpreting it to sanction the whole union's working only when willing and able, thus providing a basis for a strike. The operators wanted the clause eliminated from any new contract, while the union was equally determined on its retention.

Summarizing his own feelings, Barney said, "Just wish they'd settle things so we could get back to working a full week. This on again, off again three-day stuff stinks. Oh well," he shrugged and changed the subject. "Getting kind of chilly these days. Have you picked up that stove yet?"

"No, we haven't," I answered. "And I was wishing just this morning that we had. Some heat would have felt good."

"You got to be careful when you get it, you know. This here coal'll explode on you without any warning. You just put a little too much slack in that stove, and," here he illustrated, "bango—there she blows!"

I perked up. "Slack? What's that?"

"Oh, that's that fine stuff—coal that's nothing but sand. You wait and see."

"Thanks for the warning." Then, remembering he had once mentioned rattlesnakes, I asked, "Say, did you see that kid dangling a live rattler over his shoulder yesterday?"

"Oh, heck, that's nothing. Kids around here are used to them. Find them all the time up by the mine. Might be a good idea, though, to check the yard for snakes before you let the young one out to play.

Mrs. Nichols always did. Course they're more likely to be laying in the grass after dark. Got to be careful walking in the grass at night. Copperheads is even worse than them rattlers. Smaller, and they don't make no noise."

To think that the three of us had been down on our hands and knees, creeping around in the dark gathering excelsior!

The next ten days were busy. On Saturday, September 17, I let Bonta sleep as late as I dared since he had been out till 3:00 A.M. delivering another baby, his third for the week. It was easy to see why Dr. Meade wrote long ago that those fees for deliveries would add up fast. Nonetheless, he had to open the office on time.

The rest of the morning was hectic as could be. Payday! That brought everyone into camp, where it was so convenient to stop by the doctor's office in passing. When Eloise and Bonta finally came back to the house after ushering the last patient out, Eloise flopped down on the nearest chair. She said she was "plumb wore out" and seemed glad to accept the offer of lunch with us. Afterward she offered to stay with Susan so that I could go with Bonta on a call up Road Branch. He had driven his car up there once himself and promised he would take me with him some time. There were no office hours on Saturday afternoon, and someone had brought word that Abe Lincoln Davis needed him. The Davises lived about halfway up that hollow.

Bonta had explained that his patient population included not only the miners and the lumberjacks but also the old timers up the hollows, who had eked out a living farming since long before the mine opened. The Davises belonged to the last group.

Bonta said it had been a big mistake to take our car up that creek bed, so we parked it on the road and set out on foot with the camera and Bonta's medical bag. It was a lovely September afternoon I'll always remember. The sun was warm, even though the breeze hinted of autumn. We passed a cornfield fenced in by sagging barbed wire and stopped to take a picture of the shocks, like an encampment of little tepees with tasseled tops. Their dry leaves rustled in the wind. I thought of that mysterious power that brings the seasons around, each in its own time—how marvelous that the decay of those cornstalks in autumn was just part of an orderly cycle. They had not only produced the seed for the coming year but were about to provide room and the nourishment of their own bodies for the new corn that would come up in the spring. Death really was as much a part of life as birth, and nature celebrated by making this its most resplendent season.

Very little water trickled down between the stones of the stream-bed, for we had been without rain for a week or two. If we looked carefully, we could see two irregular ruts worn by the few cars and trucks that negotiated this "road." It was a miracle those jagged rocks didn't slash their tires to ribbons. I was glad we were walking, doubly so when I happened to think of the impasse, should two cars meet.

As we picked our way along, it was like passing from the mouth of a funnel into its outlet; the flat area near the road narrowed into a valley, and the hills rose more and more steeply on either side. Occasionally there was a stretch of footpath beside the creek, but more often we picked our way on stepping-stones in its bed. For a while we saw no sign of habitation except for an occasional hen that cackled off as we came near. Then we caught a glimpse of some blankets hanging on a line through the trees, and Bonta said we must be getting near the Hanley place. A few more steps and we saw their cabin. Several bare-foot children playing on the rickety porch stared at us, and we waved as we went on our way. We overheard someone inside calling, "Hey, did you see? The doc just went by!"

The slopes on either side were covered with young trees, though occasionally we passed cleared spaces where corn was still standing. I thought of what Mr. Ramsey had said one evening. "You know, the cornfields around here are on such steep hillsides that when it comes time to plant the men just go out with their guns, point them up, and shoot the corn into the ground."

Half a mile or so farther on we came upon a ramshackle old barn that Bonta said belonged to the Davises. Long shingles drooped from its roof, and it leaned precariously, almost as though it were held up by the vines that nearly covered it. From the cracks in the loft long whis-kers of hay stuck out. Next to the barn was a small pigpen with two noisy porkers rooting about in the mud, smelling to high heaven. A little farther on we reached their house. Its crudeness was camouflaged by the masses of golden glow bobbing in the sun on either side of the door. Clumps of brilliant red salvias vied for attention just inside the gate. At this point the valley widened out enough so that the tracks of the road ran parallel to the creek for a short distance. A bridge made of two planks crossed the streamlet in front of the house, and Mrs. Davis herself was standing on it, rinsing her broom in the water.

She smiled as she called out, "Good evening, Doctor. It's mighty nice of you to come see Abe. He's sure feeling poorly."

A small woman of undetermined age, she looked self-reliant and re-silient. Her dark hair was pulled severely back in tight braids which she wore coiled low in back. As she stood leaning on her broom handle before turning to lead us into the house, she looked as though she had somehow stepped out of the pioneering past. She limped, favoring her right leg, and I noticed a bandage around that ankle.

The front door opened into a room chiefly conspicuous for the piles of clean clothing on the bed and on several boxes. I decided they must have no more closets than we did. An old treadle sewing machine stood open and ready for use. Mrs. Davis led us directly into the bedroom beyond. Abe lay in one of the two brass beds. He had sparse gray hair and must have been in his late fifties. No doubt once strong and muscular, he now looked thin and shriveled. Punctuated by frequent ejaculations of, "Lord have mercy!" he described his multitudinous troubles in a drawl.

"Well, Doc, I worry just terrible, lying here sick, and all them things out on the hill just awasting. We can't get anyone to help, now that our boy's in the army. Silas, he lives up yonder, he can't do it all 'cause he's got to work in the mine. Seems if you're sick you just lay there, and nobody does nothing, and the corn and the cane just stands there awasting. My paw and my paw's paw kept this farm going, and now I can't even lift my little finger."

In response to Bonta's query about what bothered him most, he said, "Well, mostly I feel all wore out. Besides, once in a while I see two of everything. Sometimes when Lanny walks past the foot of the bed, there's two of her, and yesterday evening when I shined this here flashlight around, like this, I seed two lights. And I don't like it, Doc, it ain't natural." Fumblingly he set the flashlight on the little table by the bed. "No, no pain, excepting in my kidneys sometimes. It do seem awful queer to be done in this way without any pain, but Lord have mercy, I'm just plain tuckered."

As Bonta examined him, he weighed this recital in his mind, trying to match it to his findings. When he noticed that Abe had some swelling of his ankles, he recommended that Lanny stop putting salt into his food.

Abe complained, "That would sure make mighty poor eating, it would. Guess my appetite wouldn't be so good after that. Course, if you want to get well, you got to be willing to do things to help yourself." He sounded forlorn in spite of his resolute words.

I had been glancing about the room. The back wall of the fireplace grate was simply a large boulder which happened to be conveniently placed in the hill behind the house, or perhaps the house had been built around it. Light was plainly visible between the house and the rock. Over the bed were two large tinted portraits in heavy oval frames; one must have been Mrs. Davis and their newborn son, and the other, either his or her parents. They seemed slightly out of focus, but this only made them look more intriguingly antique. A vivid poster of Jesus feeding the multitude with the loaves and fishes completely dominated one wall. Scattered about the room were little signs about the size of license plates, lettered in silver glitter on a shiny blue background, with legends that read, "The world is not my home," "As ye sow, so shall ye reap," "The future is in God's hands," "Book of Life—is your name therein?" and similar sentiments. A plaster frame featuring angels and flowers entwined a yellowed newspaper clipping; it was a group picture, under which the caption read, "Family of dead faith cult leader." Could the cult leader have been a relative of the Davises? Two kerosene lamps on the bureau and two large slop pails by the bed put the final stamp of a bygone era on the room.

A peek into the immaculate kitchen revealed a shiny white coal stove (however did she keep it that way?) and huge ropes of green beans and braided onions hanging from the ceiling, along with something that looked like a string of maple seeds.

Lanny had been staying modestly in the background, but she finally admitted that she wished the doctor would look at her ankle. Bonta removed the bandage and found an angry-looking sore, swollen and red with infection.

"How long have you been putting up with this?" he asked. "And what have you been doing to take care of it?"

"Why Doctor, I had it about a week. Got a little cut poisoned by the dew, you know. Ain't been doing nothing much for it."

"Now, Lanny, it's always better to tell the truth," interrupted her husband a bit severely. "Tell the doc what you been doing for it."

"Sometimes it ain't so good to tell the truth, Abe." She cast a reproachful glance in his direction. "But if you really got to know, Doctor," she admitted sheepishly, "I been feeding it light bread."

"Feeding it light bread? What exactly does that mean, Lanny?"

"Well, you make a kind of poultice of light bread soaked in cream and some castor oil too, and, well, it's been helping draw it considerable," she ended up lamely.

"I see." Bonta took a moment to contemplate this remedy. "Well, I'll tell you what I think, Lanny. I think you need a shot of penicillin and need it bad."

"Oh, Lord have mercy, Doctor! Not that—not a shot! Oh Lord, Dr. Nichols he give me a shot once, and nobody knows how I suffered. Why, he put that needle right through my shoulder, clear to the other side!"

At this point Abe took off on a recital of all the shots he'd ever had, urging her to be as brave as he'd obviously been. Just then Silas, their neighbor, came in from the cane field where he'd been out "trying to cut the tops," and the two of them finally persuaded Lanny to submit to the ordeal.

When it was over, Bonta grinned at her. "Now tell me that was awful. Just tell me you couldn't stand it!"

"Oh Doctor, I guess it didn't really hurt at all, and now Abe, he'll treat me just shameful when you're gone, for being so scared, and all for nothing."

The conversation turned to the sugarcane. "Did you ever have the skimmings off the kettle?" Abe asked me. "No? Well, you sure would like them. They're the best part of making molasses. We'll save you some of them skimmings next time."

Bonta left some pills and careful instructions, telling them to be sure and let him know if problems continued or worsened, and we said our good-byes almost reluctantly. They seemed such gentle, hardworking folk. I admired their independence. Their life might typify the simple back-to-nature existence some yearned for, but it required more coping skills than I would ever possess. The whole afternoon was an unexpected trip into the past; it seemed a privilege to become involved even peripherally with a way of life usually found only in books. Little did I know what a different experience awaited us.

When we reached home, we found Harvey Burgess leaning on the back fence, whether by happenchance or design we couldn't decide. His height and his shock of sandy hair made him easy to spot anywhere. He must have been in his early thirties. Bonta had first met him as a member of the medical committee, and of course he had driven the ambulance the night Bonta went to Welch. He was known as a strong union member. This afternoon he wore an odd expression as he greeted Bonta.

"Hey, Doc, come on up the hollow and have a drink with me."

Bonta had nothing against either Harvey or a drink, but it was nearly dinnertime and we were tired. Besides, he didn't want to become too friendly with any one person; there were too many clans in camp to become identified with one or another. He tried his best to refuse without offending him, but Harvey persisted. "Hey Doc, I just want to give you a good time. Me and Doc Nichols, we was real good buddies, and he used to come up for a drink lots of times. Besides, I want you to sign my Masonic apron. Please! It'll only take a few minutes." His fawning tone contrasted sharply with his usual bluntness.

Harvey waited for Bonta's answer with almost childlike eagerness. As it was clear the man had already had a few drinks, Bonta decided it might be best to humor him, so he agreed to go up just to sign the apron and have a quick drink. It was with some misgivings that he invited Harvey into our car and set off toward the green camp. When they reached Harvey's home, Bonta found to his surprise that another fellow was already there, and apparently the two men had been having quite a few together before Harvey came down to get Bonta. This new member of the party was known to be a hard drinker and inclined to be vicious when drunk. Bonta tried unsuccessfully to carry on a conversation with them. Neither would answer even the most innocuous questions—whether they liked to hunt, whether they had served in the army, where they hailed from originally. All attempts were met with vacuous looks, shrugs, and "Rather not say, Doc."

Bonta quit trying for a bit and sipped his drink. Harvey ran his fingers through his hair, looked up in a meditative way, and allowed as how he sure did miss Dr. Nichols. "Him and me was real pals, we was."

Just as Bonta thought it was impossible for things to be more uncomfortable than they already were, the other fellow broke his brooding glumness with a sudden angry question directed toward Bonta. "Say, I been meaning to ask you. Why'd you charge my boy what you did for that worm medicine for his young one?"

This upset Harvey who apparently didn't want things to become so unpleasant as to drive Bonta away. The more Bonta tried to explain that this medication was legitimately an extra under the contract, the more angry the man became. Since Harvey couldn't quiet him down, Bonta finally thanked Harvey for the drink and left for home.

At dinner he mulled over the situation. He didn't believe this fellow was the type Vern would have sought out. He wasn't a particularly prominent union leader, and though Vern was pretty easygoing and friendly, his tastes ran more to champagne. Besides, both he and Mr. Ramsey had told us he was rarely in camp on weekends, so he couldn't have had much time for fraternizing. Bonta couldn't fathom what was going on in Harvey's mind. Was he just odd, a homosexual, mentally unbalanced, or merely drunk? To say the least, it made me nervous to have Bonta the focus of such uncomfortable attention from Harvey and such wrath from the other fellow. The very fact that Bonta was perturbed set the alarm bells ringing in my own mind. I didn't like it a bit, but at least the episode was past—so we thought.

I was just putting Susan to bed when we heard rattling and knocking at the back door, and there stood Harvey. This time he asked that Bonta return to sign the apron and made an oblique apology for the unpleasantness caused by his friend. As Bonta again tried to beg off, Harvey's expression changed from hurt surprise at the rebuff to outright belligerence, and he reminded Bonta again of his promise to sign that apron. Bonta finally agreed to accompany him just for that, with the understanding that he'd come right back down.

My peace of mind left with them. Maybe we were reading too much into the situation. I surely hoped so, but I spent a tense half hour until Bonta's return.

Bonta reported that this visit was much like the other one. After Bonta had signed the apron, Harvey had made some simpering remarks about how Vern had really loved him and how he missed him. We were still trying to figure things out when a car stopped abruptly behind the house. My worst fears were confirmed when I heard Harvey fumbling at the back door.

This time he wanted Bonta to ride with him out of the hollow "for a real good time." By now his speech was slurred. When Bonta absolutely refused, Harvey insisted that at least he talk with him. To prevent him from pushing his way into the kitchen, Bonta went outside, hoping to get him into the car and on his way. Harvey got in the driver's seat and insisted that Bonta get in as well, though Bonta kept the door on his side open, ready to jump out if the car started. After Bonta made more futile attempts to find out what was going on, a shadowy figure appeared. This newcomer headed for Harvey's car, and Bonta didn't know whether to be further alarmed or relieved at this new development. Then the indefinite form resolved itself into the hunched person of Dan Dubois. He came up to the driver's side of the car, in the dark not noticing Bonta on the far side. Leaning toward Harvey with suppressed excitement, he reported in conspiratorial tones, "The dog died at four o'clock today!"

To Bonta's relief this news snapped Harvey out of his drunken haze, and he responded to Dan's news with joyful amazement. Just then Dan caught sight of Bonta, and suddenly both men pretended a nonchalance they obviously didn't feel. They hemmed and hawed and tried to act as though nothing unusual was going on. They seemed only too willing to let Bonta beat a welcome retreat.

It dawned on Bonta that he had accidentally stumbled on the underground code for a strike call as it was being passed along. No wonder Harvey had perked up! Mr. Ramsey had told him once about how the union had operated in its earlier days when he himself had been involved. Communications were handled by runners who went about their business at night, getting policies and decisions from one local to another by passing on secret messages at prearranged meeting places, in dark hollows, behind a particular tree, or at the fork of a creek. Of course, methods had undoubtedly changed since then, except in places without telephones like Coal Mountain, where clandestine rendezvous and coded messages could still be useful. It sounded to me like a lot of grown men still playing little boys' games. The only trouble was that popguns had been replaced by the real thing!

Bonta had just finished telling me about Dan's remark and its possible significance when we heard the sound of Harvey's car driving off, and a quick glance out of the bedroom window revealed that Dan was headed home the way he had come. Bonta heaved a sigh and settled down to ponder the consequences if his surmise about a strike proved correct. Since both of our fathers were professionals—mine an attorney and Bonta's a college professor—we had never been directly involved with labor relations, so we had little idea about what a strike might entail. Would there be picketing? Violence?

Not half an hour later we were startled by someone slamming a car door shut, dashing up the back steps, and beating on the door. Would this night never end?

"Hey, Doc, you got to come right away. Harvey Burgess's just tipped his car over down by the beer joint, and he's hurt—don't know how bad, but he's acting real queer."

Once again I was left alone to wonder what on earth would happen next. For a long time, no clues. Bonta must have gone to the scene of the accident, for it seemed an interminable time until I saw lights on at the office. Half an hour later they were flicked off, and Bonta returned to report in a tone loaded with relief that he had sent Harvey to the hospital in the ambulance. He had been cut and bruised and seemed dazed and confused all the time Bonta was examining him. Worse, he was cussing somebody up and down the whole time—Bonta? He was both drunk and disoriented, and since there was some question about whether his pupils were equal, sending him to the hospital seemed an appropriate solution.

I stared at Bonta anxiously, wishing we were a thousand miles from here. If only we had accepted the Ramseys' invitation to go with them to see the Meades in Williamson instead of waiting around in case Mrs. Dunn decided to have that baby tonight. Besides, we might have learned something about the negotiations with the union.

To think that only a few hours earlier on that walk up Road Branch I had thought life so idyllic. This affair seemed like a nightmare. Bonta went into the bedroom and returned with the little twenty-five caliber automatic his father had given him.

"You know, honey, it wouldn't do any harm for you to know how this thing works—just in case. You never know."

My heart gave a great thump. He was as worried as I was. My own fears crescendoed. I didn't even want to touch the thing, but he insisted that I learn how to put the safety on and off, cock it, and load and unload it several times myself.

"We'll go up the strip mine road one of these days, and I'll let you practice shooting at a tin can."

When I remonstrated, he said, "Well, I wouldn't want to carry this myself, but if real trouble should ever come knocking at the door, I want you to be able to shoot past me at any would-be assassin!"

The idea was so absurd I'd have burst into wild laughter if I hadn't been so scared. I knew I'd have horrible dreams all night of having missed and hit the wrong guy.

The Strike

Miners lined up at the lamphouse after work. The miners turned in their lamps daily to have the batteries recharged and also to verify that all men were accounted for after each shift.

7. Life Goes On

The next day was Sunday, and things looked better. The bright sun helped to dissipate the night's alarms, and it was comforting to know that Harvey was gone, at least for a few days.

Susan and I went with Bonta up to the green camp in the afternoon to see Freddie Kilmer. He was the secretary of the union, a sort of wispy fellow, one minute apologizing for his existence and the next, behaving like an aggressive bantam rooster. He had a raft of kids, and his wife was always sending notes down to the office by one of them about some problem or another. Lately they had been passing head lice back and forth among themselves. I had had to hand out uncounted little bottles of Kwell lotion. In fact, the school superintendent had even come to the office, asking Bonta if something couldn't be done to keep these children from spreading lice to their classmates. Our trip was necessitated by Mr. Kilmer's attack of the kizicks. Bonta explained that the term implied some kind of respiratory problem, anything from just a bad cough to bronchitis or asthma.

As Susan and I waited in the car, I was acutely aware of the surreptitious stares through curtains in nearby houses. We could hear a radio nearby blaring that we were all going to hell in a hurry if we weren't saved. The preacher had just announced the next hymn when he was interrupted by a woman who jumped in front of the microphone. In a vindictive tone she hurriedly dedicated this to "Brother and Sister Brown—they're a pair of unsaved backsliders, and I hope this song'll be a blessing to them. Praise the Lord!"

When Bonta returned, he reported that Mr. Kilmer's kizicks had been the milder variety, and the union secretary would soon be back enjoying his proximity to power.

Mr. Ramsey came over after dinner to bring Bonta some Demerol from Dr. Meade and stayed to listen to Bonta's concerns about the previous evening. He assured us that he didn't think Harvey would be more than a nuisance and urged us not to stay in camp on the weekends anyway. He said we owed ourselves an escape from the incessant demands. His paternal attitude was very reassuring.

When we asked Mr. Ramsey about the prospects for a strike, he just smiled and said, "Well now, I don't know much more than you do!"

We could hardly wait to see whether Bonta's guess about Dan's report of the dog's demise was right. First thing Monday morning, September 19, we rushed out to the back porch to see whether the tipple was working, as we'd already been doing for days. There was no sign of activity, no noise of coal being dumped into the railroad cars, no clanking of coal cars heading down the track, no miners hurrying up the road to start the day shift. The silence was almost palpable. Bonta was right. The men were all out on strike. They would soon gather, standing by the store in little knots or squatting in circles, talking excitedly. No wonder rumors flew during a strike.

We learned later that because the contract with the union expired June 30, some of the operators had refused to make the July and August royalty payments for the UMW Welfare and Retirement Fund that were due on September 1, and this angered the union. The companies claimed they were not in default because they were no longer bound by a contract. Even those operators who paid, paid less, because production was down, thanks to the three-day week, and the amount due was determined by the amount of coal mined. The fund had dropped from forty million to fourteen million over the summer, as the miners drew on it for assistance. The UMW blamed the operators, and the operators blamed the benefit program. They pointed out that the benefits were so generous that outlay had exceeded income even before the three-day workweek began. Though we were not yet aware of it, some hospitals were told that, except for emergencies, they would receive no more payments from the welfare fund for miners or members of their families after September 17.

Then the slogan switched from "No contract, no work" to "No welfare, no work." Many of the miners were boiling mad over the loss of pensions and medical benefits. The greatest turmoil was centered around Pittsburgh and the anthracite mines of Pennsylvania and northern West Virginia, but there must have been resentment and planning in our own camp of which we were unaware. As far as we could see, the men's reaction was compounded of excitement and a jaunty certainty that they would shortly win everything John L. was demanding from the companies, which they considered evil personified. Our own reaction was chiefly a conviction that, if the strike went on for very long, the men and their families would eventually suffer more than they would gain.

Union matters were kept secret from outsiders like us, and we were so busy meeting the everyday demands of the office that we didn't always realize the significance of what was happening under our very noses.

On Tuesday, just as I started to pour Bonta's coffee at breakfast, teenaged Maggie Bannister knocked on the front door. She lived a few houses up toward the green camp, and her mother suffered chronic ill health. A fragile-looking woman, Mrs. Bannister was in her mid-forties. Bonta was never quite sure how much her problems stemmed from physical causes and how much they were related to her depressed mental state. But her distress was real, so, medical bag in hand, he went up to see how he could help this time. He was as concerned about giving her too much medication as too little. A brief examination revealed nothing alarming, so he did his best to reassure her and left.

Eloise arrived a few minutes later with a strange report. "Rick Addison told me last night it must be OK for me to get drunk 'cause the doctor was drunk last Friday in the office."

"What on earth—?" Bonta stuttered.

"Well, I told him he was crazy—that I'd never seen you take a drink, and I knowed for a fact you wasn't drunk Friday evening."

"What made him think I was?"

"Well, it was something you wrote on the ambulance slip that he didn't understand, something about a broken pelvis, and he didn't know what a pelvis is or how it could be broke, so he figured you'd been drinking too much. He's been telling everybody in camp you was drunk."

"My God, how ridiculous! What won't they dream up next? You know I sent Mrs. Mitchell to Welch after she fell partway down that cliff over Leatherwood way, and I thought she might have a fracture. The pelvis is a bone! He must have had some crazy fool idea."

I said, "Thank heaven, Eloise, you can scotch such nonsense. We're sure grateful to you for keeping us posted. And for sticking up for us."

Eloise leaned forward with her elbows on the table, enjoying the gossip. "You know, him and Freddie Kilmer and a couple others went joyriding in the ambulance and ended up over at Gilbert at the movies the other night. He's been bragging about the free ride."

Bonta bristled. "That's terrible! Why, the ambulance is supposed to be in camp all the time—for emergencies. Suppose there'd been an accident while they were off gallivanting."

"Well, I guess they figure it belongs to the medical committee."

"It belongs to the union. That's who it belongs to." He set his cup down so hard the coffee spilled. "It's not a special perk for a few guys impressed with their own importance." He considered whether he ought to do anything about it. "Well, they're union men, and Freddie's a union officer, so I suppose it's really their affair. Still, I might just drop Freddie a little note pointing out how dangerous that sort of thing is. One of them might be the one needing it, who knows?"

Eloise's willingness to serve as our eyes and ears in camp was a help, and her staunch support, a blessing. Of course, working for the doctor gave her a stature in the community that was important to her, especially since she had suffered the label Hunk. Now that her father would not be drawing any money during the strike her pay was even more important.

Shortly after Eloise and Bonta left for the office, I answered a knock at the front door. It was Tillie Toler, asking that Bonta come down to see her grandmother, old Sarah Davis, whose heart was so bad. Tillie was in an expansive mood, and when Susan peeked out from behind me, Tillie started raving about her.

"Oh, it's so pretty! It's so big and fat!" And when Susan in her usual sociable way agreed to go to her, Tillie snatched her up, murmuring, "God love its little bones!"

She kept apologizing for "looking like such a mess, hadn't even combed my hair before leaving."

Eloise's terse comment later was, "Hmph! You know what all the boys call Tillie—Queen of Coal Mountain. And there's good reasons why," she said with raised eyebrows and an emphatic nod.

True, with her short skirts, flirtatious ways, and generous bosom, Tillie could have been the model for Daisy Mae of the Lil' Abner comic strip. She had been in the office earlier to have blood drawn for a premarital test, and it took half an hour and her fiancé's holding her down forcibly to get it done.

"Lord have mercy, honest to goodness, but I'm scared of that needle!" Tillie exclaimed.

Tillie was just about to tell me what she would do, now that she was rethinking her planned marriage, when someone knocked at the back door and ruined my chance to learn all.

Promising to tell the doctor about her grandmother, I bade Tillie a hasty good-bye and rushed to the back. Through the screen door I could see a pregnant woman holding the hand of a little boy about eight years old. Unfortunately en route to the door I slipped on a wet spot on the kitchen linoleum, sat down abruptly, and slithered ignominiously half the length of the room, kicking over the garbage can and nearly sweeping all the dishes off the table with one arm. I ended up on my fanny at her feet.

Had our positions been reversed, I might have laughed out loud, since nothing but my dignity was damaged, but to my amazement, not a flicker of either mirth or concern altered the woman's expression. I probably could have fractured every bone in my body, and she would still have acted as though this were the standard way to approach a caller. Even her son stood impassively by as I got to my feet, struggling with wounded vanity.

"Where's the doc?" was all she said, and I was glad to send her across the way to the office.

That afternoon we had a chance to do a small favor for Eloise and Eva. We learned that Eloise had taken a recent afternoon off in order to borrow some money from a loan company in Welch for a sewing machine both the girls wanted. When she told Bonta about it and quoted the exorbitant interest rate they would have to pay, he offered to lend them what they needed at a minimal rate. More honorable, hard-working young women it would be hard to find. They both came over after office hours to arrange the loan.

Business concluded, Eloise asked if she could show Eva our wedding pictures. We were delighted to oblige. A friend had documented the ceremony, giving us two precious rolls of film afterward. These we developed in the zoology department's darkroom. Spending a good portion of our honeymoon up to our elbows in hypo* might seem unorthodox, but we appreciated the pictures far more that way than if a studio had delivered them to us.

The girls were gratifyingly impressed by my hoop-skirted dress. Having seen Bonta only in navy fatigues, they could hardly recognize him, looking elegant and handsome in a morning coat. It was fun to see the picture of the Vassar chapel again and of Prexy, President MacCracken, who had married us on St. Patrick's Day in 1946.

✍ The following day, after lunch Bonta and I went down the road toward the cutoff to check on the baby he'd delivered two days earlier. He said it would be OK if we were a few minutes late for afternoon office hours, and it was a good excuse to enjoy a gorgeous autumn day. The sumac was flaring red on the lower slopes, and there was an invigorating zip in the air. Luckily we met few cars. An encounter always necessitated hastily winding the windows shut against the cloud of dust trailing each one. Power windows were a luxury yet undreamed of.

On the way Bonta told me a little about the baby's arrival. "For one thing, Mrs. Hacker is in her mid-forties. A bit old for having babies. Luckily it wasn't her first. Never saw anybody more stoic about a delivery. She just lay there and grunted a little. Pushed that baby out as casually as though she did it every day. Soon as I laid it on her belly, even before the cord was cut, she asked Nelson—that's her husband—to hand her a cigarette, and she just lit up."

*Sodium thiosulfate, a fixing agent in photography

Such grit was beyond my comprehension, and I looked forward to meeting her.

The Hackers' house was definitely the most dilapidated I had entered. The wallpaper hung down in tattered ribbons on both walls and ceilings, and the floor appeared to be no more than hard-packed earth. The room was alive with children and grandchildren, dogs, and even a couple of chickens. Two fat pigs grunted just outside the door. I thought of Bonta spending long hours there. Mother and baby were resting side by side on a narrow bed, made up in haphazard fashion with faded blankets. Sheets were missing. The baby itself, however, wore a new nightgown and was wrapped in a new pink receiving blanket.

To Bonta's inquiry about her health, Mrs. Hacker answered, "Well, Doc, I'm doing all right. Got up this morning to feed the young ones, and I reckon I'll be feeding the chickens and slopping the hogs in a day or two." Her resonant voice underscored the vigor of her words. "Don't know if I got enough milk for the baby here, but I'm going to try."

Her husband, Nelson, pants torn at one knee, graying hair long enough to curl on his neck, waited for us outside. He invited himself to a ride back to the lumber camp for some supplies for the house he said he was building. At least there was hope that their situation might improve, but I wondered whether the strike would interfere. He regaled us with tales of his first wife, whose hot temper drove him out. "Now this one's a good woman. She been a right good stepmother to my five living young ones from my first wife. And now she's had nine more of her own."

My astonishment must have been obvious, for he reassured me, "Oh, she's young and strong. Only forty-four years old. Course," he added with a sly grin, "I'm not doing too bad myself for being sixty-three."

❧ The evening news etched September 23, 1949 in our memories. Edward R. Murrow reported that the Russians had set off an atomic explosion. We should have known they wouldn't be far behind us. But suddenly the world seemed a more dangerous place.

We had always talked about our future as if it were so secure: another child or two, Bonta's residency followed by a career as a practicing physician somewhere near home, maybe back to teaching for me if the opportunity should arise after the children were in school. Now it was all changed. We knew Murrow always anticipated the worst, but we still couldn't see anything but big trouble ahead. It was so much simpler right after the war, when the United States was clearly on top. A real confrontation with the Russians might be imminent. We talked it all over till bedtime and beyond. We estimated we might have about ten years' grace before some horrendous catastrophe.

So what should we do? Give up on the idea of having any more children because it would be unfair to bring them into such a frightening world? I didn't want to have sons to be sent off to war. Should Bonta get all the training he could as soon as possible so that he would have a better assignment in the navy when he was recalled? Or should we stay in Coal Mountain longer than we'd planned, make as much money as possible, and live it up while we could? The last alternative was not our style; we had been thoroughly imbued with a combination of the work ethic and frugality.

I felt somehow cheated, as though the rug had been pulled out from under us. But, though the future had become a huge question mark, we still had tomorrow to get through, and life did go on. Besides, I was not prepared to abandon my deepest desire just yet. I wanted another baby.

As a result of our discussion, I spent several evenings writing letters for Bonta to various hospitals about possible residency appointments.

By now I was very comfortable seeing patients in the office. I felt I had really arrived the afternoon I cleaned up a woman's hand, badly infected following a burn. My stomach didn't even quiver. When I had some responsibility for handling problems myself, things went far better than when I was a mere observer.

In fact, life in camp was actually going along very smoothly. I had almost forgotten about Harvey Burgess. He showed up about a week after that upsetting evening, and Bonta had a chance to talk with him, anxious to defuse any resentment Harvey might still harbor. Harvey acknowledged that some of that cussing had been about Bonta, but he insisted that most of it was about the fellow who had embarrassed him by his belligerence when Bonta was visiting. At least, after the first awkward moments, they managed to carry on a friendly enough conversation. And that helped. But I would never look at Harvey in quite the same casual way as before. I saw the car he had flipped; it was almost totally demolished.

An elderly lady came in the office on Tuesday afternoon with a "smothering" problem. She lived in Long Branch, about fifteen miles away. People in camp considered Long Branch "the other side of the tracks." Most of the people who lived there were old-time inhabitants, from long before the mine opened. The majority belonged to one of three clans, and this woman proudly informed me she was a Morgan herself. A cheerful, spry little woman, she had been patiently smoking her pipe in the waiting room.

Bonta found that her main problem was her high blood pressure. He asked her if Dr. Nichols had ever suggested she go easy on the salt. She acknowledged that he had, but that was just too much to expect of anybody: "Might as well not eat at all." She said she ate "a heap of apples, and they don't taste like nothing without salt," this with a roguish grin.

Bonta gave up on the salt angle and switched to a discussion of some pills he wanted her to take. He also told her in great detail how to treat scabies,* which he had discovered on her hands, and told me to get her a tin of ointment. She smiled amiably through this recital until Bonta casually used a term that meant something to her.

Disbelief and shock were written all over her face. "Why Doctor, you don't mean I've got the itch! Where'd I ever have got that? I just couldn't have the itch. Ain't been nowheres where they had the itch!"

Bonta assured her it was nothing to worry about. The salve would fix it up if she used it the way he described. "You tell me what you're going to do with the salve and the pills when you get home." He leaned back expectantly.

"Why, just what you told me to, Doctor, just exactly."

"I'm sure, but you tell me just what that will be."

"Aw shucks now, Doctor, you tell me. I forget so plumb fast I disremembered everything."

*Itch caused by mites

Bonta enjoyed this interview; she had such a sense of humor about her own difficulties that it was impossible not to chuckle with her. "Here, I'll write it all down for you, just what you're to do."

As he listed the steps, she watched him with open admiration. "I sure wish I could use a pen like that—so fast—and such real pretty writing." She took the note and scrutinized it, holding it only a few inches from her eyes. "Well, you see, I could read it real good if I only had my glasses. They're broke, and it sure do make reading mighty hard!"

As she left still squinting at the message, I was reluctant to see her go. I did hope she or somebody else could decipher the instructions so that she would be able to take care of herself properly.

That evening Bonta went up to see Mrs. Lambert who had shown some signs of going into labor when she was in the office earlier in the day. She was already overdue. She had followed Bonta's schedule for her prenatal visits so faithfully he was doubly anxious that nothing should go wrong. She always had some story to share about her youngsters and always asked about Susan. "I'd have knowed that was the doc's young one if I'd have seen her first all by herself down the hollow." Her husband was a foreman whom we respected as conscientious and hard-working.

Bonta returned to say nothing much was happening yet.

But no sooner had we started to drift off to sleep than Mr. Lambert arrived. "Hey, Doc, you got to come quick. Something's bad wrong!"

Bonta got back at eight the next morning. He had spent a worrisome night with a complicated delivery. Mrs. Lambert probably had a placenta previa*; this would account for the bleeding that frightened her husband. Fortunately things didn't get out of hand, but it was an anxious wait with no transfusions available, had they been needed. Bonta gave Mrs. Lambert as little analgesic as he could, but in spite of that, when the baby finally arrived, it was so lethargic he had a difficult time getting it to respond. It was their fifth girl, and they were none too happy about that, but considering everything, they had good reason to be thankful that both mother and baby were going to be all right.

*Abnormal placement of the placenta leading to dangerous bleeding during delivery

Bonta had slept just an hour when a grizzled miner came to ask him to see Clinton Witt down in Cub City. Clinton was a paraplegic who had battled a distressing urinary tract infection ever since his injury in a mining accident earlier that year, so we both set off as soon as morning office hours were over. Ordinarily I would not have gone with him, but Eloise said she was in no hurry to get home, and Bonta had been yearning to give me the thrill of fording the creek at Leatherwood.

I braced myself as the car tilted ominously, heading down the steeply sloping bank. Then we were in the stream. The way the car lurched about on slippery, uneven rocks was appalling, and the water kept getting deeper. Surely we'd stall in midstream. I had seen other cars make the crossing, and from a distance it didn't look too bad. Experiencing it was a different story. I hoped Bonta would make all Cub City patients thereafter drive him across in their own cars.

The road beyond was nothing to brag about either. It was, he reminded me, that awful road he had had to back down in the Plymouth. I held my breath as we hugged the rock wall side of the narrow passage and prayed no fallen rocks would obstruct our progress this time. I hardly dared glance to the left, way down to the big Guyandotte River. How trees managed to cling to that vertical cliff was a puzzle. Billowing white clouds contrasted with the blue of the sky, and I should have concentrated on the spectacular scenery, but my enjoyment was tempered by the thought that we had to drive back the way we had come and ford Cub Creek besides.

After examining him, Bonta left Clinton some sulfa, knowing he would be needing a lot more attention as time went by.

"Sure hope I won't have to send him to the hospital. The welfare fund wouldn't cover it right now." As we drove home, Bonta explained, "He got hurt only a couple weeks before you came. Some fellows tore into the office one morning. Yelled something about a slate fall in Number Twelve mine. And somebody being hurt real bad."

He swerved to avoid a cow in the road.

"Well, I dashed up to the portal. (Didn't know I could move so fast, did you?) Yes, I got there on the double and got on one of those little coal cars, all ready to go on in and check the damage. I was pretty excited, what with a real emergency and my first chance to go into the mine. But just then one of the guys called out on the radio and said they'd put the fellow on a car. He'd be out in a minute." He continued ruefully, "That blew my trip in. And I haven't made it yet."

He paused to concentrate on a particularly narrow stretch of road. At least my concern over the hazards of the drive were being eclipsed by thoughts of the hazards of mining.

"Sure enough, Clinton came out. Looked pretty bad, I can tell you. He was awake all right, but when I asked him to wiggle his foot, he couldn't do it. Then I pinched his thigh, and he couldn't feel that. Bad news. It looked like possible spinal cord injury. Nothing I could do right then, and he was all strapped on that board pretty well, so I just sent him to the hospital in the ambulance.

"The thing that really got to me, though, was something one of the fellows from the boardinghouse told me later. You know I've given a talk to the men about emergency care since you've been here. Well, I'd given one before. Emphasized the importance of not moving an injured man from the spot where the accident occurred—putting him on a board, immobilizing him immediately—to prevent spinal cord injury. Seems this fellow had listened real hard. He told me that class had sure helped. You should have seen how proud he was when he said, 'I sure got him on that board all right, and the only hard part was lugging him on my back the thirty feet from where he was laying!'"

"Good grief! How dreadful!" I said as the implication sank in. "What are the prospects for his getting over this paralysis?"

"Only time will tell."

"Sure takes guts to go into that hole, doesn't it?"

Our coal stove had finally arrived, and we spent hours trying to set it up in the middle of the living room. Since the pipes at the company store didn't fit, we went to Pineville Thursday afternoon. This was a very small town but a lot nearer than Williamson, and we hoped it would have the right kind of pipe and whatever else was needed to put the stove in working order. The sun was the only thing that had been keeping the house warm, and when it rained, we literally shivered.

Eloise went with us and regaled us en route with stories about her problems at home.

"Sometimes I'm so tired I could just die. You know we all sleep in the same bed, me and Eva, Nan, and Betty. Eva'll pull the blanket off me, and when I grab it back, she gets so mad she kicks me. And then Betty'll pull them all to her side of the bed off from both of us. And we both freeze. Course on hot nights it used to be the other way. Nan'd just shove them all on top of me. And I couldn't hardly breathe. Nobody can ever sleep good. We all get in each other's way."

So now I knew how they fit seven children into two bedrooms.

"Nan and Betty, they talk so cross at me and Eva because they have to clean and cook while me and Eva's away working. It's only fair, but they quarrel at us all the time."

I knew that, reluctant though they might be, Nan and Betty must do a good job, since Bonta had told me the Horvath home was so clean one could eat off the floor.

Our own house was frigid when we returned, and after a futile attempt to fix the pipes, we decided to go to bed in self-defense. We just hoped someone would take pity on us soon and help.

Barney came over to discuss the pipe installation with Bonta the next morning, but even he didn't have any helpful suggestions. "Don't know, Doc, but maybe you and me made a mistake coming down here. I didn't like Detroit real much, but at least you had a decent furnace to keep warm!"

Mr. Ramsey came in after dinner to take a quick look at it. He had only good things to say about the stove itself—ought to heat a six-room house, let alone our little place. So I was more anxious than ever to get it fixed. He was kind enough to offer to send Nick Morgan over the next day to work on it.

Saturday confusion reigned. Mr. Ramsey was good as his word. Nick arrived just as Bonta was about to leave for the office, and shortly after that Mr. Ramsey himself came to see how things were going and to help if he could. Bonta finished seeing the few patients waiting for him and returned to find out how it should be done. Skilled as he was with scalpel and needle, he was not the greatest handyman around the house.

Eloise came with him, glad to earn a little extra by working overtime. She and I rearranged furniture to accommodate the stove more gracefully, while all the men fussed over it. Then Barney dropped in to see what progress was being made and offered his expertise. His chief contribution proved to be entertaining us with the latest jokes.

Meantime Susan was running around getting into everyone's way.

In the midst of it all, Mrs. Abe Lincoln Davis came to ask for help getting her son out of the army. She confided, "I never did want him to go, but you know, there ain't much a mother can do when a boy's got his mind set on something. I remember how bad he wanted to go during the war, but, glory be, he wasn't old enough. Sure need him home now. Abe, he's still so weak he can't do nothing no more."

She had hitched a ride all the way from Road Branch, so Bonta left the stove in other more competent hands long enough to dictate a letter to me, pointing out how badly the young man was needed at home since his father's illness. We doubted it would do much good, but we both wanted to help her as much as possible. She no longer limped, and we were relieved to find that the infection on her ankle was entirely healed.

Our helpers persisted; determination and skill finally triumphed, and by suppertime we were basking in unaccustomed warmth. To my relief nothing exploded. But a fair amount of smoke and soot escaped, making it clear I would have to spend a lot more time housecleaning in the future. The stove did give off a gratifying amount of heat, just as Mr. Ramsey had predicted. Bonta hadn't dealt with coal since he was a child and helped his father dispose of the ashes from the furnace. My family never dealt with coal at all because our house was heated by steam from Great Uncle Henry's nutcracker factory.

With the stove finally working, we realized that the small supply of coal in our coal shed was being rapidly depleted. Soon we would be no better off than before it was fixed. A day or two later I stopped by the company office to order a ton, but Randall Hatfield, the office manager, said there would be none available until the strike ended. He thought that might be pretty soon, but meantime he suggested we take a little wagon up by the mine and get some ourselves. I decided this must be Randall's little joke. There were some small private mines around where people had just dug into the mountain on their own, but, being inadequately supported, these were very dangerous. So I knew he didn't mean those. But as far as I knew, there was no coal lying around for the taking near the big mines. It did seem odd to be short of coal in a coal camp.

This was the extent of the impact the strike had on us so far. The camp seemed undisturbed by it except for the unnatural peace. Miners talked by the steps of the company store, lowering their voices when either of us passed near, or sauntered up and down the road behind our house without their miners' caps when they would normally have been working. The tipple was silent, and empty coal cars stood idle on the tracks across Cub. We missed the noise of their clashing.

Bonta was not quite as busy, since fewer people came to the center of camp, but there were enough colds, minor injuries, and deliveries to keep him occupied. Of course, we would not be getting paid until the men were back at work, but we weren't worrying about that yet. He was grateful for a little time to spend reading his journals. Patients almost never commented on the strike, and if they did, it was only to chat about what they were doing with their free time.

No word of the troubles elsewhere reached us. On September 23 near Clarksburg, West Virginia, a 150-car caravan of roving pickets forcibly closed nonunion mines operating in defiance of the walk-out. They dumped tons of coal from the tipple and the nearby loaded trucks, smashed equipment, and beat up several nonunion miners. Local police were unable to stop the cars that were going from mine to mine, and by the time state troopers arrived, the pickets had melted away.

On September 29, the tenth day of the strike, a number of men were arrested in northern West Virginia, as armed pickets intensified their efforts to keep the nonunion mines closed. Nonunion workers, most of them strip miners, were digging coal with rifles at their side. Shots were exchanged in a mine near Birmingham, Alabama, and the governor of Virginia, declaring an emergency, ordered the men back to work. The UMW labeled the situation a "no day" work week.

Throughout Pennsylvania and the West Virginia panhandle, some 250,000 men had been idled, and the backlog of human misery increased as welfare and medical benefits were shut off. Many hospitals, like the one at Welch, and many doctors, like Bonta, were continuing to care for the men and their families without pay, but in spite of this, many people went without needed treatment. The miners, however, were used to long strikes and had implicit faith that Lewis would soon gain his demands for them and that they would be back digging coal. Meantime the companies were extending credit at the company stores, and few, if any, were yet going hungry.

Some of the men in Coal Mountain put their enforced vacation to constructive use. Bonta told me about the effort one couple was making to get ahead. He'd noticed that they had quite a little library when he went to the green camp to see their sick baby. When he commented on it, Mrs. Ross said, "Oh, yes, I read whenever I can get the time. Right now I'm studying to help Jack get his foreman's papers."

When Bonta asked why she was studying when her husband was the one who had to take the exams, she explained that she drilled him on the material.

"Why, after he takes that exam, I take it myself, to see how he did. He's doing right smart."

Surely such effort deserved to be rewarded.

Among other projects during the strike, some of the miners who lived over by Leatherwood built a wooden bridge over Cub Creek where we had forded it. I was glad, in retrospect, that I had had the experience of fording it before this great modernization took place. Apparently there were plans under way to hardtop the dirt road, and Mr. Ramsey said the county might build a new road into camp from Oceana on the other side of the mountain so that the company could draw on more workers once the strike was over. A general spirit of optimism prevailed around camp. Dan Dubois peered up at Bonta, assuring him, "Won't be long now. You'll see. Better days are coming."

With more men on the payroll and better roads, we might be tempted enough to stay two years after all. It was going to be interesting to find out how hard Bonta would have to work once the mine operated again on a five-day week. He felt busy enough when it was not working at all.

✎ On Wednesday Eloise bounced into the kitchen after lunch, unable to contain her wrath. "I'm so mad at Alison!"

Alison handled the children's clothing section for the company store. It was she whom Barney Glendon was dating. We'd been told that, like him, she had come to the camp only recently, and it was possible she was impressed by Barney's stories about life in the big city of Detroit. Mrs. Ramsey, our ready source of camp gossip, told us she had grown up in a tiny hamlet nearby, where she had worked in the little country store before moving to Coal Mountain. The bustle at the much larger company store put her at the heart of activity in a community she was proud to be a part of. Being entrusted with the responsibility of managing a small piece of the enterprise was a real step up for her.

"She been telling everybody I look like a gypsy with my new gold earrings. I just been to the store, and Eva says they all think it's real funny."

Eloise had finally persuaded Bonta to pierce her ears, and Alison must have been expressing a minority opinion, since there were several more requests for ear piercing after Eloise flaunted new gold hoops.

"Course, I don't care none. She's just jealous." Eloise tossed her head scornfully, making the earrings dance from side to side.

It was true that Alison went to great lengths to look as glamorous as possible. Her hair was always curled, and she even wore lipstick, very unusual around camp. I wondered if she'd been influenced by the movie magazines she kept under the counter to read whenever there was a lull in business. Attractive as she was, it was not surprising that she had caught Barney's eye.

"But she don't have no cause to be jealous," Eloise said with a touch of envy in her voice. "I heared her and Barney's going to get hitched pretty soon."

This was an interesting bit of gossip we'd missed. Apparently Barney was settling down, and we were pleased for him. We just hoped Alison was the right one. Eloise said she was a few years older than Barney, which should present no problem, but some of Eloise's reports made Alison sound very self-centered.

Bonta looked over toward the office, saw no one waiting, and suggested I go with him while he used the opportunity to make a postpartum call on Laurel Hatfield. A week earlier he had delivered her healthy baby girl. He had told me about the Hatfields' little home at the head of Road Branch, so low-ceilinged that he had to be careful not to straighten up without thinking. The only light that night came from the fireplace, a kerosene lamp, and the flashlight he used when he checked for perineal tears. Poor Laurel had had a rough time and called Bonta several unflattering names. He said her husband Marcus had been very helpful, though with his unruly hair and gangling figure he looked more like a kid himself than a new father. Marcus was a very likable young man.

Bonta thoughtfully invited me to share interesting visits when he could. Those trips were far superior to secondhand reports from him in giving me insight into life in the coalfields. I sat at home with Susan often enough to seize every chance for a miniadventure.

So we set off down the hollow after lunch, leaving Susan with Eloise.

I waited in the car while Bonta made a quick stop on the way to see Mrs. Jimmy Irons. She was recovering from a hysterectomy after the tragic death of that baby Sadie Hatfield had tried to deliver. Apparently she decided she had suffered enough and persuaded the doctors at Welch to perform the surgery that would guarantee she'd have no more pregnancies.

We parked our car on the main road at the foot of Road Branch and transferred into Benjie Hatfield's battered green truck which was waiting to take us up to the top. I was about to learn how it felt to ride instead of walk up that creek bed. Neither Benjie nor I referred to the episode we shared when I drew his blood.

What ensued defies description. I had never been so jolted and jounced in my life; it was like being in an automatic paint shaker. We couldn't have missed a single one of those rocks we had seen on that afternoon walk.

But at the end of the line, we found ourselves completely surrounded by the mountains freshly decked out in their autumn dress, flaming reds, russets, and golds, with enough green to blend them into a rich brocade. The sumac cascaded down the hillsides like wine-colored foam. Many people had better houses than Marcus and Laurel did, but, just as Bonta had told me, nobody on earth could have a more breathtaking view. And they had it all to themselves. They grew what they could use themselves: sugarcane, potatoes, corn, even a little tobacco. They raised their own pigs, a few sheep, and a couple of cows. They were almost self-sufficient, but Marcus worked in the mine like most of the other men.

We found the baby and Laurel, a big buxom girl with wavy blonde hair and a cheerful smile, both doing well. She had no recollection of having cussed Bonta out for not making things easier for her and was much embarrassed to see him after her mother told her all she had said. She had thought very little of him that night. It was really quite funny, and she needn't have worried. Laurel was wearing a short-sleeved flowered cotton dress in bed, and that embarrassed her, too, since she hadn't seen us in time to put on her nightgown. As we left, we found their adorable little sixteen-month-old girl toddling around the yard which was full of mud and cow dung. She turned to wave bye-bye to us and at that critical moment down fell her diapers.

Benjie drove us back down, taciturn as usual, grunting assent to Bonta's request to allow us a brief stop at the Davises' house on the way. Mrs. Davis was scrubbing up basins and other equipment used in making molasses. Mr. Davis was sitting on the porch and looked a bit better.

"Now, Doctor, I got out of bed, and I'm setting in this here chair. But, Lord have mercy, I'm weaker than a sick lamb. It's my back. Hurts like a toothache."

Bonta checked him over again, gave him some pain pills, and prescribed heat treatment for his back. Whenever Bonta made house calls, he was apt to pick up other patients in addition to the one to whom he was responding. This trip was no exception. The Davises' retarded daughter, who was rocking rhythmically near her father, had several badly infected sores on her legs. Bonta recommended hot soaks for these, as well as for her father's back. All this meant more work for poor Mrs. Davis, who was running the farm, making molasses, cooking, scrubbing, and doing the laundry. She was hardly a rugged soul herself. I did hope the army would bend a little and send their son home to help.

After we finished the professional part of the visit, they insisted on giving us a large jar of molasses so that we could "have some skimmings." I was sure they picked out the best, the one with the most "skimmings." Mr. Davis assured us that it was "a mighty fine jar of molasses" as we accepted it. Then he told us of the dreadful experience he had endured the day before. He had tried to help with the molasses making, which involved pouring water from a barrel into one end of the trough full of cane which they had crushed in their mill, heating this to boiling by a wood stove at one end, and draining off the finished product through a hole at the other end.

"I was trying to put some more wood on the fire. Got to keep it real hot so as the water boils the cane good. Then, Lord have mercy, I was took with a fainting spell. I like to have fell right into the boiling vat! It was a miracle I didn't. But just then one of the horses slipped his halter and ran into a mess of our bees. We keep a couple hives by the fence over yonder, you know. Lord have mercy, that horse was like to bolt right at me and me helpless as a newborn baby!"

We couldn't help smiling at the picture he painted in this drawn-out recital, forgivable, we hoped, since he had, after all, survived.

We were ignorant of the events elsewhere that afternoon. John L. announced his terms: the eight-hour day must be reduced to seven, the royalty of twenty cents per ton increased, base pay of $14.05 raised to $15.00, and work spread evenly among all union members. (Lest it sound as though the miners were grievously underpaid, one must realize that this wage scale was higher than that for most heavy industries at the time, in recognition, no doubt, of the greater hazard.) Meantime violence continued to flare elsewhere. Trucks were overturned and three tipples dynamited in Pennsylvania while we were enjoying the pastoral peace of Road Branch.

8. Susan

Eloise and Susan had become the best of friends, and no wonder: Eloise spoiled Susan outrageously. Eloise played house with her and taught her songs, which Susan tried to sing for us without much success. Eloise dressed Susan up like a doll and took her for walks around the camp. Sometimes they wandered over by the railroad embankment, where Eloise showed Susan how to launch a cloud of silvery parachutes from the ripe milkweed pods.

On visits to the company store, Susan was granted freedom to explore wherever her curiosity drew her. There Eva often sat her on the counter by the cash register, teaching her to push the button that totaled the cost of the customers' purchases and allowing her to hand out the slips. Everyone in camp knew "the doctor's young one."

One day Eva noticed that Susan was enchanted by a little red rocking chair, lugging it around until Eloise said they had to go home. Bless Eva, if she didn't buy it for her. Next day when Eloise took Susan over to pick it up, Susan insisted on staggering home with it herself. Of course, it was a very small chair, and she was a very determined young lady. She spent the rest of the day transferring it from one room to another, and it was her favorite seat for listening to stories as well as for rocking dolls.

Eloise often took Susan up the hollow to visit Mama Horvath, as she taught Susan to call her mother. Mrs. Horvath was almost always in bed those days, and Susan's cheerful jabbering was a bright spot in her long days. Susan loved nothing better than entertaining her, playing the clown, flirting and winking, thoroughly enjoying an appreciative audience.

Before long Eloise began to understand Susan's jargon as well as Bonta and I could. It was sometimes fortunate that no one else could, for Susan's favorite occupation on a pleasant day was to stand on the bottom rail of the fence behind our house and hail passersby. She waved enthusiastically to all who came down the road, and she sometimes held court for groups of neighborhood youngsters who were kind enough to stop and listen. When miners occasionally came by straight from the mine, she greeted them with stern cries of, "Doy! Doy!" Only we knew that meant, "Dirty! Dirty!"

When one of the men once asked me what she was trying to say to him, all I could think to answer was, "Oh, she's just talking about her toys. She broke one this morning."

She was fairly resourceful at entertaining herself when necessary. She loved to walk around her small fenced domain alone, and I welcomed requests to let her out to "walk 'round," until the day she slipped in a cowpie left by the Davises' holstein. Her distress was nothing compared with mine, and unfortunately this was not an isolated incident. The cow should never have wandered in our yard, but that back gate had never been fixed. Once when I glanced out to find the cow there I took Susan out to see it; she was both thrilled and appalled by this close encounter. From her point of view, there were always new things to marvel at. Occasionally a horse or one of the two donkeys that enjoyed the freedom of the camp paid us a visit.

One of the neighbor's hens took a liking to a packing box partly filled with excelsior, which we put out on the back porch before throwing it away. Susan liked the hen because it had pretty feathers and cackled. I liked it because it laid an egg in the box every morning for several weeks. I became addicted to truly fresh eggs for breakfast, and, not knowing whose hen it was, I suppressed the guilt I might have felt.

To give Susan something living of her own, we purchased two goldfish. These were of great interest, but I must have slipped up on their care and feeding because their life was all too brief. We let Susan put the little corpses in the brook, "back in their 'ome."

She gave her dolls countless baths in a pail of soapsuds on the back porch, and I even interested her in finding pretty stones to wash when

Eloise with Susan and me in the backyard of our home in Coal Mountain.
Eloise was our helper in both home and office, one of our main links to the
community, and a good friend.

the dolls lost their charm. When I felt she really needed some new toys, I ordered some modeling clay, fingerpaints, and a little red telephone from the latest Montgomery Ward catalog. I had become as dependent on wishbooks as everyone else in camp. The package duly arrived, and I put the telephone by her crib as a surprise when she woke from her nap. Eloise reported that it was an instant success. Susan spent the rest of the afternoon having imaginary conversations and ringing its bell. However, Eloise added, "Now Susan's little phone don't ring no more. She wanted me to play calling her up on it, and I did till I got plumb tired out. Then she got so mad she throwed it on the floor and the bell broke." Hard lessons for a little girl to learn.

With the toys came a pair of little duck slippers. Susan was overjoyed when we showed her how they quacked when pinched. But when she discovered she lacked the strength to do it herself, the thunderclouds rolled in. Her wrath at such times was positively Churchillian. With her fat little cheeks, she often reminded us of Sir Winston.

Though she seemed to be well adjusted to this new way of life, there were times when the daily separation from Mommy overwhelmed her. She had spent the first year and a half of her life in a one-room apartment with me while Bonta was in the navy, and I danced attendance on her constantly when we were in Herkimer waiting. So it was something of a shock to her to have me disappear half of every day and sometimes longer. I had to adjust to our increasing separateness, too, as work in the office occupied more and more of my time and energy. Occasionally she demanded that I hold her when I came back in the late afternoon from the office, and I confess I got dinner more than once with her in my arms. In retrospect I realize my mother was right—I probably did spoil her.

When she was tired or stressed she reverted to her babyhood dependence on her kitty blanket. Sucking on a corner of it still soothed her to sleep; clutching it to her breast gave her courage to meet the unknown. The state to which this constant use had reduced the blanket had been my mother's despair. She had more than once threatened to rip it in two so that half of it could always be in the laundry.

Late one evening I heard Susan calling from the bedroom, and it sounded as though she said something was spilling. When I investigated, I found her description quite accurate. She was a pathetic sight, having thrown up all over the bed. When she next called, " 'Pill! 'Pill!" I responded on the double.

Whenever she saw Bonta and me kissing each other, she promptly ran over for her turn, looking like a little bird begging its parents to feed it. I sometimes wondered how such a tiny being could fill so much space in one's life. I was grateful Bonta could share in her development to a degree never possible with our later children, when he was a busy surgeon. In spite of his erratic schedule in camp and frequent lengthy calls, the proximity of the office meant that he was in and out of the house more than he would ever be again.

As every young mother can appreciate, it was a source of great joy to watch Susan growing into a little person, learning to communicate better each day. Coal Mountain helped her change from a baby to a sturdy two-and-a-half-year-old, who felt the world was full of wonderful surprises, all designed for her benefit.

9. Eloise

Life kept throwing new challenges in Eloise's path.

One morning she was writing on Mrs. Carson's chart as Bonta dictated. Mrs. Carson, who was all of seventeen, was due to deliver in about a month, and she wasn't feeling very well that morning as she lay on the examining table. Bonta suddenly became aware that she was about to throw up and called out to Eloise, "Pail! Pronto!"

Eloise didn't move quite fast enough. She arrived with the pail just in time to catch it all down her skirt. Poor Mrs. Carson was embarrassed. Eloise was horrified. She fled the scene and could be heard running water in the lab full force. She scrubbed and rinsed and rinsed and scrubbed again and finally took off for home and a change of clothing.

She told us indignantly after lunch that her father was anything but sympathetic. In fact, he was convulsed with mirth over his fastidious daughter's discomfiture. Poor Eloise had been even more sheltered from this aspect of life than I had been. Having a baby at least forces one to confront some of the less attractive realities.

Eloise had a hard time doing some of the things Bonta expected of her. Whenever he did a vaginal exam, he asked her to hold a flashlight so that he could see what he was looking for, since the room was poorly lighted. But this was more than Eloise could manage. She simply could not bring herself to look. She aimed the flashlight in the general direction of the perineum and kept her gaze steadfastly on the view out the window. Bonta had to catch a glimpse as best he could whenever the beam of light wobbled in the right direction. No matter how often this situation arose, she persisted in this practice until he was forced to get an auxiliary light.

One day when things were quiet at the house the subject of getting pregnant came up. We assumed she understood the basics from some of her jokes and her matter-of-fact comments.

"Found rubbers in the road this morning. Janie and Ward, they was parking last night right in front of our house. Can you beat that?"

We couldn't have been more wrong. We had a wide-ranging talk, from dogs to people, and all the way to birth. I happened to have a booklet with some diagrams, which I gave her. She took it home to educate her sisters. We heard later that her father had snorted that he didn't need any such book, and Eva couldn't be convinced it really happened that way at all.

We thought part of our responsibility in camp was to promote greater understanding of the basic facts of biology and health. It seemed so strange that some parents I met shooed their children out of the room the minute adult conversation included any reference to menstruation, but nobody seemed surprised or insulted at the suggestion that their teenage daughters might be pregnant or the victim of a sexually transmitted disease. Such inconsistencies really troubled us, but we had to be very careful in any attempt to change patterns of thinking or correct medical misconceptions, since such attempts were all too easily construed as unacceptable criticism.

We hoped we weren't leading Eloise into trouble with her family as we tried to teach her some of these fundamentals about reproduction. I had the feeling that she enjoyed her sisters' shocked reactions when she shared her newfound knowledge with them.

She also carried home such new practices as leaving her sisters lists of things which needed to be done, like those I left for her. This precipitated a minor rebellion.

Eloise was definitely nervous about the prospect of being an old maid. Here she was at nineteen without a wedding band. She was currently interested in a young man who worked in the grocery department at the store. Tommy seemed nice enough; in fact, the more I heard of the way he treated her, the more I thought of him. His future seemed very limited though. He wanted to work in the mine where the pay was much better, but there was a rule that store employees couldn't transfer to the mine, so even that was out. We envisioned a more exciting future for Eloise. We admired her quick intelligence and hoped someone would come along who would appreciate this and give her the opportunity to grow beyond Coal Mountain. We always called her our diamond in the rough.

But Tommy it was for the present, and one Thursday in mid-October Eloise put on her best dress and her gold earrings and went off with him to meet his family in Kentucky. We were immensely relieved when she reported to work Monday morning, still single. She told us later that she was amazed to see how Tommy's family treated him. He was clearly adored by his mother, and his little sister even sacrificed the contents of her piggy bank so that he could take Eloise to the movies.

"That could be a hard act to follow," I warned her.

Whatever the future held, it was good to see her so happy. That Monday afternoon she sent a note to me at the office, courtesy of a youngster walking past the back gate. The note asked if she might take a bath at our house, providing she went to the store for a towel and washcloth; she had a date that night and not enough time after work.

I sent a return message—"Of course, any time, but for goodness' sake, don't buy a towel; there are clean ones on the shelf." I thought with contrition about the faucet on her family's back porch as their only source of water and wished I'd offered long before. On the other hand, such an offer could have been misconstrued. At least now she might feel free in the future.

When I got home, she told me that her family lived in the green camp because her father wanted it that way. Because of his seniority he had been offered a house in the white camp.

"But Daddy said he's always gone outside, and by God, he wasn't going to start going inside now." Eloise gamely insisted, "Oh, I'd rather live in the green camp, too. Course, I wish them green camp houses had a bathtub. Sure did like having a bath here."

She paused on her way out the door and smiled as she said, "You know, Daddy says I spend so much time down here, I might as well bring my clothes down and stay!"

Eloise was an accomplished seamstress, but she had always sewn by instinct rather than by the instructions that come with patterns. She liked the fabric I had ordered when I sent for Susan's toys and decided she wanted to make a jumper just like the red Indianhead version I was finishing. When I asked her to hang this for me, using a yardstick to measure the length from the floor, she commented, "Well, I never did nothing like that before."

"Really? How do you get the hems of your dresses even, then?" I asked.

"Why, I just cut the bottoms off and sew them up!"

She planned to order three yards of material for her jumper, even though the pattern she intended to copy called for five and a quarter yards. I had faith, however, that she would somehow work it out.

As though that weren't enough, after watching me knitting a sweater for Susan, she decided she should learn to knit a sweater for herself. So we worked on the basics.

"Just don't forget. You're going to tell me what them instructions mean. And when I get it all mixed up, you're going to fix it."

Since she had apparently done very little cooking, I introduced her to the intricacies of following recipes. Baking cupcakes was her first venture, and she was so full of self-doubt that I promised she could take some home if they turned out well. She was surprised and pleased at the result but a little embarrassed when it developed that taking one for each of her family left less than half the batch.

She hid her pride. "I swear, they'll all be coming to the office tomorrow, sick."

One day I asked Eloise to simmer a beef tongue. I told Bonta, "You never saw anyone more shocked when I unwrapped the tongue. She stared at it and asked incredulously, "You mean you and the doctor's going to eat that thing?"

And as she left afterward, she commented with a wry smile, "Hope you enjoy your supper!"

About a week after Eloise's trip to Kentucky, Bonta went up the hollow to see her mother. She was getting progressively worse, as more and more fluid accumulated in her abdomen, and he had to send her in the ambulance to Welch for yet another tap to relieve the pressure and pain.

Later Eloise remarked impatiently to him, "Why can't they make

Mother get better? I just know she'd be all right if only they'd get rid of that queer lump in her stomach."

"But you see, Eloise, that's just the problem." Bonta went on to explain what a cancer is. As gently as possible he told her what it signified for her mother.

Eloise was dumbfounded. "You mean—you mean, she ain't going to get better?" She burst into tears.

We had both assumed Eloise and Eva understood what cancer meant and had been a little surprised that they talked about it as casually as they did. However, we thought that they had simply adjusted philosophically to the inevitable. We realized now that no one in the family knew what was going on, including Mr. Horvath.

As the weeping subsided a little, Bonta began to talk to her about what this would mean to her and to the others at home. She would have to assume more and more responsibility for her younger brothers and sisters and become a source of strength for her father. If her mother was to stay at home, she would need ever more nursing care, and Eloise was the logical one to give that support.

The conversation drifted into prospects for her own future. Bonta talked to her about marriage and the commitment and maturity it requires of both partners. He asked her to think about that hard as she contemplated marrying Tommy. I'm sure no one had ever talked to her like that before, and she was more than willing to listen. One of Bonta's strengths has always been his ability to talk over people's problems and explore their options with them.

Since her eyes were suspiciously red, he asked her to join us for lunch. Perhaps she wasn't yet ready to face her family with this new insight.

He told me she considered his offer a minute before she stood up, squared her shoulders, and said firmly, "No, I'm going home. Got to think about this some more before I tell the others, though."

When she saw me after lunch, she started crying afresh. It hurt to see her so devastated, but all I could do was hug her tight and let her cry. We all talked about it a little more, and the sobs gradually quieted down. By the time I left for the office, Eloise had started playing with Susan and was outwardly her sunny self.

Next morning, however, her grief was renewed. She had just told

Eva, who was equally shaken. Moreover, at the hospital the night before her father had been told what was in store, and he was taking the
news very hard indeed. It was a great pity to see such a fine, close
family faced with such tragedy. They would need all the support they
could give each other before the sad affair was played out.

10. All in a Day's Work

Eloise wasn't the only one who was learning lessons; I had a few to learn, too. Bert Teller came to the office on a Friday in early October complaining of passing blood in his urine. I had met him when we stayed at the boardinghouse, a wizened old miner in baggy pants and a dark wool shirt patched at the elbows. His fatalistic attitude was reflected in everything he said. Bonta asked me to see that he provided us with a specimen. Bert at least understood what I wanted when I handed him an empty jar, which was more than some of the younger men did—a few times things had become a little awkward.

As he took the jar from me, he commented, "Before this puts me six foot under I figured I might as well see if the doc has any ideas."

When he shortly afterward handed me the partially filled jar, I let out a small gasp. The urine was not only bright red, it looked as though it was starting to clot. When I handed it to Bonta in Bert's presence, I commented with some feeling that it looked as though he really did have a problem.

After he left, Bonta came into the lab where I was working on the daybook. "Honey, what were you trying to do—scare poor Bert half to death? He already knows he's got a problem or he wouldn't be here. No matter what condition a patient's in, we have to play it deadpan, act as though it's perfectly routine, certainly nothing to be alarmed about. Our job is to reassure people, not make things worse!"

I must have looked crushed. He gave me a comforting pat on the shoulder and added, "Well, don't worry. No real harm's been done.

Bert's a tough old bird, and I straightened things out with him. It's just a bit of insight for future reference. Lots to learn about this business, and you're doing fine. Just give it a little more time."

That Saturday was supposed to be quiet; we were just waiting for Mrs. Carson to have her baby. Though she didn't call us, it seemed as though everyone else did. Even though there were no office hours, Bonta spent half the morning in the office seeing people who just waited by the door.

When I finished hanging out the clothes, I crossed the creek to get something from the office myself and found Mrs. Lambert in the waiting room. I hardly recognized her for a minute, now that she was no longer pregnant. When I congratulated her on having come through that difficult delivery, she startled me by asking without preamble, "Is the doctor a Christian?"

I told her he wasn't a born-again Christian as they defined being a Christian down there, though he was a confirmed Episcopalian.

"He been calling on the Lord mighty hard when the baby wouldn't breathe, and we all been studying on it since that night." They were most impressed by his distress. "Oh, his hands was just shaking, he was breathing hard, and sweat pouring down his forehead!"

I wouldn't have been surprised if at least a little of this were true. He really did sweat over that one, and he was apt to say, "Oh, my God!" under stress. But they might have taken some of his remarks more seriously than they were meant.

Our lunch was interrupted by Rick Addison. He usually drove the ambulance when it was needed—according to Eloise, even that time when it was needed only for a trip to the movies. He basked in the limelight shed by this responsibility, and he was always first at any emergency, genuinely trying to be helpful. But this Saturday he was upset because their baby's teeth weren't coming in the way he thought they should. There wasn't anything Bonta could do about this; perhaps Rick had only needed an excuse for a visit. Anyway it turned into a long confidential chat. Rick was always confidential. If Bonta just waited patiently enough, all the undercover information Rick was dying to spill would eventually trickle forth.

Rick was a tall, lanky fellow with a gaunt face. He thrust his hands deep in his pockets and leaned a little nearer as he said sotto voce, "You know, folks been mighty impressed by how much you been learning about taking care of young ones since you been here. I know some folks said they wasn't happy a while back, but things is different now."

This was the same story that Bonta had heard from Harvey Burgess that night he went with Mrs. Morgan to Welch.

It did make us wonder. A few big words, a confident manner, a pill with a fancy name, all were more effective than simple candor. This was a lesson Bonta tucked away for future use. We later found it served as well in New York or Michigan as it did in Coal Mountain. People can talk all they want about wanting to know the truth—wanting the doctor to level with them, to treat them like an equal—but deep down some of them really want a little magic and an authoritative father figure to trust.

While Bonta was away on a house call in camp, a young miner I recognized as Overt Blankenship yelled from across the creek, "Hey, Doc!" holding up the goriest pair of hands I ever hope to see.

I rushed over, taking Susan along, clad only in diapers and duck slippers.

"Cut myself in the creek while I was hunting minnows. Lost my footing and fell right on some broken glass."

I tried to clean things up in a preliminary sort of way, meantime sending the fellow who had driven him there to get Bonta. I managed to apply enough pressure to stop the bleeding by the time Bonta arrived. Gentle soul that he was, Overt was a brick about the whole thing and seemed grateful for the little I could do. When there was no one else to turn to, some things just had to be done. But it was a great relief when Bonta finally came and sutured the wound.

Once Overt's problem had been taken care of we decided to call on our new neighbors. The report Eloise had shared about Alison and Barney Glendon getting married proved true, and they had just moved in next door. We wanted to offer them our best wishes and see how they were doing. They looked pretty settled, and Alison seemed pleased by our visit. We looked forward to having Barney as a neighbor, friendly fellow that he was. Nothing ever seemed to get Barney down. He was always whistling, whether working on his old car or heading up to his shift at the tipple. I hoped Alison and I could become better acquainted, too.

Bonta decided to enlist Barney's help in a campaign to let people know that if they pestered him with problems that weren't urgent when the office was closed on Saturday and Sunday they might drive him away on the weekend, leaving no one to take care of genuine emergencies. We felt sure Barney would spread the word.

As we left, Bonta turned to me and said firmly, "We're just going to leave next weekend, no matter what."

But I noticed that about half an hour later he said, "If Mrs. Carson hasn't come through yet, guess you and Eloise'll have to go out for those errands without me next weekend."

Bonta had four other pregnant women on the waiting list, too. None were due in November, so possible deliveries wouldn't keep us in camp on the weekends. But by then the men would probably be back at work, which would of course be good, and Bonta would be too busy to leave. Since these women counted on him, he refused to abandon them. They couldn't very well go to the hospital since medical benefits were so uncertain, and even more important, they wanted to have their babies at home. He could have left them to call on Sadie Hatfield, but of course he didn't trust Sadie.

A week later Mrs. Carson still hadn't had her baby. This was the third weekend we had stayed in the hollow, expecting that one of the women who were due would deliver. Our supply situation was becoming desperate. We might have to patronize the store in camp more extensively than I wanted to; things were so much more reasonable on the outside.

We had talked over the merits of saving time and buying groceries and supplies from the company store. But we decided the price differential was too big to ignore, and it would be worth an expedition every couple of weeks to go out the fifty or sixty miles to stock up. Besides, produce at the company store tended to be limited in variety, and all too often items like celery and lettuce were a bit tired. There were some things, like milk, that couldn't be bought way ahead, but there was no doubt it was good economics to get canned goods, cleaning supplies, and such things outside. In addition, a trip outside offered a welcome change.

The miners all had cars, and it seemed strange that they didn't take advantage of the savings outside, too. But the real reason undoubtedly was that they couldn't sign a slip against their future earnings anywhere but in camp. A song that has meant a great deal to us over the years is Tennessee Ernie Ford's rendition of "I Owe My Soul to the Company Store"; we understand what it means.

Cash was not a commodity the miners dealt with. They bought almost everything on credit, just signing slips against their pay. This of course was why the company store did so well, also why medical bills and those at the store were paid so reliably. The company simply deducted what was owed from the miners' paychecks. Actually so long as the strike went on there were neither paychecks nor deductions; the debts were just accumulating. Bonta let patients sign slips against the future for extra charges they owed him; in the meantime he received no pay, neither the regular monthly withholding nor the extras. It was fortunate for us that the lumber camp continued to operate as usual.

Perhaps it was just as well we didn't try to go out that weekend, since I was fighting a cold. I spent a wretched night, apparently going over in my sleep the previous day's session of unpacking the drugs Merrell and Company had sent—100,000 aspirin tablets, including some 15,000 one-grain tablets for children. It seemed as though every minute was a one-grain aspirin tablet, and I accumulated huge piles of them which I couldn't use.

While Bonta took Susan with him to get the mail, I indulged in an afternoon nap, from which I was awakened by his calling from somewhere outside that he had a problem. I looked up groggily to see a chicken he was holding up at the window. That woke me in a hurry. He explained that Eloise's brother Jimmy had brought it down for us. He carried it by the feet and presented it to Bonta without saying so much as a word.

So Bonta was left to circle the house with this raucous creature, trying to figure out the next move. A consultation was in order. There seemed little doubt about what we had to do, since we couldn't hold it by its feet forever. We deposited Susan in the house to shield her from the gruesome proceedings. She had been petrified enough already by its hysterical flapping.

We had never faced this situation but decided to behead it on the stump beside the house. Bonta vaguely remembered his father doing this. We tied a cord around its neck for Bonta to hold with one hand,

and I stretched the chicken across the stump by pulling on its feet. With his other arm Bonta brought the ax down smartly and severed its head. Not very pretty. What we hadn't counted on was the ability of the corpse to flap around the yard. I let go in a hurry the minute it started to kick. It ended up under the coal shed, whence we retrieved it with some difficulty, its white feathers all befouled with blood and coal dust. Somewhere in the recesses of my mind I had a conviction that we should dip it in boiling water to make plucking the feathers easier, so Bonta carried through on that. I was elected, as resident zoologist, to clean out the innards.

No chicken dinner was ever fresher. We soon recovered from our initial reservations and agreed it was very tasty.

11. What Routine?

All up and down the roads that mid-October the men were out with their long guns. The squirrel-hunting season just opened, and this had been the target of much planning and excited anticipation for weeks. The men seemed actually pleased that the strike freed them to hunt all week long.

They were probably as unaware of developments elsewhere that would determine their immediate future as we were ourselves. The situation in Virginia had deteriorated so far that the governor was threatening to impose martial law to protect the miners who obeyed his order by returning to work.

Mediation efforts by the government had failed. Some people expected Truman to start implementation of the Taft-Hartley Act by appointing a fact-finding board, a first step toward an eighty-day injunction. Lewis was quoted as hinting that the men would refuse to work in spite of an injunction, even though he, as head of the United Mine Workers, would by law have to order them back.

Reports circulated that some operators and some miners wanted to get back to mining coal, and the operators indicated their willingness to accept government intervention. Lewis, however, was vehemently opposed to the idea. He belonged to the small company of old-style orators and made his case very clearly: "We don't want the government to indicate that it will use the infamous Taft-Hartley Act to bludgeon our people like galley slaves back into the mines, and seize the moneys which these men placed in the treasury of their union by loading coal in coal mines, in wet places, under dangerous rocks, in bad air, many of whom died, while the government gaily takes its money as a punitive action to force us to agree to the operators' terms."

A few weeks after this speech the Supreme Court dealt the union coffers a severe blow. It refused to hear the union's appeal from a contempt charge that stemmed from its refusal to obey a government order to end an earlier strike in 1948. This meant that the union had to pay a fine of nearly $1.5 million. It was that strike that had won for the men their hundred dollar per month pension.

◆ On Tuesday, October 18, Maggie Bannister once again came down the road to our house and knocked on the front door, and once again she caught us at breakfast. We knew what she was about to say before she opened her mouth. "Mother wants the doctor to come see her before he goes to the office. She ain't feeling so good."

Bonta went but with the uncomfortable feeling that her problems were such that he might not be able to do much to help her.

In response to his sympathetic inquiry about her condition, Mrs. Bannister poured out some of the reasons for her unhappiness. She wanted more children, but a complete hysterectomy a few years earlier effectively ruled that out. Bonta made a mental note that early enforced menopause might be causing some of her difficulties. She explained that Maggie and her two sons, now in the service, were children of her first marriage. This had been a very unhappy union to a man who subjected her to a good deal of physical abuse, and she was thankful that her present husband, Gillis, was good to her. But she stewed about her boys, and she fretted over her inability to give Gillis the child he really longed for.

She was also upset because she hadn't been able to go to the revival somewhere near Pineville, which Dan Dubois had urged her to attend. As her near neighbor and an active churchgoer, he had taken an interest in her problems and felt she would benefit from some spiritual assistance. Bonta wondered briefly whether Dan's concern stemmed more from genuine religious devotion or from his tendency to be a busybody.

Bonta found all he could do was listen to her problems sympathetically and give her something for her headache before leaving for the
office.

I spent some time that morning pleasantly browsing around the
store with Susan. We needed some milk, but Tommy explained to me
that there wasn't any because milk came in only late on Tuesdays and
Fridays since the strike had cut down demand.

Since Eva was not busy at the moment, we stopped by her cash register to chat. She was grateful for Bonta's visit to her mother the night
before. While carrying out some neurological testing to check on the
facial paralysis Mrs. Horvath complained of, he asked her to wink at
him and move her lips as he directed.

To her question, "Why" he answered, "Oh, I just like to flirt with
pretty women!" This apparently made her laugh for the first time in
weeks. Eva appreciated the exchange, even though it could distract her
mother from her problems only for the moment.

Mrs. Bill James happened to be looking over the produce section.
Ever since our friendly encounter on my very first afternoon in the
office, I had had a special regard for her. I went over to say hello,
remembering how Bonta had told me that she'd become increasingly
frustrated by the daily chores since her miscarriage in the early summer. When he questioned her about her other interests, she said she'd
always liked to design things and paint. So he had encouraged her to
put some real effort into this.

When I asked her whether she'd started on this new venture, she
put down her bag of onions and said in a confidential tone, "Why,
that's sure nice of you to ask. Course I ain't no good at it, but I got
me some paints and India ink, and I'm trying."

"What sorts of projects are you working on?"

"Well, I figured I like printing, too, and I might try to make a sign
for a friend of mine over in Pineville who wants to start a hair-cutting
business. Pretty it up like for her."

She nodded hopefully as I wished her luck.

That afternoon Barney went to the post office for the mail on his
way to the office to see Bonta about a little rash on his arm and
thoughtfully picked up ours, too.

Mail was incredibly important, both outgoing and incoming. Sometimes it seemed we spent hours each day just getting ready for the one and recovering from the other. I looked through the assortment of drug company fliers, forms from the County Health Department, serology reports, and the inevitable bills. A Christmas catalog was a reminder that the fall was passing swiftly by. At the very bottom of the pile was an envelope addressed in my sister Mary's familiar hand.

She wrote that she was planning to visit us the last weekend in October. Her bus would drop her off at Logan that Friday noon unless she heard from us to the contrary. I couldn't wait to see her, our first visitor from home since Barbara left.

Mary was always curious about everything, and her job as reporter on the *Louisville Times* had only broadened her interests. I knew she would be fired up by all we could show her. What fun! We were anxious to let someone from home share our experiences. Mary was also just the one for a real bull session about all the issues: atom bombs, strikes, socialized medicine. We might not always agree, but that was what made visits with her so interesting.

The only thing worrying me was that this meant I would have to screw up my courage and take the car out myself to meet her. I dreaded the trip, especially because of the rainy spell we'd been having, but after all, it was precisely for this that we'd bought the blue car. If the weather cleared up, it shouldn't be too bad, and I'd have company on the return trip.

That evening our coal supply ran out, and a fire was a high priority as the mercury plunged. We had developed a neighborly relationship with Barney and Alison, and Barney had already offered to let us share his more ample supply of coal.

Eloise still had her reservations about Alison. Once she said something about the importance of partners being the same age, and I pointed out, "Alison's being a few years older than Barney needn't hurt their relationship."

"A few years! Pooh!" she scoffed. "She's eight years older than he is, and she goes around acting like she was still twenty. Why, she's old enough to be my mother!"

I wondered if Alison was really that much older than Barney and, if so, whether that much of a difference in age along with the difference in their outlook—he from Detroit and she to whom Coal Mountain was big time—might eventually create a problem for them. They were very much the happy newlyweds so far as we could tell.

Concern for their marriage was farthest from my mind that night as I buttoned my jacket and headed for the coal shed. Feeling rather nervous, I filled the coal scuttle from their side of the shed by the light of our flashlight. Not knowing of our agreement, anyone who chanced to see me would surely have drawn the wrong conclusion.

🦢 The following Sunday we were just finishing a leisurely breakfast when we heard a knock on the back door. Sadie Hatfield, the midwife, had sent for Bonta the day before to help her with a delivery down toward Long Branch, but by the time he arrived, the baby had been born, the couple's twelfth child. Things appeared to be under control, so he made only a rather superficial check of the woman's condition, being reassured by Sadie that all was well. Now Mrs. Harrington was doing poorly—in fact, very poorly, her brother reported. So we packed Susan and some toys in the backseat and set off together, glad the place was this side of Long Branch Mountain.

On the way we passed Leatherwood and discovered that the bridge was finished. It was plain that it had not been built for the ages, and it looked as though it might actually be safer to ford the creek as before.

A little farther on we came to a large "meeting." The small church-house with its peeling white paint was surrounded by a collection of surprisingly good-looking cars. I wondered if the people were handling rattlesnakes inside. We had heard this was not too unusual down in Long Branch.

The rocky road up the small hollow to our destination was almost as bad as the creek bed at Road Branch—steeper but luckily shorter. Bonta parked the car in front of what could only be called a shack, with a roof that looked as though it would cave in at any moment. I didn't know how anyone living there could survive a winter with all those cracks; the floor would be cold, too, since the front of the house was supported on stilts.

We had to jump a smelly ditch to reach the boards that served as steps up to the sagging porch. Six or seven adults and at least as many children were clustered on it. I marveled that it hadn't collapsed.

Mrs. Harrington lay in one of the three beds that filled most of the main room. The midwife's ample form overflowed a straight chair at the foot of the patient's bed. The most conspicuous feature in the room was a coal stove without a door, in which a fire was blazing. Mrs. Harrington was obviously in great pain, lying under a heap of tattered blankets, though the day was hot and the coal fire hotter. Although she was still bleeding, she wore no protection.

On the bed next to hers a little four-year-old boy was sleeping; a swarm of flies hovered over him, crawling around his eyes, nose, and lips. I winced at the sight. His angelic little face was corrupted by those revolting flies, a Dali-esque image I mentally titled, "The Decay of Innocence."

Besides us and the patient, eight adults were in that stifling room; three of the women were nursing babies of assorted ages. A lively group of barefoot children were playing on the floor, their legs and arms marked by scabs and mosquito bites. Sitting off to one side was the woman's husband, wearing a shapeless wide-brimmed hat over his long, curly gray hair and peering at us through thick lenses, when he wasn't perusing various documents at a distance of about two and a half inches from his eyes. He was Preacher Harrington, probably about sixty-five, and now and then he addressed us with an erudite phrase replete with biblical references.

We stayed what seemed like a long time because the poor woman appeared to be quite sick. The midwife told Bonta how she had given Mrs. Harrington quinine the day before to speed her labor. I hoped she was using it more cautiously than before. It was this practice that had led to the premature delivery and strangulation of Mrs. Irons's baby, and too big a dose of quinine could even cause contractions severe enough to rupture the uterus. This morning Sadie had prescribed a dose of castor oil. Bonta looked dismayed. Nothing could have been worse for someone in her condition, except perhaps turpentine, which her neighbors had also given her because she was doing so poorly.

Bonta spent a long time examining her, going over her symptoms and trying to decide just how sick she really was. Whatever measures had been taken to ensure a clean delivery undoubtedly left a lot to be desired, so it was not too surprising to find some postpartum complications. Was it an ordinary infection amenable to antibiotics, or could it be something more serious, even a ruptured lower uterine segment as a result of the quinine? She also kept coughing up sputum, which she inelegantly removed from her mouth with her fingers and tossed against the wall.

Very hesitantly, after considering all the circumstances, Bonta decided to try to hold out for a while and avoid sending her to the hospital just yet. The Harringtons were destitute, and the Welfare and Retirement Fund would not help them out at this time. He believed she wasn't quite as sick as she appeared and as all the fuss being made about her would lead one to believe. He hoped the penicillin and sulfa he gave her would get her over the crisis. So, after his emphatic instructions to keep him posted, we returned to the car and Susan.

The poor child was drenched with perspiration, and I was conscience stricken at having left her so long in the hot car. I had looked out periodically, and she was always bouncing around, apparently happy enough. But the car was like an oven, even though the windows were half open. Bonta told me I would only make her feel sorry for herself if I acted so upset about it all. After all, she was all right, greeting us with open arms, much more interested in the chickens and cows as we drove off than in her own discomfort. So I simmered down (simmered was the word). I supposed he was right. But it could have been worse, and I vowed to be much more careful in the future.

On the way home we detoured up the lumber camp road to a deserted spot for that promised practice with the handgun. Bonta was concerned about the gun; it was so old he even wondered if it might explode. We found some tin cans for a target, and he fired it. There was no problem with the gun, only with his aim. I thought the whole idea so preposterous I wasn't about to take it seriously, until I realized Bonta wasn't looking at it as a game at all. He had been pretty good at target practice with a rifle, and now he was intent on learning to handle this gun so that he could use it if he had to. I overcame my distaste enough to shoot a few times, discouraged by my poor marksmanship.

Susan held her hands over her eyes, inappropriately enough, and shouted, "Boom! Boom!"

While we were still at it, a fellow who had been spreading unpleasant rumors about Bonta through the lumber camp happened to drive by. He slowed down to see what was going on, and Bonta was pleased that at least he now knew we had a gun and knew how to use it.

I wondered how he would interpret our little session: that we were just enjoying hitting tin cans, we were paranoid and preparing for any eventuality, or what? It would be interesting to hear any repercussions. I just hoped he didn't notice that the tin cans hadn't suffered too badly.

We hadn't been home long when someone came for referral slips for the hospital and the ambulance to take Mrs. Harrington to Welch. The person said she had become delirious and certainly seemed worse, so Bonta signed the permits. We hoped the hospital could help her, but I thought about what she had to return to if she did recover.

✌ We were delighted when Freely Browning came a few days later to say his wife was in labor. We would be able to check off at least one delivery from the list hanging over Bonta's head. I was pleased that I could go along with him before office hours, since Eloise had come early and the Brownings' home was not far away. I was interested in how the people I met in the office actually lived, what their homes would reveal about their interests, and how their children behaved at home. I knew only too well how a few of them behaved in the office.

The Brownings' house looked comfortable and neat. Mrs. Browning was sitting up when we arrived but retired to a bed already prepared with new, not merely clean, sheets so that Bonta could examine her. Since she was in the very earliest stages of labor, we left, Bonta promising to return in a little while.

Later I spent another of those long evenings reading alone while Bonta was taking care of Mrs. Browning. A miner from the green camp knocked at the back door and asked where the doctor was. He said that his baby had suddenly gone blind and deaf and desperately needed medical care.

He suggested that perhaps I could come up. "You're a nurse or something, ain't you?"

People simply didn't know how to take me. They vaguely thought I was more important than a nurse, but then again, I wasn't even a nurse.

Since I couldn't help him, I sent him to the Brownings' house. Bonta was able to take the time to check on the baby, and it turned out that it had a mild case of tonsillitis. Did people really believe in those flamboyant symptoms they described, so totally removed from reality, or did they think that was the way to get immediate help?

Bonta got home about 3:00 A.M., after delivering the Brownings' baby boy. Though it wasn't a large baby, he said Mrs. Browning would have torn without an episiotomy, so he performed his first one there. It must have been pretty scary—nobody to provide an extra pair of hands, no real sterility, and, as it turned out, a pretty wild patient, restrained only with the help of three other people. A neighbor assisted, and her mother-in-law gave the anesthetic. The mother-in-law was very calm about the whole procedure, and the patient's husband was downright phlegmatic.

From the way Bonta described the various deliveries he attended, it was clear that each woman handled childbirth in her own unique way. Some were unbelievably stoic, and others created havoc. The families expressed their concern in such different ways, too, from the withdrawn hostility the Clines had displayed when Bonta and Barbara were there, to this very matter-of-fact approach. I hoped for some firsthand experience; I had yet to be on hand for a delivery myself.

12. A Visitor

My sister Mary arrived on Friday, October 28, full of curiosity about this place, and anxious to learn. Six years my junior, she was a fairly recent graduate of the University of Michigan where she'd espoused the liberal views of her colleagues on the *Michigan Daily*. She approached new situations with wide-eyed earnestness and sometimes seemed a little breathless with amazement at the world around her.

We took her over to the office to experience a bit of coal camp medical practice for herself. I hoped some of our more colorful patients might come in; I was not disappointed. Mrs. Clay Morgan, a favorite of mine, arrived for her six-week postpartum check, full of concern lest she be pregnant again already. It was she whom Bonta took to Welch in the ambulance that night. She vowed she didn't want another child—ten were plenty, even if only eight were living. She chatted cheerfully with Mary and me about the strike while waiting for Bonta.

"Clay, he's fixing our old car while the men ain't working. There's lots to do. We bought some lumber, so he'll be building us a new house pretty soon. Going to have six rooms, and Lordy, do we need them!"

"The plans are all ready?" Mary asked with interest.

"Plans? You mean drawed out? Shucks no, he's just going to build it!"

When Mary looked a little dubious, Mrs. Morgan reassured her. "Oh, it'll turn out all right. He built the one we had when we lived over in Clear Fork, so I know he can do it. You just come back and see," she added cheerfully.

She turned to me. "You know, I'd sure like to catch a chicken for you, so as you could have it while your sister's here. Don't know if I can grab one, though. Have to catch them in a net while they're roosting. They're so wild."

As Bonta came into the room, she turned to us ruefully and confessed, "I'd rather take a beating than have the doctor look at me." I thought to myself any woman going in for a pelvic would have understood.

The next patient was a faded, worn-out twenty-nine-year-old woman, Mrs. Ransom, whom Bonta had described earlier as tense and unhappy. I had been in their home, and considering the conditions under which she lived, I felt it was no wonder. A slight, pale woman with mousy, unkempt hair streaked with early gray, she wore an oversize sweater over her cotton dress. In spite of the chilly morning she had nothing but sandals on her feet.

As we sat in the lab waiting for Bonta, she explained, "I'm passing chunks of meat, and Lord, they smell terrible. I'm just so miserable I can't hardly stand it." She turned to Mary. "You see, my husband is older than I am, and he had a family when I married him. Three of his kids live with us in this little house that's falling apart. I guess it's always hard to bring up young ones that ain't your own. Course we got two of ours besides, so it's pretty crowded."

Knowing how far beyond Long Branch Mountain she lived, I asked her how she'd come to camp.

"Oh, I caught a ride on the bread truck. I'm going to go back on the mail truck, if I'm lucky. Why, last time I come to Coal Mountain I hitchhiked. Do you know once I had to pay somebody five dollars to bring me?"

That sounded like sheer robbery to me.

Bonta examined her carefully and found little objectively wrong. He told us a little bit about his conversation with her. Every symptom he had mentioned she suddenly acquired. He gave her some estrogen and spent a long time talking to her. She was very depressed, probably more depressed than physically sick. Her biggest worry was that she might not be saved. Bonta listened sympathetically to her many problems, trying to reassure her as best as he could, and she did seem a little more relaxed when she left.

I felt it was a shame her religion brought her more grief than comfort. I tried to imagine what it would be like to be in her shoes. Having been spoiled by all the privileges that had come my way, I wasn't sure I'd even survive. I wondered if she yearned for the things that mattered to me: education, contact with stimulating people, travel. Or were those things altogether beyond her ken?

Mary was amused by one miner's brief call. He came in for some salve because his son had a rash. When Bonta asked if there was any swelling along with it, he answered, "No, nowheres excepting under the rash, where the hide's hooved up."

Being a career woman herself, Mary was pleased by my involvement with the office, and I was happy to tell her about the things I did: ordering supplies, keeping the daybook, helping with patient records, and dispensing the medications Bonta ordered. The office might not be fancy, but we were pretty proud of what we were able to do in it. As she looked around the tiny lab, she asked, "Don't you get lonesome here? I can't imagine a more godforsaken spot!"

I swatted a couple of tired flies still buzzing at the window before answering.

"Oh, it would be pretty grim if Bonta hadn't encouraged me to help the way he has. As it is, I'm learning a lot. Yes, we sure do need each other down here. But I've actually come to love this place. You may smile, but I look up at the mountains and think of the psalmist. They've been just glorious this fall. Not many people have a chance to live in a coal camp, in a place that's so out of the way it's not even on the state map. Oh sure, Coal Mountain has its drawbacks—lots of them—but I look at it all as a big adventure."

"What about the people here? Are the two women we talked to typical?"

"In a way. Most are friendly, many are generous to a fault. Most of them have grown up without much formal education and almost none of the comforts we always took for granted. There's only one person around who graduated from college, so far as I know anyway, and that's the principal of the school. He lives quite a ways from here, so unfortunately we hardly ever see him.

"Some, like Barney next door, have worked in Detroit or other big cities before deciding coal offered more. I know one miner who served in the army where he received some extensive legal training. Spent over a year in Europe but chose to return to the mine and lives in a modest house down beyond Guyan.

"Some of them are poor, but by no means all. Many of them have fairly comfortable homes and good cars.

"So you can't generalize. We're getting to know quite a few people. After all, we're all worrying about the strike and when it'll end. Common problems really bring you together.

"It's a rough life for many of the women—hard work, too many kids. You should see how quickly some of them age. Women come into the office with stretched, wobbly bellies at the ripe old age of twenty-five or so, having had seven children already and never any time to take care of themselves. Some women I would place at thirty-six turn out to be twenty-four, and one who I swore must be postmenopausal proved to be thirty-three. I wonder how old they think I am.

"There's a lot of difference between those who've lived in the hollows since long before the mine opened and those who've come in since. The old-timers lead a much more marginal existence.

"True, sometimes their ways are hard to understand, and I don't always know how to take them. I confess I've even been frightened a couple times." I told her about that strange evening when Harvey Burgess pushed Bonta to be his drinking buddy. "Luckily that seems to have cooled down. Some pretty strange rumors float around, but maybe that just goes with small town living anywhere."

Mary lit a cigarette, inhaled deeply, and then said thoughtfully, "You sure hit the coalfields in the middle of a mess. How's the strike affect you personally?"

"Not much at all so far." I shoved an ashtray on the counter toward her. "Of course, we don't get paid while the men aren't working, but sooner or later that'll be straightened out. We do feel like frontline observers in this battle between the union and the companies. For weeks we've checked the tipple every morning to see if the men are working, and we do try to keep track of developments as best we can. For the most part the miners are very secretive about it all, and Mr. Ramsey is pretty discreet, too. Not having newspapers, and only occasionally getting network news, we don't always get the big picture."

She said, "Of course, everybody's been expecting Truman to use the Taft-Hartley Act to stop the strike, but he seems reluctant to. Claims the situation isn't really critical yet. Still, a lot of railroad and steel workers have been laid off, and they say coal supplies are getting pretty low.

"But tell me, how did you find the house you're living in?"

"Oh, the company built the camp when it opened up the mine seven years ago. So it owns everything in sight and supplies the doctor with a house and office for a very nominal sum."

"How do you mean, nominal?"

"Well, like all other tenants who live in the white houses, we pay eighteen dollars a month for our house, and the office rents for twenty a month."

"Boy, I wish I could find a place that cheap! So how much does their medical care cost the miners?"

"Here it's three dollars a month—a little more in some other places. It's simply deducted from their paycheck. The union actually makes the contract with the doctor even though the company brings him in. The men negotiate the monthly deduction and the charges for extras like deliveries and shots. All these prices are pretty uniform around the coalfields."

Bonta joined our conversation, and as we walked over to the house, he told Mary how the negotiations had actually gone. "I'd been working about three weeks when the union's medical committee paid me a formal call at the office. There was a lot of throat clearing and boot shuffling. Then one of them informed me they'd come to hire me to be the doc for the union. They needed 'to make a contract about it.' So I asked how I could be sure they were really empowered to make it. Well, this stumped them until Freddie Kilmer came up with the answer. He pulled a torn sheet of paper out of his pocket and laboriously spelled out, 'You will reconize only the follering as medical committee.' He signed the names of the three men there, Harvey Burgess, Mark Hatfield, and himself as 'Sec.' He handed this to me, downright triumphantly, and we started negotiating.

"I asked them what they had in mind, and they looked real blank. So I suggested we might start by looking at Vern's old contract. I'd been using it all along anyway, on Mr. Ramsey's advice. Soon as I said that, they came up with some changes 'the body of men' wanted.

Not surprisingly, they didn't like the twenty cents a mile charge for calls outside the camp—which I hadn't been charging anyway—and this precipitated a lot of discussion. As you can guess, calls outside camp are a lot more time consuming than those inside. But we didn't get anywhere deciding on camp boundaries, so we dropped that. Instead they said I could charge a dollar for any house call after office hours that wasn't an emergency. Then they OKed the usual charges for shots. It took some bargaining, but we finally agreed that thirty-three dollars was OK for deliveries."

"Thirty-three dollars!" Mary echoed his words in astonishment. "What about pre and post care? Surely they're extra?"

"Oh, no, that thirty-three dollars includes everything, whether the delivery takes one hour or twenty-four. Well, when we had it all settled, I suggested they put it into a formal contract and I'd sign it. Did that ever fluster them! 'Oh, no, Doc, you write it up, and we'll sign it.'"

This contract didn't cover the foremen, who represented the company. They paid their three dollars through individual agreements. Bonta treated them and their families—the definition of family was very loose, sometimes including grandparents, aunts, and uncles—just as he did the union men.

While I fixed dinner, Dan Dubois came to the back door, asking for something for his wife's headache. Feeling that he was one of the most involved union men around and quite articulate, Bonta took advantage of the opportunity for Mary to talk to him. He introduced her without mentioning that she was a reporter. They ended up by the back fence where so many social exchanges occurred. Most of the story Dan related went over Mary's head, since she didn't understand the intricacies of administering the Welfare and Retirement Fund. But we explained it to her at dinner, perhaps in more detail than she had bargained for.

The gist of Dan's report was that Mr. Harrington, the curly haired preacher from Long Branch whose wife was so sick and went to the hospital, had recently applied for reinstatement in the union so that he could become eligible for benefits. The local union refused him, since he hadn't worked in the mine for years. Undaunted, he wrote John L. Lewis himself. John L. replied favorably, so at the next union meeting, he stunned the gathering with this directive from the supreme authority, which they simply could not ignore.

Dan said that the local union officers had talked it over and decided the national union must be padding the union roll with these old-timers just so they could claim the Welfare and Retirement Fund was inadequate and, in spite of the big treasury on hand, demand bigger royalties from the company. That union officials would come up with such an interesting theory we found intriguing.

We explained to Mary what the Welfare and Retirement Fund was, emphasizing the significance of this relatively new benefit the union had obtained for its members. Of course, payments had become erratic since the strike. Sometimes the fund paid the miners for hospitalization and sometimes it didn't. Now the men wanted it to pay their three dollars a month for the doctor as well as their hospital bills. There was no doubt that the fund was a godsend for them.

As with every good thing, there were a few who abused it, or tried to. One day Bonta had come home fuming because one of the union officers had asked him again for a medical excuse from work for no discernible reason.

"He's asking me to say he's eligible for long-term disability, and I just have the feeling that he's trying to use his position as an officer to exploit the fund. I want to protect the fund—after all, I take the union's goals seriously. This new program should funnel resources to people genuinely in need. If it were anyone else, I'd have no qualms about refusing, but I hate to cross one of their own officers. It bothers me, too, even to be taking his position into account in my thinking.

"As it is, since you can never be medically sure about reported backaches, I sometimes end up giving him an excuse for the day."

So Bonta continued to give him excuses one day at a time and avoided any long-term commitment. But because you never knew what the consequences of thwarting anyone might be, this whole problem made me uneasy.

After dinner we adjourned to the living room where the small fire in the stove took the chill off the evening. "Almost as good as sitting by a fireplace—it's just that you can't watch the flames," Mary said. "Now tell me about this miner we were talking to. He fascinates me."

Dan was someone not easily forgotten. Somewhat handicapped

though he was, he was an active participant in community affairs and appeared to relish his role in camp. He didn't seem to miss much. His dark complexion, thick hair, and heavy eyebrows gave him a swarthy appearance. I could easily imagine him, stooped as he was, as an alchemist in a long black cloak casting spells.

We told her about the slate fall that had injured his back and the help he'd apparently found in the church. She was impressed to learn that the company found a job for him he could handle.

"Is he married?"

"Oh yes. His wife's a bit older than he is," I said. "She strikes me as rather austere. Her teenage son Alvin lives with them and works at the lamphouse. There have been reports that Dan's unkind to Alvin. Supposedly he charges things at the store to Alvin's account, putting him in debt. They say Dan'll make Alvin buy gas for the car and then refuse to let him drive it. Who knows? If so, perhaps this is an outlet for his frustration, or perhaps he just doesn't like the boy because he's not his own."

"Hmm, I hadn't heard all that," Bonta said. "My impression is that Dan's a loyal union man—was president of the local once—and seems to be a bit civic minded. I certainly enjoy talking with him. He's always got an opinion about things."

The conversation touched on a dozen topics, the most stimulating discussion we'd had since Barbara left. Our own tended to become ingrown, and the challenge of different viewpoints was welcome.

Finally Mary steered it in a direction dear to her heart. "You know I've been in favor of socialized medicine for a long time, and I don't think you have been. Now you're actually practicing it. Have you found anything wrong with it?"

"Well, I suppose prepaid care could be called socialized medicine, even if the government isn't involved." Bonta took another sip of the sherry Mary had brought as he thought about her question. "Oh, one thing that can happen is that some people begin to think they own the doctor—view him as sort of a hired hand—because they've paid for his services in advance. I even ran into a little of that in the navy, where medical care was free to servicemen and their families."

"Any way to stop unreasonable demands?" Mary's eyes always bored right into the person she addressed.

"Well, you might charge a token amount for a visit, just enough to make them think twice before running to the doctor." Little did Bonta dream that he would be facing that very problem years later when he became director of medical affairs for a health maintenance organization, a far bigger prepaid group than the one in Coal Mountain.

Mary mused, "What would happen if the company brought in a doctor who wasn't very well qualified—or was lazy? Any way the people could protect themselves then?"

"They couldn't do much but complain a lot to the superintendent. Oh, I suppose they could break their contract with him. The kind of care they get in a place like this really depends on the competence of that individual doctor—and his conscience."

As I knitted on Susan's navy blue cap, I said to Mary, "Hmm, if it's conscience that counts, Bonta's got more than his share."

He glanced at me in acknowledgment, shrugged his shoulders, and got up to shovel some more coal into the stove before continuing the discussion. "One problem is that lay people aren't usually in a position to judge the quality of care. They just don't know enough about medicine, and they tend to judge by the wrong things. You know, whether the doctor makes them wait or not. Or whether he's friendly. Some awfully incompetent doctors can be very friendly."

On Saturday, a little girl interrupted our late breakfast. Mrs. Morgan must have been quick with the net; anyway she had caught that chicken. Here it was, legs tied together but wide awake and full of energy. We asked her daughter to thank her for us and put the chicken out on the back porch in a large box. I couldn't help feeling guilty accepting gifts from people who had so many mouths to feed and so little to put in them.

When Bonta returned from a quick trip to the office, he startled us by saying, "Congratulations! Didn't think you had the nerve to kill that chicken without me."

"Don't be silly. That's the last thing we'd do. The chicken awaits your pleasure."

"No, it doesn't. It's not in the box where we put it, anyway."

A frantic search of the yard failed to reveal any stray chickens. We wondered if a dog had grabbed it and felt chagrined and disappointed until Mary spotted it on Barney's side of the coal shed. It made a wild flapping dash for freedom as we closed in, hopped on both legs at once and fluttered along, got under the fence and down the road toward the clubhouse. We finally surrounded it as it started down the bank toward the creek; Bonta made the capture. We were smarter about the execution this time, tying cords around both neck and feet, so the poor decapitated thing could flop only as far as the string attached to its feet allowed.

Mary was nonplussed. "I never expected to see you playing an animated corpse like a big fish!" As we continued our job, "Nor you, Bonta, lost in a cloud of chicken feathers."

The afternoon went to showing Mary all the unusual things that had originally fascinated us as outsiders. We started with the most significant feature of the camp, the mine itself. She was glad to learn this mine was not gassy, so less dangerous than many. And as I had anticipated, she was surprised it wasn't a deep shaft mine. In spite of the strike, no barricades blocked our way to the portal. Obviously Mr. Ramsey did not expect sabotage.

We explained the operation. The long chutes down the side of the mountain from the high-grade mine slid the coal from the coal cars directly to the sorting house. The chutes from the other mine sent the coal to the washing house, where compressed air floated the coal while the slate sank.

To show her the alternative mining method, we took her down to the lumber camp and the strip mine road beyond. The road was rutted from big coal-carrying trucks. This method really did strip the mountain. The stratum of coal was exposed by huge bulldozers which shoved the overlying earth down the mountainside. Then the miners scooped up the coal and loaded it into monstrous trucks. The denuded earth below the layer of coal became an extension of the road.

Though this operation had been halted before we came, the results were all too evident. The desolation appalled us all. How could mere men wreak such havoc? Strip mining had started landslides which had isolated little wedges where trees still survived, but that only accentuated the wasteland of shale, soil, and uprooted vegetation that filled the lower valley and threatened to cut off the little creek entirely. The bare bones of the mountain were exposed above the road the miners

The two mines above the camp at Coal Mountain: unlike deep shaft mines, these were tunneled into separate horizontal strata. The coal was sent down by chute or cable car to the tipple.

had made as they removed the stratum of coal. As we drove along this road, we saw that in places the edges had started to crumble. Rounding one big curve, we suddenly saw that the road ahead had slid right down the mountain. Tire tracks indicated that two different cars had skidded to a halt not more than twenty yards from the gap. We backed gingerly away, found a place to turn around, parked the car, and returned to gawk. It looked as though the whole mountain might slide if we so much as threw a big rock at some of the unstable margins.

On our return we discovered that our coal shed had been unexpectedly filled while we were gone. Barney told us that some of the men had helped themselves to the coal in a partially loaded coal car in the tipple, and he was kind enough, neighbor that he was, to see that they filled our bin, too. Mr. Ramsey was well aware of what was going on but winked and looked the other way. I thought this was very decent of him. He ran the camp in a firm but sympathetic way. Knowing he was boss made me feel good.

Susan performed for her appreciative aunt, singing her latest song— one Eloise taught her—"Mine Buckdet Dot a Hole in It!" Mary looked on with tolerant amusement at Susan's delaying tactics at bedtime, but I suspected she was too polite to tell me I ought to put a stop to all the rituals—potty, drinks, kisses for the doll, kisses for herself, retrieval of her blanket, potty again.

We talked into the small hours, since Mary asked so many questions. She wanted to write a local color article on the strike, and we debated at some length about the material she could include without jeopardizing our position. We knew how sensitive people were hereabouts: very proud and very private. I told her about my first day in the office when I had commented on the lunchpail belonging to one of the miners who was waiting to see Bonta. Later through Eloise I found out that this had offended him. I should never have mentioned anything so personal. Mary promised to be discreet and offered to send us a clipping if her story was ever printed.

13. Is This Progress?

✿ Mary left on Sunday. On Monday Bonta stayed late at the office attempting to help a miner whose little girl had active TB. The father had been out of work for some time himself with what might well be the same problem. Pale and emaciated, the child with her long straight hair and pinched little face was a wan Alice in Wonderland. A sanatorium had offered her father a place for her, but he had no transportation. Bonta went to the company office to verify the reservation in Welch and then took them over to ask Dan Dubois whether the union could arrange the trip for them. Dan was only too glad to cooperate. Having gone through so much himself, he was sympathetic to others in trouble, and he also enjoyed wielding his power in the union, where he served on the ambulance committee. The organization did look out for its own. When Bonta first described the problem, I was ready to drive her to Welch myself. Denying a child medical care for so trivial a reason as lack of a ride was unthinkable.

Eloise and Eva had expressed an interest in our photographic setup in the kitchen with blankets over doors and windows to keep it dark, so we invited them in for an evening session of developing and printing some pictures of the first aid class and of Eloise and Susan. The pictures were not outstanding, but the girls were intrigued to see how it was done. While the prints were in the hypo, we caught up on the latest camp news. Among other things, Eva told us that the miners then owed the store some six thousand dollars; the store did a charge business of fifteen hundred dollars that Monday alone. During the last strike the company hadn't allowed them to charge, and things got pretty desperate, so she was much impressed by the bill the company let them pile up this time. For all the adversarial relationship between management and labor, this company at least seemed to adopt a sort of paternal attitude toward the men, and the men weren't above taking advantage of whatever favors came their way.

It was Halloween. We'd been warned that it was celebrated enthusiastically in this territory. Unless something really devilish was done during the early morning hours, it looked as though we might get off with nothing worse than a little soap on the car windows, which we discovered when Eloise and Eva left. But then, as we were turning out the light a little before midnight, some men arrived to say a woman was aborting at seven months down Reedy way, of all forsaken, faraway places. Bonta had to go, but fortunately the men offered to go along with him. They said it was pretty bad, that on Halloween several cars were better than one. They had had a hard time getting through themselves, but around Long Branch the justice of the peace and somebody else were patrolling and promised to try to keep the road clear until the doctor got through. I didn't know just what the problems were, but they sounded ominous.

Bonta got back around 4:00 A.M., so mad he couldn't get to sleep when he finally did get to bed, so I fixed something for him to eat while he reported on the night's troubles. The men escorted him to Reedy all right, but they didn't offer to escort him home. He ran into all sorts of roadblocks which he had to clear away, some of them small trees and brush, some of them rocks. But down near the lumber camp he came upon a huge oak tree which had been felled right across the road. He woke Mr. Arnold, the superintendent of the lumber camp, and together, with the aid of a truck and chain, they cleared that away. But there were nine other roadblocks between that camp and this. Mr. Arnold was kind enough to stay with Bonta, and the two of them worked for what seemed like hours just to go the relatively short distance between the two camps. Bonta said he would never go out again on Halloween without a guaranteed escort both ways.

Such games struck me as neither funny nor intelligent. Suppose some real emergency had come up and the ambulance had had to make a fast trip out.

In the morning we discovered someone had removed the bridge between our house and the office, leaving only one precarious plank over the creek; for half its length most of that was missing. It was like walking a tightrope just to get to work.

The road had been cleaned up from Halloween by the next night when Dacie Ransom knocked about bedtime. (People do get frightened late in the evening.) He was the husband of that depressed young woman Mary had met in the office. His sixteen-year-old daughter by a former wife apparently had appendicitis and couldn't be moved, especially not in their rattletrap car, which had one headlight and no battery. This meant a trip all the way to the other side of Long Branch Mountain.

I suddenly decided to go along, so we routed Susan from bed, bundled her into the car bed, and set off. I just felt like being with Bonta. We gave Dacie and his friend a push to get their car going and then quickly passed them.

The narrow beams of our headlights only emphasized the utter darkness. Occasionally they revealed the massive bulk of cows asleep in the middle of the road. Luckily it was wide enough so we could detour around them. We felt as though we were the sole inhabitants of this silent world, and as night erased the landmarks we knew so well, the familiar route grew mysterious. Crossing Long Branch Mountain, we found ourselves in the heart of a low cloud, and the mist removed us from earthly time and space altogether. It was a night to snuggle closer to Bonta and be glad we were together.

At last one dimly lit window visible through the haze signaled that we had reached the Ransoms' home. By flashlight we puddle-jumped our way to the porch. Since we were last there, they had replaced the missing rung of the ladder that served as steps and rechinked the walls with mud in preparation for winter. Mrs. Ransom was all dressed up—clean checked dress, hair neatly combed, even lipstick—as she invited us into what she ironically called her "nice house." By the light of the kerosene lamp, I could see that the main room was like so many others, papered with pages from Sears's and Ward's catalogs and UMW newsletters. Seeing a package of pills on the table with my own handwriting on it gave me a small jolt. It seemed unreal that something of me had found its way into such an unlikely place. I wondered about all the other strange destinations I'd never see, to which my little envelopes must have gone.

One of the two beds in the other room was occupied by four children, probably two to eleven years of age, all piled like so many jackstraws at odd angles. The two older children, a boy and a girl, woke up while we were there and disengaged themselves so they could see what was happening. Those two and the patient must have been the stepchildren. The boy tried to monopolize the conversation, talking about his dog, his school, and his plans to become a farmer. The nine-year-old girl had nothing to say but casually lit a cigarette and spit into the stove at intervals. This stove was the most remarkable thing in the room, a small potbellied model without a door, radiating enormous amounts of heat, and glowing bright cherry red like a small sun in the darkened room.

The girl Bonta had come to see lay in the other bed, shaking with disease and fright. She did have an acute abdomen, and Bonta tried to decide whether she had appendicitis or PID.* At first she denied there was any possibility of her having such a thing as gonorrhea. Finally Bonta asked the girl if she'd had intercourse a couple weeks ago or more recently, and she broke down and said it was about ten days ago. This meant he could treat her with penicillin to cure the infection without a trip to the hospital.

I couldn't get used to seeing those young girls with lives blighted by casual sex before they had really finished childhood or could appreciate the consequences of what they were doing. She might well be sterile now. I did wonder which was worse—having no children or having fifteen.

Meantime I visited with Mrs. Ransom. When we arrived, she was reading her Bible by the light of the one kerosene lamp. Now she was eager to tell me about her own illnesses and those of the young boy.

"Why, he like to have passed right on one time we was at a Decoration!" In answer to my puzzled look she said, "Oh, a Decoration is when you put flowers on the graves, and then you eat your lunch there."

I asked her how long she had lived in this house.

*Inflammation of the pelvis caused by sexually transmitted disease

"Oh, I been here three years. It's better now than it was when my uncle lived here, too. They was twelve of us living here then, and it was pretty cramped up. We pay Azel West ten dollars a month for it, and I'm hoping that when this here strike gets over we can move to Guyan. I'd sure like that."

She was much happier than I had ever seen her. She'd lost that forlorn look she wore whenever she came to the office. The makeup helped and perhaps the kerosene lamplight, too.

"I been feeling some better. Them pills what the doctor give me, they helped a lot." She paused to turn up the wick in the lamp. "Yes, lots of folks, they say that doctor down there ain't no account, but he sure helped me more than anybody else."

I thought about that backhanded compliment. I wondered who and how many called that doctor no account. Clearly, you couldn't hope to please everybody, but it was sort of deflating. I recalled Eloise's report that the postmistress had stood up for Bonta when someone was comparing him unfavorably to Vern Nichols. You could take neither praise nor criticism too seriously. Either one could change before sundown.

Anyway I was really glad to see her feeling better. And it was both comforting and pathetic to find her reigning over her impoverished kingdom with such dignity. She thanked us as we left.

On Wednesday Mrs. Rollins, a young woman from the lumber camp, brought her four children to the office, and while she was waiting to see Bonta, she and I had a chance to chat a bit. The youngsters were just a year apart, she told me, all born in July or August, the youngest just a few months old. The oldest was a shy little girl with snarled curls, who tried to hide behind her mother. Mrs. Rollins drew her forward and said severely, "No, Lissie, now you show the lady that red mark on your arm."

I felt sorry for Lissie who was clearly embarrassed at being on display but took a look at the irregular dark red patch.

"Now ain't that the queerest thing?" Mrs. Rollins asked. "Course it was cause I had such an awful fright when I was carrying her. They come down from work telling me a tree'd fallen right on top of Jake.

I like to have passed clear on! I finally come to, though, and it turned out he'd only been cut some and shook up, not really hurt bad at all. But it made that mark on Lissie there, plain as day."

"I see," I said, uncertain as to whether or not I should try to explain that prenatal influence of that sort was simply not possible. I'd almost decided it would be best just to listen politely when I noticed some raised spots on Lissie's arm that had nothing to do with the birthmark. "Oh, what's this?" I asked, checking to see if there were more. "Had you noticed these?"

She bent to see what I meant. "Oh, them! Well, sure, she come down with the chicken pox last night, that's all."

Such a casual attitude toward a contagious disease was a shock until I realized the other children would get it sooner or later anyway, and I supposed it might as well be sooner. True, you didn't have to fall apart if your child got sick. Of course, some of the parents around there did, and I hadn't been tested yet myself.

Mrs. Rollins continued her thumbnail sketch of the little girl's medical problems.

"Had trouble with her all along. First that there mark. And seemed like she was always pretty mean as a young one. She had a bad cough, and then if she didn't get the worms. One day she vomited up a great big one, long as this," and she held up her forefingers to indicate a worm about six inches long.

I shuddered involuntarily. Ascaris in the zoology lab was unattractive enough, but the idea of a child vomiting up a specimen that big was enough to make my stomach turn a somersault. No wonder Bonta didn't want Susan to play in the dirt. "Laced with cow dung, pee, and worm eggs," he said.

"Oh, I knowed just what to do," Mrs. Rollins hastily reassured me, having no doubt observed the expression on my face. "I put three drops of turpentine on some sugar and made her eat that and rubbed turpentine on her stomach, and you know, she ain't never had no trouble since. That one there, though," and she indicated the next to youngest, crawling on the floor, "he's got them, cause I found them in his pants, and the turpentine didn't seem to help him so quick. Ain't never seen none on the other boy, but I reckon he's got them too. He fusses at night when he ought to be getting to sleep. And he always gets worse during the light of the moon." She turned to me, adding matter-of-factly, "Course you know that's a sure sign of worms."

I'd listened to this quietly as long as I could. My conscience kept prodding me to tell her something about how worms were passed within a family. I hesitated though, knowing through Eloise how angry such an explanation had made another young mother. On the other hand, Mrs. Rollins seemed willing to listen, so I launched into a little speech about how worm eggs were discharged into diapers or at the outhouse. If the children's hands weren't clean, they might touch food that someone else ate, and so the worm eggs would be passed around.

Mrs. Rollins in her turn listened politely but just as incredulously as I had listened to her. It was a relief when Bonta appeared to end the conversation. I hoped Eloise wouldn't bring back another report like that earlier one: "That no account doc said I kept a dirty house!"

After a late call in camp the following Saturday, Bonta stopped at the Ramseys' house for a quick visit. While he was there the men got into a serious discussion. The prospects for improving the camp which Mr. Ramsey outlined set Bonta to thinking about our own future again, and we were up till the wee hours looking over our correspondence and applications for residencies. We both agreed that a residency was the first essential, whatever else. That was a given, something Bonta had counted on ever since he started medical school.

But strangely enough, when we talked about leaving this place, my mind conjured up all sorts of reservations. It had become our own little kingdom. We relied on each other for help and for fun as well as for love. When we were married, I thought I knew what love was about, but Coal Mountain showed me there was more. I learned to know Bonta so much better. I saw how he dealt with people, how he coped with problems, how honest and conscientious he was. I felt so blessed because we had each other, and I hated the thought of losing some of this sharing, as I would, once we left Coal Mountain and our paths diverged.

It went without saying that this place offered a great experience medically for Bonta, furthering his long-term goal of becoming a competent and compassionate physician. It provided a real education for me, as wife of a physician. And the money it enabled us to save was important because it would make the long-term goal possible. If the mining operation should expand, all the pluses would probably just get bigger.

No need to enumerate the disadvantages. In some ways they were just the other side of the same coin: isolation, no cultural advantages, no opportunity to interact with other professionals. As for the physical aspects, the dust and/or mud, the bad roads, they were still novel enough to be an interesting challenge. Of course, in the long run we didn't want Susan to grow up thinking this was the whole world. We wanted her to have the opportunity to appreciate all the things we cherished back home.

🙞 The first Sunday in November was delightfully different. We helped the Ramseys celebrate their anniversary, leaving the hollow with them for a noonday dinner. It was a crisp, cold, sunny day—a fitting postlude to the night's brilliant moon and hard frost. Bonta put on a white shirt for the first time since we had been there, and I wore the brown taffeta dress he said made my brown eyes look even darker.

On our way out Bonta remarked that he had forgotten to stop at Guyan to check on a patient there, but Mr. Ramsey advised him to let the patients come to him, not the other way around. This admonition not to treat them too paternally intrigued me, especially considering his own attitude, which I interpreted as nothing if not paternal. Perhaps his stage of paternalism was more advanced than ours. He was more willing to let them face the consequences of their own actions; perhaps we were still overprotective. To be honest, at least some of our concern was selfishly motivated; Bonta didn't want to be responsible for any medical problems that could have been headed off.

Mrs. Ramsey told us she was working to reconcile the Holinesses and the Baptists so the children in camp could have a well-organized Sunday school. She said, "As it is now, while their elders are preaching and shouting, the young ones are playing marbles off in the corner. If nothing else, they should learn respect for the Lord's word and them that preach it."

She planned to go up to the churchhouse that evening to see that they did. She was a very determined woman, and this was her current project as first lady of the camp. I admired her for using the influence of her position in the cause of peace and progress. As she was clearly a product of this culture, she understood the people and could say things for which an outsider might be shot.

We went to a combination drive-in/sit-down restaurant just opened in Pineville, which offered good food and even pleasant music from the jukebox. It wasn't exactly the Waldorf Astoria, and at first it struck me as odd to make a big deal out of dinner at a drive-in, but it was the best within thirty miles, and it seemed heaven to me. After all, the event was what you made it. It was with regret that we headed back to our hollow.

Mrs. Bannister came over at noon the next day to tell us one of the men who had been to the hospital in Welch Saturday reported that Mrs. Horvath was sinking fast—that they had the "death curtains" around her bed. This set her poor husband to "shaking like a leaf," to quote Eloise later, and he hurried to find someone to drive him over.

Like so many other stories around here, this, too, was unfounded. She was no worse than before, and I imagine she was on the bedpan, hence the curtains.

We picked up another rumor, too. Supposedly the doctor wasn't taking care of anyone until the men went back to work. We were fast learning we couldn't take everything we heard seriously, but many did, and trying to put out all the fires was hard.

Mrs. Clay Morgan, donor of our last chicken, came to the office, and after I had thanked her for sending it, I asked how the diaphragm I had helped her with a couple weeks earlier was working out. She confided that she really hadn't used it yet. "I'm scared to, but someday I might take a notion to try it. Clay, he don't know I got it."

I tried to remind her tactfully that it wouldn't be very effective so long as it stayed in the bureau drawer, but I wasn't sorry when she changed the subject.

"We're lucky we're living on a farm while the men ain't working. Leastways our family ain't going hungry." As we'd had no inkling that hunger was a problem, this remark added a new dimension to my understanding of the seriousness of the strike. Most of the patients who came into the office seemed to be getting along one way or another. Nobody had mentioned lack of food.

"I heared one teacher down Long Branch way is bringing food

Two of our neighbors preparing their hillside garden. Most of the inhabitants of Coal Mountain farmed to some degree; during the strike these gardens acquired an added importance.

for some of the young ones who come to school without breakfast or lunch."

I could see how some people might suffer real hardship, if they neither grew enough of their own food nor worked at the mine, where credit was so readily available. It was fascinating to realize that the company was in a way subsidizing the strike against itself, giving the miners enough credit to keep going. Of course, the men would be heavily burdened with debt when it was over.

Mrs. Bill James came in later to get some cough syrup for one of the children. As she turned to leave, she announced with a mixture of pride and self-deprecation, "You know that sign I was working on for cutting hair? Well, I sold it! Ain't that something!"

The look on her face was worth a lot.

On Tuesday Bonta had to make some arrangements with the physicians at the hospital in Welch, so we suggested that Eloise come with us so she could see her mother. She jumped at the chance, and the visit cheered both of them up, for the moment at least.

The doctors were cordial and showed us around the hospital. They complained at length about the additional paperwork necessitated by the Welfare and Retirement Fund payments. The hospital had to hire extra secretaries and keep abreast of frequent changes in the regulations.

Wards and waiting rooms at the clinic were segregated for blacks, although the hospital did hire black nurses. I had been amazed all along by the fact that there were no blacks in Coal Mountain, while they were numerous in most of the coal camps in the area. It was clear there was a high level of intolerance in our own community for any outsiders, be they black, white, Hungarian, or what have you. I didn't know whether the absence of blacks was happenchance or whether Mr. Ramsey had responded to the mood of the camp and avoided hiring them to keep from unpleasant confrontations. Some things he didn't discuss.

Strike's over! Wednesday, November 9—a red-letter day! Still without a contract, Lewis ordered the miners back for a three-week truce. That was all we knew at the time. We learned later that some believed he had become fearful Truman would invoke the Taft-Hartley Act to end the strike and impose a settlement if he didn't act to defuse the tension. There was some speculation that he needed to quiet the growing restiveness of his men. Some men had threatened to go back to work Monday, regardless, and some observers openly wondered if Lewis might be pushing the miners beyond their endurance in spite of their fierce loyalty.

I heard a recording of his announcement midmorning on the radio. He deplored "the contemptuous arrogance of the operators," denouncing them as "brutal, with a sordid and mercenary appetite, users of deceitful stratagems, conspirators to destroy the UMW welfare fund."

I dropped everything and dashed over to the office to tell Bonta the big news. He couldn't picture the men working again without a contract. It sounded to us like an admission of weakness on the part of the union.

Since Bonta asked me to take something over to the company office for him, I had the fun of telling Randall and the others the big news. They didn't believe me at first. "What kind of radio do you listen to, anyway?"

Word spread like wildfire. I ran into Mr. Kilmer, excitedly shouting to the men in front of the store in his high-pitched voice, "Hey, you better get your hats on! We're working tomorrow!"

The prospect of work and a paycheck was cause for general rejoicing. It would be the first full week's pay since June 30, when the old contract expired. Eloise shared the jubilation at first but sobered as she said, "It still won't be enough for a good Christmas, will it? And everybody owes so much."

It was indeed an insecure return. The union still had no contract, and Lewis might pull the miners out again when the truce ended in three weeks. We later learned that all the walkouts and slowdowns had cost each miner approximately twelve hundred dollars he would otherwise have earned. The September-October strike had idled thirty thousand railroad workers and nine thousand in other industries. Midwest states were rationing coal for home and hospital use. In spite of everything, many believed that Lewis could still rule the men "by a wink or a nod."

The office was busy that afternoon as some of the men came in for back-to-work slips. A new sense of purpose pervaded the whole camp.

Reflecting on it later, for a purely selfish reason I felt relieved that things would be back to normal. I had the feeling that the miners had been getting pretty edgy as a result of all the uncertainty about work. Who could blame them? But baseless rumors like that one about Bonta's not taking care of anybody during the strike bothered me, and I was concerned about their exaggerating any small dissatisfactions.

Friday, November 11, turned out to be an important date to me. Bayliss Carson called Bonta before breakfast; after all those weekends we'd stayed in camp waiting for her, Mrs. Carson was finally going into labor. She was the young woman whose upset stomach had caused Eloise so much distress.

I was doing the usual morning tasks at home, just starting the laundry, when Eloise came to the house. She was wearing a new pink sweater with a soft gray skirt, but her mood was not as upbeat as her appearance. She looked glum and depressed. When I asked what was on her mind she seemed relieved to unburden herself.

"I just don't know what to do. Tommy wants us to get married, and I do like him. There ain't nobody else around here, and I do want to get married. I'm almost twenty already!" Her tone was one of near desperation. "But Daddy'd be real mad if I left."

I didn't find that hard to believe. From what I heard Joe wanted all his girls to stay home forever.

"Then sometimes Tommy and me'll get fighting. For instance, he don't like me telling him what the doctor says all the time. He asked me right out what the doctor has that he don't have. I told him, 'He's got two cars, and his mama ain't paying for them, and he's got an education, and he's not a mama's boy!' He didn't much like that."

Trust Eloise to have a quick and fulsome comeback. She could put a sharp edge on her remarks when she felt like it.

She returned to her problems with her family, growing more pensive. "And course there's Mother to take care of. Seems like everybody expects me to do it all. Poor Mother, she thinks something's poisoned her stomach, and she don't know why she ain't getting better."

There were no easy answers. All I could say was that she ought to use her head as well as her heart in making the decision about Tommy, that she was exceptionally intelligent, and that she owed it to herself and others to use her talents wisely. We'd already pointed out to her that Tommy didn't yet have a secure job and that waiting a bit looked like the sensible course.

Her mood changed abruptly as she apparently tired of the discussion. "I heared you're going up to the churchhouse to teach the girls in Mrs. Ramsey's Sunday school class how to knit."

That was the first I'd heard of it. "Where'd you get that story?"

"Oh, Opal next door, she heared it from one of the girls, and Nan told me, too. Mrs. Ramsey, she told them all last Sunday."

I was more than willing to cooperate, but I couldn't help thinking it odd that Mrs. Ramsey hadn't mentioned it to me before making a public announcement.

Eloise had a sudden idea. "Say, the doctor's gone to the Carsons'. Long as the office is closed, why don't you go down there and help him? I can stay with Susan."

"Me, help? Don't be silly!" Then I thought again. This might be my one chance to be involved with a delivery. Most of them seemed to happen at night when I couldn't leave Susan, and I remembered how badly I'd wanted to take Barbara's place at the Clines'.

So off I went in our new car, feeling very bold and independent. Since the company had just scraped the road, I whipped along at thirty miles an hour and made good time to Guyan. But as I got nearer, I began to worry lest I barge in at some inopportune moment and feel like an idiot. Or perhaps it would be all over, and I'd meet Bonta returning and feel just as foolish.

As it happened, I arrived at just the right time. It took quite a bit of courage to knock, knowing I would be walking into the midst of things. Would they think I was just a busybody, or would they accept me as someone who came to help? Needless to say, Bonta was surprised, but he very kindly allayed any momentary awkwardness by asking, "What's the matter? Don't you trust me?"

He was just putting his gloves on, so I was in time to hand him instruments. Then while the patient's husband supported one leg, I held the other. A neighbor administered whiffs of chloroform as Bonta indicated. Mrs. Carson did a great job, working hard and pushing when told. Here she was, only seventeen, having to grow up so fast. Everyone seemed quite calm about it all, though the minute the baby was born I could feel the hidden tensions drain away.

I was most impressed by how natural it all was and how wonderful that she knew as much of what went on as she did, so different from the way it was when I had Susan. She heard the baby's first cry and began talking about whose nose he had before Bonta even severed the umbilical cord. Bayliss was real sweet and bent over and kissed her fondly the minute the baby emerged. The baby was a cute little fellow. After having talked about it in embryology lectures, I was intrigued to see the protective vernix* smeared all over his dusky little body. He rapidly turned pink, and we had him cleaned up in no time.

Before I arrived, Bayliss had given Bonta a nice lunch. He had actually gone across the street to the little general store in Guyan to buy some bacon and eggs and offered him bread and homemade jam. Bonta felt bad because he had asked for a knife to spread it, only to be told they didn't have one.

They had just moved in, and Bayliss had obtained something like $600 credit at the company store; this he'd used to buy a stove, refrigerator, chifforobe, and bed, and then he blew $265 of it on a radio-phonograph! The latter reposed in the living room in solitary splendor. I couldn't help wondering what he was going to play on it. The records I had seen in the area stores carried the same music I heard on the radio day after day. How wonderful my Beethoven records would sound on such a super instrument. I promised myself we would get those records out of storage someday and buy ourselves a decent phonograph.

Bayliss said he had made more money working for Ford in Detroit than he made here but had nothing like the security the coal miners had. I couldn't help thinking, "What security now?" With great courtesy he saw us right to the car in spite of all the mud and expressed appreciation for Bonta's help. He even thanked me for coming.

At the post office later I bumped into Mrs. Bill James. It occurred to me that she might be willing to help us with an artistic project we were working on.

---

*Cheesy material covering the skin at delivery

"How's it going? Have you sold any more signs?" I asked.

"Oh, no, but I'm hoping. Course I can't do anything real good."

"I don't believe that for a minute. I'm glad to see you because I wonder if you'd be willing to help us out. We need a little white paint and a brush and thought you might be willing to lend us some." I explained our plans for a photographic Christmas card with Susan asleep in her crib, dreaming of Santa reading his list. I needed the paint for adding "Merry Christmas."

"Why, sure, sounds real interesting. You can stop by and pick them up any time. You know where we live in the white camp near the Bakers. You just got to promise to show it to me when it's done."

The afternoon mail brought a letter from Mary, with a clipping of her article from the second section of the *Louisville Times*, datelined Coal Mountain. We were most interested to see it:

> "Striking Miners' Long Rest Is Wearing Thin, Despite Squirrel Hunting, as Funds Dwindle" by Mary Brush, *Times* Staff Correspondent—Coal Mountain, W.Va., Nov. 1
>
> While the nation's coal supplies and their own funds dwindle, the miners here are off squirrel hunting. Most of them will tell you they would "like to go back to work tomorrow." They're beginning to feel the pinch economically, and their long vacation is wearing thin.
>
> Tucked away in the mountains just across the Kentucky border, this mining camp is fifty miles from Logan, the nearest good-sized town. And that's over narrow, unpaved roads, blasted into the mountain-side or left by the strip miners, with a sheer drop below. So they don't go "out the holler" much. Some took off as soon as the strike began, but the rest are left with time on their hands.
>
> The day the squirrel season opened two weeks ago was a big event. Some of the men even spent the night out in the mountains to get an early start at dawn. At night they came back with squirrels slung from their belts.
>
> Other strikers are repairing their two or three room shacks, built of boards or logs chinked with mud. To keep them dry without cellars, some of the houses are set on stilts, sometimes high enough for the children to play underneath on rainy days. Some of the men are leveling land for new homes. Some are tinkering with their cars and trucks. Some of them stand around and talk to each other. And the camp doctor has received a number of good-natured warn-

ings: "Just wait till nine months from now, doc; you'll be plenty busy then."

The miners here aren't hungry. They buy food on credit at the company store, run by the Red Jacket Coal Corporation, as they did before the strike. But some, whose bills are running too high, aren't allowed credit for gasoline any more. Even for the thriftiest, the reserves are running low. It has been six weeks since the day they passed the word, in a sort of fraternal union lingo, that "the dog died at four o'clock."

Sometimes, the strikers go back to mining, unofficially, for awhile. They run out of coal, too, and when that happens they scoop a little out of the veins along the mountainside and carry it home.

That was it—the whole of it. Short and innocuous, we were glad it didn't seem to present any problem.

The Ramseys dropped by after supper to get something for Mrs. Ramsey's cold, and we persuaded them to stay and visit. Mr. Ramsey even had a little bottled cheer in his coat pocket to improve the Cokes we offered. The conversation went from stories about other doctors here before us to the subject of worms in young patients. Mr. Ramsey heartily approved our efforts to educate people about the way they're spread, even if some of them were initially upset by the implications.

We suddenly remembered Mary's article and thought they might find it intriguing. Mr. Ramsey was amused.

"That's interesting all right. But she might have mentioned those shacks are privately owned. Not the kind the men get from the company."

Mrs. Ramsey had reservations about the whole thing. "Hmph! If folks had known she was a reporter, you better believe they'd have clammed up right away."

I had the distinct feeling that she felt Mary (and, by implication, we, too) had intruded on the privacy of the community.

Monday brought the welcome sounds of the tipple working once again; cars clanked once more down the track—all reassuring, constructive sounds, bonding the whole camp in a single important enterprise. I didn't even mind the extra laundry from the office, now that the miners were coming in again, many of them grimy with coal dust. Bonta had several preemployment physicals to do. Apparently Mr. Ramsey meant what he said about hiring new people once the strike was over.

Bonta spent another morning delivering a baby. One might think all he did was deliver babies, but that wasn't so. Most of the time he treated sore throats, cuts and bruises, backaches, and people who claimed they had tired blood or were just worried about things. Of course, he also had some seriously ill people like Mrs. Horvath, and he worried about some who had bad heart trouble and high blood pressure, like Sarah Davis, who still insisted on lugging the pails of water from the well, and old Brett Morgan, one of the patriarchs of the Hatfield-Morgan clan.

Those deliveries were such major events because once Bonta was called out, unless the woman lived in camp, he stayed until the baby was born. If she were nearby, he could check her progress by repeated short calls. It did seem as though most deliveries took him far away. Without telephones to keep him posted, he felt obligated to be there till the end. He probably wouldn't have trusted reports anyway. People tend to be panicky when they're excited and nervous. Furthermore, chasing back and forth on those roads was no pleasure.

Actually he enjoyed deliveries. Each new baby was another miracle, and it was enormously rewarding to help when the outcome made everyone so happy. For a while his experiences at Coal Mountain made him rethink what he wanted to specialize in; surgery had been his first love, but he wondered if he should switch to obstetrics.

Our discussions brought up some other kinds of questions— whether the amount we would probably have saved in a year would see us through either kind of residency. Our conclusions finally led to our filling out applications for surgical residencies at several places, including the Ohio State University Hospital at Columbus.

Physical problems were not the only kind his patients brought. He discovered far more mental and emotional distress than either of us expected. At least as many anxieties flourished here as anywhere else. This rural life was far from idyllic, and deprivations took their toll.

One pathetic young woman came to the office every payday "smothering." I could hear her breathing heavily in the waiting room.

Special pills "just for smothering" helped her through the two weeks till the next time. The big pills were nothing but calcium carbonate, and I did wonder whether it was right to deceive her into thinking she was really getting something potent. But what else could Bonta do? They gave her the strength to cope with her problems, and there was no way anyone could successfully address all her very real difficulties. That would take redoing her entire life!

I had a chance to talk to a badly disturbed young woman myself one afternoon. On an earlier visit she had kept Bonta for an hour and a half listening to all her problems while I was waiting for him for lunch, and I confess to having been impatient with them both. Everything had gone wrong that morning. I'd smothered the fire, Susan was cranky, and the washing machine had flooded the kitchen floor. I had fixed a fancy soufflé for lunch, and by the time Bonta arrived, it was fallen and cold. I found myself wondering why I'd ever married a doctor anyway. This time I found the same young woman in the waiting room, looking so frightened and unhappy that I asked her to come into the lab, hoping I could do something to help while she waited till Bonta could see her. She willingly followed me in and sat down on the stool beside me, shaking all over; her eyelids quivered, and she clasped her stomach in acute misery. Never had I seen anyone more pathetically upset.

"I just sit and worry about myself all day long." She was silent a moment, staring fearfully at the door. "You know, I look in the mirror, and I look at my eyes. They look just like the eyes of a crazy woman I saw. They was taking her away after she tried to hang herself with a belt. I keep seeing her."

I asked her if she had any aches or pains in addition to these troubles.

"Well, lots of times I feel kind of numb and queer all over. And then I'll forget what I was saying right in the middle of talking."

"Do you eat well?"

"Oh, I eat all the time. Ain't nothing much else to do."

I could hardly believe this, since she was slender and looked perfectly normal. In fact I thought with her big gray eyes, ivory skin, and long dark hair she was beautiful indeed. Though Bonta said her husband seemed like a very decent sort, she didn't trust him.

"I'd sure like another baby. You know, I lost one a while back. But

I can't stand Tollison near me. No, I ain't had relations since I lost the baby."

All this spilled out almost nonstop. I wanted so much to say something helpful but felt woefully inadequate. All I could do was listen sympathetically and hope that was enough to convince her someone cared. Her trust was touching. No wonder Bonta was late for lunch the other day; nobody could possibly cut off a recital of such wretchedness until it wound itself down. What was a fallen soufflé weighed against all this misery!

After Bonta had seen her, I asked him what he thought could be done for her. He said he was much puzzled by her symptoms: manic-depression, postmiscarriage melancholia, or schizophrenia? He had been alternately treating her with mood elevators and sedatives and wanted very much to get her to a competent psychiatrist as soon as the Welfare and Retirement Fund would again permit. He felt she had gone downhill alarmingly just since he first saw her.

Talking with her myself made me far more understanding of Bonta's sympathetic response to his patients' problems. It was a revelation to recognize the difference that circumstances made in my attitude toward her. When she kept Bonta from lunch, I resented the time spent on her worries, but when she was pouring her heart out to me, no amount of time was an imposition. This was an insight that helped me to become more graceful whenever patients' needs disrupted personal plans.

⁓ Thanksgiving morning found me stuffing our chicken and about to start on the pumpkin pie when Mr. Ramsey arrived to invite us to have dinner with them. Receiving such a casual invitation for Thanksgiving dinner was disconcerting for a moment, especially since I'd made all the plans for our own dinner. But it was more than kind of them to want us, and of course we accepted. Mrs. Ramsey outdid herself; everything was delicious. Fortunately when Susan ate enough turkey to embarrass us, our hosts seemed pleased.

Mrs. Ramsey and I had fun singing hymns together at the piano. It reminded me of those long-ago Sunday night hymn sings, which were a tradition at Thousand Island Park where my family had a summer home.

Bonta asked Mr. Ramsey what he thought about Laredo, a coal camp larger than Coal Mountain, which apparently needed a doctor. Mr. Ramsey said he didn't believe Bonta would be ready to tackle such a big job until he understood the people here a little better. Mr. Ramsey believed we were still too easily rattled by some of the rumors that flew around. His insight into our thinking was impressive. We expected people's behavior to conform to our own idea of what was rational and didn't quite know how to handle some of the things that looked unreasonable to us. He was right. We couldn't toss those things off as easily as he thought we should.

Mr. Ramsey didn't venture any opinion on the likelihood of the strike being resumed. He seemed glad to put all those worries out of his mind. He just wanted to enjoy the holiday.

We celebrated Bonta's twenty-seventh birthday on Saturday, November 26, by leaving the hollow midafternoon. We needed a number of things, including some aureomycin for Jimmy Morgan. Injured in the mine a year earlier, he was a paraplegic, in Coal Mountain on a temporary release from a UMW hospital in California. After the accident he had been sent there for rehabilitation by the union, treatment made possible by the new Welfare and Retirement Fund. Now he suffered from a chronic kidney infection, and Bonta was working hard to keep it under control. Sometimes when Jimmy's need for care seemed overwhelming, we reminded each other that there'd come a day when we'd beg for patients!

Having finished our shopping, we decided to celebrate our freedom by going to a drive-in movie on our way home, our first since coming to Coal Mountain. It turned out to be a corny affair about horse racing but provided enough laughs to make it worth the dollar it cost and the miles we drove. Susan woke up toward the very end of the second race as the right horse was winning and became wildly excited over the "Hoy" who was running so hard. She couldn't get over this, talking vehemently all the way home about the Hoy, then saying "dog" and shaking her head emphatically, for she knew it wasn't a dog; it was a Hoy!

The fire was almost out when we reached home, and the house felt like a barn. The weather had turned bitterly cold, and we were thankful the coal shed was full. Sometimes the wind blew the light snow almost horizontally, and it howled around the house, rattling the windows unmercifully. Luckily Bonta was able to revive the fire without smothering it, a disaster that had occurred all too often in our eagerness to warm the house up after trips.

I hadn't yet mastered the knack of keeping the fire going evenly. One Saturday while Bonta was out I spent the afternoon working on the budget. I was trying unsuccessfully to balance a bank statement with the checkbook when I realized I was half frozen. I'd completely forgotten about the fire, and it was almost out. From the lumps that were still glowing, I managed to start a few coals blazing, but then I became impatient and dumped in too much new coal, some of it rather fine. It smoked like fury for a while, and I kept opening the cover to let air in and see what was happening. I had just turned my back on it to return to those numbers when it ignited. With a fearful bang the whole thing went up in flames. The lid of the stove jumped up to release a mushroom cloud of soot. It billowed up to the ceiling; the fallout reached every nook and cranny. The mess was indescribable. Everyday cleaning was a chore, because whenever the lid was lifted to feed the fire it belched soot and smoke, but this was catastrophic. It took hours to make the place livable again. Well, Barney had warned me!

Susan thought it was hilarious and talked about the big boom and the dirty coal, as though the show had been put on for her benefit.

On Sunday I went to see Mrs. Bill James to return the paint and brush. I was struck by the Jameses' relative affluence. She showed me some new slipcovers and silverware she had recently purchased, and I couldn't help wondering whether they'd saved up for these things or had taken out a loan as Mr. Carson had done.

The conversation turned to the problems of bringing up children and avoiding the chicken pox that was going around.

"I remember when Doc Nichols told me to put our Sally in a tub with a lot of baking soda in the water. Didn't help her much, but she got better by and by."

This reminded her of something else about our predecessor. "Oh, it was plain scandalous. Him and Mrs. Nichols, they wore shorts when they was sunning in the yard when they first come. Everybody was talking about it. That was bad enough, but they even went down to the beer joint in shorts!"

I wondered what tales would later be told about us.

I left, promising to send her one of our Christmas cards when they were finished.

✒ As the three-week truce drew toward an end, everyone in camp hung on John L. Lewis's words, anticipating a renewal of the strike. He had set midnight, November 29, as the time for a big announcement. We didn't see how he could possibly call the men out again, so near Christmas, considering all the debts they had accumulated and the likelihood that Truman would invoke Taft-Hartley. The men were fed up with this on-again, off-again business with no new contract in sight. They wanted it settled, preferably without another work stoppage, but if necessary to win that contract, by a long strike. They wanted assurance that when they did go back to work there would be no chance of their being called out again.

Dan Dubois shared his thoughts on the matter with us when we met by the back gate.

"Yes sir, the way I see it, Lewis'll call the men out for a couple days, but then he'll send them back to the pits with a three-year contract in his pocket." He beamed at the thought. "Yes sir, that'll be good enough to make up for all the time they've lost already. That Lewis, he's a smart one."

"But do you think there's enough demand for coal to keep all of them working five days a week?" Bonta asked.

Dan glanced around to see whether anyone might overhear. "Looks to me like there's getting to be too much coal around. Why, over there in Europe, they're beginning to mine the stuff again, and they don't need ours the way they did right after the war. You want to know what I think?"

Of course, we nodded, and he continued with supreme confidence. "Well, now, what we got to have is a guarantee of so many days' work a year. And if that makes for too big a stockpile, well, we need a fund to pay for some of them days a man can't work. Yes sir, the union and the company both ought to pay into that there fund. Why, there's lots of mines that won't make it unless we spread the work around."

I thought it remarkable that he had done so much thinking about policy and the big picture. I didn't realize at the time that all this came straight from headquarters.

It was noteworthy that Dan was so willing to share the limited work among all who needed it. We had long been impressed by the apparent solidarity of the union, the seeming lack of competition among the men, and their spirit of "all for one and one for all."

However, that attempt Bonta had described to tap the welfare fund when it was not justified made me realize that not all of the members were beyond exploiting union resources.

If the men should strike again, things might be pretty quiet around camp. In that case we might go to Columbus for the weekend to see about a residency at the University Hospital. The radio said at noon that Lewis had called off the third meeting of the union policy committee, and we didn't know what that signified.

14. Nothing's Easy

On Thursday, December 1, a special radio bulletin reported that Truman wouldn't invoke Taft-Hartley immediately against the UMW. The next bulletin was from Lewis himself. This was the big announcement everyone had been waiting for, expecting him to call for a renewal of the strike. The miners were prepared for the big showdown, much as they wanted to work. Instead he asked the men, still without a contract, to continue work Monday on the old three-days-a-week schedule. This was a stunning development!

Not only that, but individual unions were authorized to negotiate contracts with individual companies, which to me sounded like a real admission of defeat. Mrs. Ramsey, on the other hand, told me she thought that was a smart move on his part. That way companies which could afford higher royalties would have to pay them, and this would enrich the Welfare and Retirement Fund more than a compromise industrywide figure.

The men were despondent. Dan Dubois was discouraged. I had given him the report on my way to the office to tell Bonta. He said, "Well, guess you might as well give up. Sure, we all want a chance to earn a little money, but we was counting on something better than this—or else the big fight. Lewis sure let us down this time."

The depth of his disappointment was revealed by this criticism of his idol.

Reaction to the news varied. In Harlan County men had put work ahead of the fight for the contract. Rumor had it that if Lewis had called a strike and union officers tried to enforce it there the men there would have gone to work with guns if necessary. So they welcomed Lewis's pronouncement. The local radio quoted the story going the rounds that John L. had killed Santa Claus. Another commentator called it a poor sop and no gravy.

It struck me as a real shame that the men were unwitting pawns in a big power struggle between Lewis and the operators. Their fate was essentially out of their hands, and they were suffering for it.

Old Fred Blankenship came in that afternoon looking very subdued. While I packaged the cold pills he needed, he leaned close and asked confidentially, "What would you take for a whole jar of that there itch salve? Ain't got no money, but I could sign a slip." He confessed that the entire family was suffering from scabies, himself, his wife, and all eight children.

When I told him how expensive it was, he looked so blue that I put up eight ointment tins for him and almost cleaned out our supply. Fred always reminded me of Tweedledum and Tweedledee with his baseball cap, round belly, and normally happy disposition. How many times had he breezed into the office with the request, "Hey, Doc, how about lending me a fiver? Just kind of short this evening. Oh, I'll sign a slip, and the company'll pay you back—just soon as I get back to work anyways."

Bonta usually complied, knowing full well Fred's income would never catch up with his debts, but his naive optimism was irresistible.

꙰   We did spend the weekend in Columbus, where Bonta looked into the possibility of that surgical residency. While he talked to the doctors there and watched an operation, Susan and I went shopping.

It was a treat worth the ten-hour drive (no superhighways in those days) just to be in a real department store again. I spent some time staring at the well-dressed women shopping and wandered happily among the racks of clothes and the counters with their endless temptations.

Since I had planned to do our Christmas shopping on this trip, I'd come well supplied with money. This was not hard to do, since the lumber company paid us at the end of each month in cash. For some reason they favored hundred-dollar bills, a couple each time. I'd never even seen one before. We always had a hard time deciding just what to do with them until we could get out of camp to a bank. Usually we tucked them into the toe of a shoe or a dress pocket in the closet till we could deposit them. This trip, however, we took several along for my shopping spree and the hotel expenses.

Having finally decided on a briefcase for Dad, a robe for my mother, and several other things, I presented one of these bills to the saleslady. She gave me the merest suggestion of a sharp look and disappeared with it. Apparently her superiors decided it was not forged, and she returned with the most deferential smile imaginable to ask in what way she might be of further assistance to me.

When Bonta returned from his interview with a big grin on his face, there was no need to ask how it had gone.

"Looks as though there's a good chance for an opening in a year and a half. Everybody was real friendly. And boy, was it good to see a big hospital again!"

"I'll bet. What's their residency program like anyway? What's the nights on/nights off schedule?"

"The program's fantastic, but the schedule's not so good. Just three nights home a week, I'm afraid."

"That makes our own little rat race seem not quite so bad, doesn't it?"

"I suppose that's true. Ours is just so unpredictable, and things gang up on me. But we do have a lot of time together."

At dinner he continued his report. "Oh, I talked with a young surgeon who's just finished his residency here. Trying to set up a practice. And he's having a rough time. Too much well-established competition."

"That must have been a little discouraging. At least where we are we know we're needed."

"Oh, it just takes patience. Nice thing about this, though. The slot will open up at the end of our second year at Coal Mountain, just when we'll have saved enough to swing it."

"Good planning. By the way, what do they pay their residents?"

"You know better than to ask that," he said with a smile. "This is a topflight residency with Zollinger, biggest name in surgery. They don't pay anything—same as at Reese. Board, room, and uniform."

But he looked so enthusiastic that all obstacles were swept from his thinking. Apparently our course was set.

Dinner in the dining room was almost too good to be true, and Susan behaved like a lady. It was wonderful to have a weekend all to ourselves away from the distractions at home. We reveled in the hot showers and thick carpeting of the hotel room.

Our return trip on Monday was highlighted by one unforgettable scene. As we neared home, in the darkness we saw a red glow in the sky ahead. We rounded a curve above a little valley, and across the creek and railroad track we saw that a house was going up in a roaring blaze. An adjacent building had already caught fire, and this in turn threatened the church. Perhaps two dozen people were gathered on the tracks, silhouetted against the flames. They had piled their belongings there, and some of them were bringing pews out from the church, which seemed sure to go. Their efforts to fight the blaze were pitiful. They had organized a bucket brigade and were passing pails and dishpans of water up to the young men on the roof of the building which had just begun to burn. Smoke billowed up through broken windows and a hole in the roof, swirling about and partially obscuring them. A large tree near the house had been charred to ghostly whiteness, while blanched smoke poured from all its branches to mingle with the darker clouds from the house. Here and there a tiny flame spurted from a branch only to sputter out like a candle running out of wax.

One of the eeriest aspects of the tableau was the complete silence. We were too far away to hear the shouting or smell the smoke. We watched till it seemed they might save the church after all, thanks to a shift in the wind. Human despair, helplessness, courage, and endurance all seemed epitomized in this one brief scene. That picture would haunt me for a long time.

☞ Twice on Tuesday Bonta was called to see Mrs. Bannister. He'd seen her so often over the last several weeks and simply didn't know what to do for her. I found myself wondering if there'd have been fewer calls if she hadn't lived so nearby. It was all too easy to send Maggie down to get Bonta. In a quandary he'd sent her to the hospital at Welch eight days earlier, but she had just walked out after a week, saying they weren't doing anything for her and she'd much rather have Dr. Hiscoe take care of her at home. This time he suggested they might see if the doctors in Bluefield could find an answer to her problem.

At lunch Eloise shared Eva's latest report from the store. Apparently Alison was busily selling the special boxes of candy one of the other buyers had ordered for her own gifts for Christmas. She was also showing off a box of panties embroidered with the days of the week. Though this might have been a popular item, she'd ordered only the one box for herself. Neither Eva nor Eloise seemed to squander much affection on Alison.

At the office the following Monday Mrs. Lambert brought the baby in to show us how alert and healthy she was in spite of the scary delivery and her unresponsiveness that night. Then she wanted to know whether we were really leaving. She had heard we'd already made arrangements at the hospital to leave the first of the year. I assured her that was furthest from our plans. Rumors were born and matured before the basis for them was even conceived! She and I had covered a number of subjects in the past, including even Bonta's religious affiliation, so I asked her how these stories originated. She was pleased to share some other choice examples.

One was that Bonta had never delivered a baby before he came to Coal Mountain. Another was that he was too scared to go into the mine to treat Clinton Witt after the slate fall. Still another concerned some unspecified delivery, during which children were running around the room and men were peering through a nearby window. Then Bonta supposedly handed the afterbirth to somebody who put it out on the porch and the pigs ate it. Of course, who knows? It was possible he did ask someone to dispose of the afterbirth, and they might have left it where the pigs could have found it. I didn't think children had ever been running around during a delivery. Children asleep in the same room, yes, but only nursing babies awake. What the men outside might do was up to them. Bonta was usually much too busy to pay attention. Whatever went on in camp was bound to be embroidered in the telling.

Mr. Ramsey came in with a representative from the Compensation Commission. He looked serious and said he had to see Bonta about a very important matter. He explained that the inspector was checking on the safety record of this mining operation. Mr. Ramsey took great pride in the fact that injuries had always been kept to a minimum, and one of his greatest ambitions was to get the state's award for a year without any serious accidents. This year things had gone exceptionally well, marred only by the slate fall that injured Clinton Witt. Everything hung on his condition at the moment. Bonta didn't realize just how much depended on his answer when the inspector asked him whether Clinton must be considered completely disabled or not.

"Oh, there's no doubt about his being completely disabled. He can't move his legs. There's some question as to whether he'll ever be able to. Of course, you never rule out the chance of some improvement, but I'm not overly optimistic in his case."

Mr. Ramsey looked crestfallen, positively crushed. "Well, you've just settled a big issue for us. This means Coal Mountain doesn't win that top safety award for the year. My father won it once, and I was sure hoping this was my year."

He looked anxiously at the inspector, seeking what he knew wasn't there, some indication that the verdict wasn't irrevocable. Finding only an expression of sympathy and regret, he was forced to accept the disappointment. His shoulders sagged, and he sighed deeply. "Poor Clinton! Well, I guess we'll just have to hope for better luck next year."

Those last forward-looking words were belied by the look on his face.

✎ We celebrated Susan's second birthday on Friday, December 23, starting at breakfast with the arrival of Eloise and Eva with a pink dress. Susan could hardly eat for "hubbing" it. Two candles were duly blown out at dinner, and we managed a couple of pictures of the big moment, with Susan holding her hands over her eyes because of the "bite 'ight."

She had been difficult to handle lately, good enough with Eloise, but demanding that I "ole" her the minute I returned from the office. Perhaps this was the start of the terrible twos the books warned about. I kept reading them to see what a good parent ought to be doing at each stage. I wasn't sure I believed everything they said, but it was reassuring to know I wasn't the only insecure mother around. Luckily

Susan seemed to be making pretty normal progress. I hoped this phase was as short-lived as some of the other ups and downs had been.

It was two days before Christmas, and we still had no proper Christmas tree! One of the men, Harry Hutchinson, very thoughtfully brought us a tiny table-size tree with a few thin branches. Much as we appreciated his kindness, we put it in Susan's room and schemed to get a bigger, fuller one for the living room. We'd both grown up with Christmas trees that reached the ceiling, and we wished Susan could have a big one like those. Since the last thing we wanted was to hurt Harry's feelings by being seen with another tree, any expeditions to find one had to be undertaken after dark.

We had tried unsuccessfully to find time to go hunting for one earlier. This was hardly the ideal night; it was pouring as though the heavens had split, but the date made the situation critical. So on went our rain gear. Bonta wore the big leather boots he'd bought because Vern had written he'd need them for tramping around the rattler-infested hills. Though he probably should have worn them on some of his calls up the hollows, he hadn't taken the trouble to put them on. They were, however, useful that night. With heavy coal stove gloves, ax, and flashlight we set off, with Susan in her car bed in the backseat.

As soon as we left the few lights in camp behind, the night became impenetrably black. The roads were slippery as a skating rink, but we wanted to drive slowly anyway, looking for the right tree with the help of the headlights and flashlight. We were surprised to find that our impressions were all wrong. Countless suitable trees did not grow right along the roadside. We drove for miles before we finally spotted one that seemed about the right shape and size, and it was at the top of a twenty-foot embankment on our left.

We parked the car close to the edge of the cliff on our right, and Bonta set out to scale the heights, ax strapped to his belt and flashlight in hand. Somehow or other he scrambled up in spite of greasy clay and sliding rocks, only to discover that distance had deceived us about the size of this tree. It was really huge, much larger than he'd imagined, but it was the only one we'd seen that came even close. It was raining, and we'd come so far already that he decided to cut it down anyway. He chopped it off about three feet above ground, hoping that would cut it down to size. It was a struggle hacking away under the branches in the dark, but he finally toppled it. It came crashing down into the road, gathering mud on every branch as it rolled. Then I, too, saw how big it was. Bonta slithered down after it, and we held a hasty consultation in the downpour.

"We'll never get it through the door!" Bonta's expression was rueful, but he sounded a little proud of what he'd accomplished.

"No, and if we did, we'd never stand it up unless we chopped a hole in the roof."

We stood there in the rain, helpless with laughter over our predicament. How could we have misjudged so badly?

I held the flashlight for him in one hand and my umbrella in the other. While the water ran in a little stream from the tip of his nose, he wielded the ax, finally shortening the tree by three more feet. This eliminated a circle of boughs that spread almost the width of the road.

Somehow we hoisted our muddy prize onto the roof of the car and tied it down with soggy ropes, while Susan inside bounced from side to side, demanding to " 'ee big dee!"

We prayed nobody would see us driving home with it, especially not Harry. The bad weather was in our favor. When we got home, we lifted it onto the back porch where we had to wash the mud off with uncounted buckets of water. We put Susan to bed before we lugged it, still dripping, into the living room and set it up. Its symmetry was marred by a gap or two among the branches, and its circumference was still ridiculously large. It represented an achievement, however, and the fun of trimming it, thinking of Susan's excitement the next morning, was sufficient reward for getting cold and drenched.

✻ The morning of the twenty-fourth Susan toddled into the living room, wide-eyed with astonishment at seeing the tree with lights, tinsel, and bright balls, filling a third of the room with woodsy glory. She clearly thought our efforts to make Christmas an overwhelming experience were a success. Eloise tactlessly burst out laughing when she saw it. Suddenly embarrassed, she was relieved when she realized we thought it was as funny as she did.

Knowing of our interest in photography, Dan Dubois had asked us to take pictures of the outdoor service at the community tree after supper. He had assumed the responsibility of managing the appropriate ceremony for the camp. The tree stood in the open space across the creek where the revival tent had been. During the night the weather had turned frigid, and the rain had changed to snow. Now the ten-foot pine made a brave show with its colored lights glinting on the thin dusting of white.

We found Dan with about a dozen hardy adults and children, gathered in the biting cold to hear the preacher exhort them not to forget the Christ in Christmas. Although he could have carried on a quiet conversation with the few of us there, he used his most impressive rhetorical style, asking that even those of us who were unsaved might acquire at least that much grace.

By the light of several cars strategically located, we photographed the tree and the cluster of people. Dan was most anxious to get this picture in the coal company newsletter so people would know that, remote as we were, "we got civilization." Four little girls lingered, and Dan asked them to sing "Silent Night." Their thin soprano voices might have been a bit off key, but they sang all three verses in a touching conclusion to the ceremony.

That had to serve in place of our usual Christmas Eve communion service. I visualized the banked poinsettias behind the altar, the candles glowing in every darkened window, the swelling chords of the organ as we all rose to join the white-robed choir processing to "Come, Oh Come, Emmanuel." Just thinking about it brought a wave of homesickness. But I reminded myself that this was home now, and I did appreciate the chance to participate in the service I'd just witnessed. The form might be different, but there was no doubt about its sincerity.

Before going to bed, I stood for a chilly moment on the front step, warmed by the glow of Christmas lights from houses along the road toward the green camp.

Wonderful as it was, Christmas quickly receded into the background. Dan was pleased with the pictures we had developed and printed, and he proudly took them over to the company office to Mrs. Doug Blake. She was both a secretary and the camp reporter for the *Red Jacket News*. She promised to see that our celebration was duly acknowledged in the next issue of the paper.

Mrs. Bannister needed medical attention again. She had gone to Bluefield, but no answers were forthcoming there either. This time she was suffering a recurrence of her lower abdominal discomfort, worse than usual, so Bonta gave her some oral medication and hoped this would be sufficient. She told him she'd felt bad on Christmas, too, but had refrained from calling so that she wouldn't disrupt our holiday. He thanked her for her thoughtfulness.

She told him how much she appreciated receiving our Christmas card. "Oh, that'll go in my album for sure. It's such a cute picture of Susan and Santa Claus. Can't believe you made it right here!"

The office was incredibly busy as the year drew to a close. One afternoon I rushed back home for some vaccine stored in our refrigerator and all but collided with the Davises' cow. She was munching garbage from the barrel just inside our fence, and I never looked up from jumping mud puddles until I was upon her.

On Friday, December 30, a man came in very angry because Bonta hadn't answered an urgent call to see a sick baby up Road Branch. Finally convinced that the message had never been delivered, he just pleaded for help now to save the baby. Impressed by his desperate sincerity, Bonta managed to see those who were waiting with the most urgent needs in record time, told me how to take care of the last few, and left.

Tragically the baby had died several hours earlier. It was Laurel and Marcus's little girl whom he'd delivered two months before. Bonta was shocked! She had been the picture of health when last he saw her. Poor Laurel was in a state of collapse and required sedation. Marcus didn't even know about it yet, since he was out hunting. Laurel's mother said they hadn't realized the baby was that sick. They'd just asked a man to tell the doctor on his way to the store. If only they'd brought the little thing down then, Bonta might have sent it by ambulance to the hospital in time. But who knows?

They asked him to look the baby over to see why it died. He did a sort of symbolic examination, but there was nothing he could find to explain the sudden death. They'd prepared it for burial with a little handkerchief tied around its head and under its chin and two pennies on its eyelids.

When he told me about it later, he said, "I can't figure out the significance of the scarf and the pennies."

"Don't you suppose the scarf might have been to prevent its little jaw from sagging and the pennies to keep its eyes closed?"

Such isolation meant handling situations alone that we'd never even thought about. It was pitiful, yet it made me realize that people could and did cope when there was no alternative, that life did go on. They planned to bury the baby in a pine box out in back of their little home.

Bonta felt just awful about it. It was one of his babies—and he was so fond of Laurel and Marcus. He was only thankful it hadn't been the result of any unnecessary delay on his part. With all the cries of wolf around here, it frightened us to think it might have been.

Unnecessary calls were a problem and could be a danger to others. Early that very morning we'd been treated to one such call. About six-thirty somebody yelled, "Hey, Doc!" outside the window and banged on the door. "Hey, Doc, you got to come quick. Jake Hawley's poisoned, drinking bad liquor, and like to die! He's took fits and can't talk. Ain't no time to lose. Just follow us out to Leatherwood. And hurry!"

Bonta wasted no time getting dressed in spite of skepticism about the urgency of the call. By the time he arrived, the patient was sound asleep; his only complaint on being awakened was that his back ached. Bonta refrained from lecturing him but did say he had backache pills only in the office. He gave him a shot of Demerol, charged him $2.50 for that and $1.00 for a nonemergency house call. That was the first time he charged that dollar, so far as I knew. He had been reluctant to do it because he knew people were pretty touchy, but he did feel this call was inexcusably inappropriate, having to go all that way before breakfast just to find a fellow sleeping off a night of drinking.

꾳 Inspired perhaps by the success of the Christmas Eve pictures, Dan Dubois decided on a photography project for the youngsters in camp and came by on New Year's Eve to enlist our cooperation. Since we'd already participated in one of his community ventures, we'd apparently become part of his circle. He needed some supplies—developer, hypo, and paper—enough to see whether there was sufficient interest to pursue it. Mr. Maynard from the grocery department at the store was to pick up the packet we'd put together and help Dan with the experiment. Dan said they'd be using the Boy Scout hut up on the hill right behind Bonta's office, and about eight boys had promised to come.

Just as I was going to bed Maggie Bannister came over with word that her mother had taken a turn for the worse. I told her where Bonta was, and apparently they asked Sam Dean, another neighbor, to find him, because shortly Mrs. Dean came with instructions from Bonta for me. I was to give Mrs. Bannister a shot of Demerol. Mrs. Dean planned to stay with Susan while I went to the office for the supplies and carried out the mission.

Mrs. Bannister apologized for her dirty house, which looked spotless to me. She was most grateful for the relief the drug brought and managed to tell me a little about her two sons, whose pictures I admired. They obviously meant the world to her.

As she relaxed, she felt more like chatting. "You know, I wanted to crochet something for you both for Christmas, but I just weren't up to it. Something like that pillow cover on the big chair."

I thanked her for the thought, noting not only the intricate pattern of the pillow cover but the crocheted ruffled edging around two pictures on the wall and a gold and brown lacy afghan on the couch.

Next day Bonta sent her once again to the clinic at Welch, since he still didn't know what to do for her. That proved unfortunate, for she returned, a pathetic, weepy figure, saying that they'd done nothing for her, and one of the doctors had told her she ought to be ashamed of herself—she'd break up her family with her complaints and big medical bills. Where was the answer?

Later that week Eloise reported that Dan Dubois had led a small group of church members in a service at Mrs. Bannister's home. He had concluded that she didn't have much longer to live and took the responsibility of arranging this ministry. Apparently it was a very emotional affair, culminating with her receiving the Holy Spirit and being saved.

Eloise's story was later confirmed by one of the women who was there, who described the scene. "Oh, she was saved good, wailing and talking in tongues, and all. Guess each to his own way, but I can't see that kind of thing myself."

It wasn't my way either, but I certainly hoped it would help Mrs. Bannister.

✿ On January 8, a Sunday, one of the men told us we were lucky we'd ordered our coal when we did, so we inferred the miners were going to renew their "no day workweek" the next day. In Illinois fifteen thousand were out on a wildcat strike, and in Indiana hundreds walked out after emptying their water pails at the portal. This was a symbolic ritual signifying contempt of the company. From the radio reports it was plain that there was much dissatisfaction in the union with the prolonged three-day workweek that Lewis was still promoting. But in Coal Mountain the majority of men straggled in.

On our way to the office the following morning we stopped to chat with Freddie Kilmer, swinging jauntily down the road, dressed for work in the mine. He was all fired up about the possibility of a strike. In his high tenor, even higher because of his excitement, he told Bonta, "You just wait. Could be a different story around here tomorrow!"

Because of his position as secretary of the union, we took his hint a little more seriously than we might otherwise have done.

We wondered if the time had come when the men might go out on their own just to precipitate a settlement. Most were convinced that no contract would be forthcoming so long as John L. kept them on this three-day week, though their loyalty to him was still as fierce as ever. Eloise told us that someone who ventured to criticize him was almost beaten up by a group of miners.

Mr. Kilmer spoke in a manner that suggested he knew he shouldn't be telling union secrets to an outsider, but the temptation to display his inside information was too great to resist. "Yes, sirree, Lewis, he's a smart one, he is. He can't come right out and tell us to strike, cause they'd slap a big fine on him if he did. But if we all just walked out spontaneous like, that might do the trick."

Mr. Kilmer explained, "This here three-day week's mighty hard on the men. Keeps them sore all the time. They get stiff from working, then they get laid off long enough to get soft. And then they got to start digging again. Don't make no sense."

The radio reported that railroads were ordering big cutbacks in passenger travel. So if lowering the stockpiles of coal was Lewis's goal, he had already succeeded.

❧ Regardless of union crises women kept right on having babies. Bonta was out half the night on Thursday with a delivery way over in Reedy Creek. Ronnie Witt, the young husband, came for him early in the evening. Tildie was not one of the women on his list of expected deliveries. When he found she had hardly started her labor, he didn't stay, but they called him out again about 1:00 A.M.

After he left, I vainly tried to go back to sleep. First the mattress was too soft; then it was too hard. I thought I heard Susan calling, but when I checked, she was sound asleep. The house was so cold I snuggled under the blankets again. But the wind made strange noises, and I got up to see if something was loose and rattling around the front door. Nothing seemed amiss. I sat on the edge of the bed wondering if I should just stay up and do something useful. Since it was too cold to work in the kitchen, I put a little more coal in the stove. Then I decided to read in bed until the place warmed up a bit, and I must have fallen asleep.

When Bonta staggered in at 6:00 A.M., he was surprised to find the bedroom light on. "Afraid of the dark?" he asked. "Well, move over. I'm going to try to get a little sleep before Tildie gets going in earnest. I just waited around too long expecting some progress, but nothing happened."

It did seem as though he had had more than his share of deliveries recently. If he only had the routine office problems and local house calls, he'd have been busy enough. But these deliveries usually came at night, and he still had office hours all day. He was badly in need of sleep.

I was dressing Susan when Eloise came by to report that Jesse Davis had stopped her on her way to the office to say his wife was about to come through. Bonta had been caring for her, and she had been very faithful about her prenatal visits. I had to wake him with that news.

He grabbed a bite of breakfast and told me to come along to help any way I could, since he had to take care of her before returning to Reedy.

The Davises lived only a few houses up from us—it was their cow that kept coming through our broken gate and perhaps their chicken that laid eggs in our box. A wobbly calf was mooing in the yard as we arrived.

Mrs. Davis had been in labor since 4:00 A.M. but hadn't even called for help until now. Bonta told her he had another woman working on the same project over in Reedy Creek, so half kiddingly he added that he hoped she'd be a good gal and get it over with for that woman's sake as well as her own. It was highly unlikely that this suggestion had anything to do with her progress, but whatever the reason, she did the job with amazing efficiency. I couldn't imagine a better patient. She said hardly a word, held perfectly still, and there came the baby inside an hour! I'd obviously never seen anything like it nor even imagined such a stoic, businesslike birth. Probably the fact that it was her sixth made some difference in the way things went, but it was impressive.

We left in a great rush as soon as we were sure both she and the baby were all right, saying we'd be back after the other delivery to fill out the birth certificate and give her instructions. Eloise cleaned the Kelly's pad while we restocked the medical bag at the office. I grabbed two bananas to add to the lunch I'd put up for Bonta the night before, still in the car.

Since Ronnie had come pounding back from Reedy to get Bonta only a few minutes after we went up to the Davises', we positively flew down to their place. I was tense, hoping we'd get there before the baby did. Though Bonta was inclined to be casual about being on time for things, even he drove as fast as he dared. But when we arrived, it was plain that nothing much was happening; several people clustered outside the little house with its weathered boards, just visiting.

Tildie, the focus of all the excitement, lay under masses of faded cotton quilts, in one of the three double beds in the biggest room. She was only seventeen, and this was her first baby. She moaned a lot but never spoke two words until late that evening. The poor girl reminded me of Markham's "Man with the Hoe." She just endured. Perhaps she was hard of hearing like her totally deaf mother.

The older woman was a pathetic, emaciated creature, shooed out of the way by everyone else there. She looked worried about Tildie, and her eyes were inflamed either from weeping or an infection. It did seem as though Tildie's mother ought to be the most important helper there, but she seemed banished to the barren, dark kitchen, reached by a short ladder down from the main room.

I think the women in the room might have been more casual if Bonta had been there alone, but I had the feeling that they thought I was his chief assistant and they shouldn't butt in. Anyway, since nothing was happening and everyone was too polite to presume to talk to us, I spent some time discreetly looking around. The room was papered in part with newspapers so yellowed with age that I could just barely make out the date—1943. Besides the usual calendars and religious posters, there were several large fascinating ads from some New York concern selling "Ladies' dresses, sizes 12–20 used, good condition, $.15 each; Ladies' evening dresses, used, excellent condition, $1.15 each; and Maternity dresses, used, $.65 each." These were illustrated by the most ravishingly dressed models.

Eight women occupied the three straight chairs or sat on the other two double beds in the room when we walked in. Jeana, a large-boned woman with bold features, had come all the way from England to Long Branch. I learned later that she had grown up in a coal camp in Wales, so perhaps she didn't feel as out of place as I first thought she must. Jane was the most friendly. She was the first to respond to our overtures in a comfortable way. I recognized a huge fat woman, dark hair, no teeth, from trips to Long Branch. She was always there, no matter what the crisis. I thought of her as a sort of Greek chorus; Madame Defarge also crossed my mind. Still another with straggling hair partially covered by a bandana held a sickly baby in her arms and kept up a steady flow of chatter in a squeaky voice. An older woman wearing a long gray skirt retreated periodically to the kitchen where I saw her smoking her corncob pipe.

This was the merest sample of the people who drifted in and out of that room the whole long day. At one time fifteen people crowded into the room, and when the baby was actually born, twelve, in spite of attempts to send out all but those actually helping.

As the day wore on, however, I began to appreciate their presence. They were patient and sympathetic, ready to help if needed. When Tildie let out a particularly loud groan, one of them would go over to see if they could help her. Ronnie stayed close to her, lending encouragement throughout the long ordeal.

Since Bonta found that she hadn't yet made any real progress, he decided he had plenty of time to check on Ronnie's sister-in-law whom he had delivered two nights earlier. So we left, promising to be back in an hour or so. Actually it was good just to get away from the tension and the closeness of the room.

We finished that call and were on our way back when Ronnie met us in his truck. He had called the midwife while we were away, just in case. Sadie had done a vaginal exam, without benefit of sterile gloves— no gloves at all, in fact. On discovering that the baby was presenting with one foot first, she sent for the doctor posthaste.

Bonta had suspected that it was a breech from his rectal exam, so this was not startling news, but he was distressed by her contamination of the birth canal. He had taken pains to keep things as clean as possible, borrowing some soap from a neighbor so he could scrub her perineum.

We returned to another interminable wait. Bonta was worried. He had to decide when to start interfering. He wanted to be sure that Tildie was fully dilated, of course, but even more important, that the baby had come down far enough. Handling a breech was very tricky business. Since Sadie's report on the complication, there had been some discussion about the advisability of sending Tildie to the hospital, but Ronnie insisted he wanted his baby born at home, and he wanted the doc to catch it.

Bonta knew that he had to appear confident, even though inside he was churning with anxiety. Relatively inexperienced as he was, delivering a breech alone under those circumstances was frightening. But he had to keep everyone else's courage up. At all costs general panic was to be avoided.

He went outside for a while, pacing up and down, mentally rehearsing his plan over and over, even talking to himself aloud. As the hours wore on, weariness took the edge off his anxiety, and he just wanted to have it over, whatever might happen.

Every time he gave Tildie a shot for pain, her contractions stopped entirely; he even had to give her some pitocin* to start them going again at one point. I empathized with the long waits when he was out all night on one of these calls.

*Hormone to induce uterine contractions

Meantime I knitted on Susan's sweater, and Bonta even leaned back in a chair and tried to catch a few winks of sleep, in spite of the crowd and the moans from the bed. We sneaked out to the car just before dark to get another breath of fresh air and eat our bananas and that half sandwich left from his lunch. We split a blessed tangerine, the only liquid we had all day. We'd had nothing to eat or drink since that hasty breakfast hours before. Nobody offered us anything, and if they had, we probably wouldn't have been tempted. The condition of the kitchen suggested that they'd been without soap for quite some time.

Tildie's contractions finally started in earnest, and this untied her tongue. "Shit, you're just fooling me. You all want to kill me. The baby ain't even there any more."

Rick and several other men arrived with the ambulance; word of the complication had spread. In clearly threatening tones they demanded that Bonta send her to the hospital. They implied there had better be a live baby, or else. By then Bonta was committed, since the last thing he wanted was to deliver her in the ambulance en route. Luckily Ronnie stuck by his guns; he wanted that baby born at home.

Eventually Rick drove the ambulance back to camp, but some of the men lingered across the road, talking among themselves and just waiting. They had been hunting and still had their rifles. With their slouched hats and distrustful attitude, they were a menacing presence the rest of the evening. What had promised to be a routine delivery was developing alarming overtones. Worry about the baby was bad enough; Bonta was clearly tense about that. But now I began to stew privately about our actual safety. Maybe that was foolish, but I didn't know how far those men would go if the baby weren't right. Bonta kept any concern about that to himself. He was concentrating on making sure they had no grounds for complaint.

Meantime everyone was "cheering Tildie on," telling how their labors had gone and saying encouraging things like, "Course your back hurts, Tildie. Going to hurt lots worse before the baby comes!" Or, "Now, don't waste your miseries crying. Bear down! Now's the time you can help yourself!"

Poor Tildie responded, "Shit, you all, shut up! I'm doing the best I can." And once when her husband told her to take it easy, she cried out, "Take it easy, nothing!" I couldn't have sympathized with her more! She begged, "Get me out of this shape! You Christian people, pray for me."

And many in the room did, audibly.

Her Aunt Erna had come in shortly after things began in earnest. She was a strong-willed, take-charge sort of woman, who'd had eleven children herself, so she spoke with authority on the subject of childbirth! She took Tildie in hand. "Don't waste your breath crying. Course your back's going to hurt. Use every bit of your miseries and help yourself! If you'd done what was good for you, you'd been out of this way before now." She continued her lecture after a brief pause. "And don't handle dirty words in front of the doctor! You just bear down and keep still."

Tension mounted. The unspoken fear in the minds of everyone, Bonta and me included, was, of course, for the baby. Would it live? Would it be normal?

As the minutes dragged on, Sadie began to whisper to first one and then another, "That baby going to die. Going to be born dead, just like the one Mrs. Jimmy Irons had—I should know."

I mused, "Yes, and if you hadn't been in charge, things might have been different." I thought of Barbara's shock at the scene.

"Its head got stuck. That's the way 'tis when they come feet first." Sadie shook her head lugubriously. "Too bad, her first and all."

The women hushed at the thought of the impending tragedy. They cast awestricken glances toward Tildie and Bonta.

Bonta gave Tildie a pudendal block* to lessen the pain. The size of the needle brought an involuntary gasp from the onlookers. It horrified me as much as it did everyone else. Waiting was hard for Bonta as well as for Tildie, much harder than doing something. He kept checking her.

Finally the baby's foot and lower leg became visible, all swollen from Tildie's pushing. The baby was now down far enough. Bonta confirmed that the fetal heart tones were good up to that moment and let me listen, too. The time had come to do the episiotomy and precipitate the delivery, a decision that took all the courage he had. Sadie wasn't the only one thinking of Jimmy Irons's baby.

*An injection of a local anesthetic to block the nerves to the floor of the pelvis

Bonta gave Tildie a local in preparation for the episiotomy. Then he turned to me. "Now I want you to time me carefully. Here's my watch." Though low, his voice was urgent. "I figure I've got three to four minutes to get a live baby out, once I start breaking up this breech."

He put on his gloves. "Now hold the flashlight so I can see what I'm doing."

In the ceiling outlet the seventy-five watt bulb we'd had to borrow from Jeana's house gave a feeble light.

Bonta alerted Sadie to be ready to push down on the abdomen to help push the head out and had Ronnie and Jeana each brace a leg. My heart was racing. His certainly must have been.

He made the incision. He reached in, broke up the breech, straightened out the feet, and swung the arms down.

I reported, "Only twenty-five seconds." He let out a big breath. That was better than he'd expected. Each second had seemed like an eternity.

He pulled and Sadie pushed. Ronnie and Jeana held the screaming girl. I wondered if the tiny body could survive the tugging. Then the baby emerged. It was dusky but looked normal except for the left foot. We all held our breath waiting for it to breathe.

At its gasp the tension burst. "Praise God, bless Jesus's name!" Down on their knees with, "Glory hallelujah! Blessed God!" Jeana quietly cried her eyes out. Several others did, too, and I must say I had a big lump in my own throat.

The women figured it was all over, and most of them disappeared. The rest crowded around, admiring the baby and getting in the way.

For Bonta it was plainly not over yet. It looked to me as though poor Tildie was hemorrhaging badly; her pallor matched the sheets. I recalled those impersonal words in the textbooks—"Hemorrhage is the chief cause of maternal mortality"—and prayed Bonta would be able to stop it. Whether it was really excessive or not, it looked frightening to me. She continued to lose blood, and the placenta was slow to come. Bonta and Sadie both pushed on her abdomen to speed the process. That, too, was finally delivered. Next he had to repair the episiotomy, and I held the flashlight for that.

Tildie was a pitiful sight, staring in stoic disbelief at her baby, while

Bonta worked on the little vernix-covered body, dangling it over her belly with a trickle of blood running down its face, encouraging it to keep breathing. After the cord was cut, Bonta gave Tildie a shot of ergotrate to contract the uterus and limit further bleeding.

When things finally seemed to be stabilized, we helped Tildie to a more comfortable position. The poor girl had been lying with her hips over the edge of the bed and her knees hooked over two chairs. I cleaned up instruments while Bonta talked to Ronnie about caring for both Tildie and the baby. The foot that led the way had seemed swollen as it became visible during contractions, but it looked much worse after the delivery. Now it was twice normal size and almost purple, but there was nothing to be done but wait and let nature take its course. By now everyone but Ronnie and Tildie's mother had vanished. The show was over. We gathered up our things and slipped out into the night.

The cluster of waiting men had melted away at news of the live birth, and we were grateful to be alone and on our way home.

As we talked over the trials of the day, I told Bonta how much I admired his coolness under pressure. And I added my heartfelt conclusion, "When it comes to medicine, you can have it! I wouldn't want that kind of responsibility for all the coal in Appalachia!"

This admission on my part proved somehow reassuring to him. Though I'd been unaware of it, perhaps my career before we were married had been something of a submerged, but real, problem. He had felt the need to establish some territory exclusively his own. I've always credited him with strengths I don't have and never will and had taken it for granted that he knew this. Apparently my voicing it did matter. To be sure, while I valued my past, I had never dwelt on it. Joyfully and optimistically I had traded a career for marriage and the family we had started and felt not a moment's regret.

I had no idea then that years later that career would revive, with an opportunity to teach in a great midwestern university.

15. Rising Discord

The knitting class in the churchhouse was scheduled for mid-January. I had looked forward to it since Mrs. Ramsey finally broached the subject, and I wholeheartedly agreed with her that teaching the girls a useful skill was a good idea. We decided they should start on something simple like pot holders. Both she and I had some odds and ends of yarn to help the cause along. She asked the girls to bring their own needles.

I was keeping an eye out for her car when I heard her honking for Susan and me. Mrs. Ramsey negotiated the back road, and we deposited Susan at the Horvaths', next door to the churchhouse, before joining the girls who had already arrived.

Much like other green camp houses on the outside, inside the church merely lacked the usual partitions. A coal stove in the middle, some benches around the periphery, a typical Sunday school attendance board on one wall, and a huge paper cutout panorama of a Palestinian village on another—that was it.

More girls drifted in, most of whom I'd seen in the office one time or another, and the lessons began. It was hard to make much headway teaching them to knit. There were over twenty, which meant individual instruction was limited, and they were not used to following verbal instructions; a few were just too young to manage anyway. I was pleased that Nan Horvath was there, and Maggie Bannister, and a few others I knew reasonably well. They even helped some of those who weren't making such good progress. The little Kilmer girl was among the very young ones, and when I held her hands to show her how, I couldn't help thinking briefly of the Kwell ointment I'd put up for her infectious scabies. The girls seemed to enjoy the project, though the conversation was clearly more interesting to them than the knitting.

The lesson ended, and Mrs. Ramsey brought from the car a chocolate cake, some Dixie cups with vanilla ice cream, and a thermos jug of cocoa. She set them on one of the benches, and while she cut the cake, she explained, somewhat accusingly, "Well, there won't be enough to go around. I sure hadn't expected so many of you. After all, last Sunday there were only three of you in class, and now look—twenty-one of you come here tonight. I just won't be bothered with you again if you don't come to Sunday school. And another thing, this is for big girls. If you're under twelve, just stay home."

The girls listened passively, and one nudged her neighbor, casting a disgusted look at their hostess.

"And you all better start paying in to the treasury if you expect to get birthday cakes and presents. I sure can't do it all myself every month. Fact is, I made this cake partly for myself anyway, cause my own birthday's coming up next week."

The ideas were reasonable enough—it was the tone that grated. I couldn't help wondering if she ever talked to Mr. Ramsey that way.

   Bonta had had so many long, difficult deliveries in the recent past that people were actually beginning to sympathize—at least so long as they didn't require his services themselves.

He responded to an urgent call from way up Leatherwood to see old Brett Morgan at lunchtime on Tuesday, January 17, delaying afternoon office hours and upsetting the people waiting for him by the office steps. From the excited report of the two men who'd come to get him, he concluded Brett must be having the heart attack that Bonta had been dreading as he monitored Brett's blood pressure over the past weeks. He jumped in the car and raced all the way there in a downpour, only to find that all that was troubling him was a sore arm. Since treating him for a sore arm was far from an emergency and he was a private patient, Bonta charged him three dollars for medicine and a dollar for an unnecessary house call.

He told me he'd been fairly emphatic as he pointed out that they could just as well have brought Brett to the office. He explained to the men that he'd dropped everything and whipped down, thinking it was a big crisis. I couldn't blame him a bit, but I hoped the men wouldn't think he was talking "right smart"!

One of Bonta's classmates in medical school was a family practitioner in Kingsport, Tennessee, and had invited us to visit him and his wife whenever we could find the time. So that evening we went to the Ramseys' home to ask if Bonta could use their telephone. He wanted to call to see if it would be convenient for us to spend the next weekend with them. Luckily Jack was in and said he and Phyl would be delighted to see us.

When the phone call ended, Mr. Ramsey invited us to stay and visit a while. He indicated one of the overstuffed chairs, and Mrs. Ramsey brought out cokes and some crackers and cheese. Mr. Ramsey doctored his coke generously from his flask, offering Bonta some for his drink.

Bonta shook his head. "You never know when I might be called out. Thanks anyway."

Mr. Ramsey was in a mellow mood and started reminiscing about the old days in the coalfields. He leaned back in his chair, crossed his legs, and looked at the ceiling, as though the pictures he called to mind were painted up there.

"Yes, I worked in a mine in Logan County. Ran a coke-making operation. I was only eighteen. Didn't know the first thing about making coke. One of the Negroes working on the furnaces had known me since I was a little tyke, so I went to him. Told him how we had to turn out better coke, or the company'd shut down, and we'd all lose our jobs.

"This fellow said, 'Well, Master Johnny, not my fault. I keep the furnaces burning right, but the other fellows, sometimes they dump in too much coal, and sometimes they don't dump in enough.'

"So I told him OK—I'd check on that. The next fellows said they didn't weigh the coal any more because the cart had lines on it for the right load; that was good enough. I asked them to start weighing it again, because the size of the lumps could make the weight of a load vary. So they promised. Wasn't their fault anyway, because some of the other fellows cooled it down too fast. Didn't care how much water they poured on.

"So I went to them, and they said they'd be more careful, but it wasn't their fault—well, you get the idea. I tried to correct the mistakes at each step in the process.

"Anyway, later the inspector showed me two lumps of coke and said this was a good one and that was a bad one. I couldn't have figured out which was which. So I asked him to explain the difference. He told me one was all burned out, but the other one was full of little bubbles of brown stuff. And the inspector ended up, 'This good one came from your ovens.'"

Mr. Ramsey's managerial talent surfaced early.

Warming to his appreciative audience and fortified by a refill from the flask, he embarked on another story.

"Yes, that was a nonunion mine, and by and by the miners in the counties round about decided we ought to be unionized. We didn't like their butting into our affairs, and we meant business. But they did, too. I led thirty-five Logan boys up Blair Mountain* myself one night, guns at the ready. Our fellows all wore white arm bands so we could tell who was on our side. Man, that was some fight. When the fracas was over, a bunch of the union men were dead. Us Logan boys didn't do all the killing either. When anybody acted like they didn't want to take a chance getting hurt doing the union's dirty work, their own buddies didn't hesitate to shoot them. Yes, the others'd drag their bodies back and dump them in some neighbor's yard." He nodded emphatically. "Rough business."

It was hard for me to believe that people like those I saw every day were capable of such violence.

Mr. Ramsey turned to Bonta with sudden earnestness. "But I'll tell you something. It's still rough business. I respect these men, and I

---

*A landmark attempt by the UMW to unionize the nonunion bituminous mines of southern West Virginia. Federal troops were brought in to quell the fighting, and the attempt failed.

watch myself around them. Far as I'm concerned, every miner is a potential killer. The only way to keep them under control is to show them you're not scared of them. Guess it works. One of them told me the other day I'm the only person they're afraid of."

Mr. Ramsey dropped his voice as he leaned forward. "Just a suggestion. You need to keep your mouth shut sometimes when you'd rather not. And be wary up some of these hollows. If anybody thought you were talking to him right smart or something, he wouldn't hesitate to get his gun out and use it."

Bonta looked very sober, and I knew what he was thinking.

"There are a few fellows in the union I'd keep an eye on, if I were you. One's the treasurer, Elton Jamison. He'll talk with you real nice to your face, but next minute somebody'll turn him right around and he'll talk against you just as hard. Then there's Dan Dubois—same story. He can sound real sincere, and his churchgoing makes you think he must be real honorable, but you can be fooled real easy if you aren't careful. Or take Doug Blake. He's a very sharp guy but radical—bears watching. If he's with you, you've got a strong ally, but if he isn't, you're in trouble."

As we turned out the light in the bedroom that night, Bonta said uneasily, "You know, I've been thinking it over, and I kind of wish I hadn't charged Brett Morgan that dollar."

❧ Eloise was despondent when she arrived for work Wednesday. Tommy had left camp. He quit the store, and since policy forbade hiring ex-employees into the mine, he went to look for a job back home in Kentucky. His promise to come for her as soon as he had things under control didn't help much. Tommy would probably be better off in the long run in something other than mining, but jobs were scarce in the whole area.

Poor Eloise. Tommy provided the happy excitement that counteracted the somber atmosphere at home, and now that he was gone, life looked grim indeed. There was nothing we could say to cheer her up.

Before afternoon office hours we drove to Reedy to check on Tildie. The countryside was supersaturated with water after all the heavy rains. Water gushed from every tiny crevice in the hillsides, spouting down into the little streams like miniature waterfalls and swelling Cub into a torrent. The road was a sea of mud.

Amazingly enough, Tildie didn't remember much about her delivery, and she seemed very happy with her little boy. Probably one reason Bonta could be more objective than I could be about the pain these women suffered was because he knew from experience they wouldn't remember much. They were in more of a fog at the time than I realized. Incredibly the baby's once swollen, purple foot looked perfectly normal. Tildie's mother looked more cheerful and seemed to hear better, too. Ronnie was loud in his praise of the way Bonta handled it all. Said he'd had a "stiff argument" about whether the men should take Tildie to the hospital or not—used real strong words with them! In light of what we'd been hearing from Mr. Ramsey, I thought that very brave of him.

But bad news, too, on our return. Eloise had gone to the store while we were away and reported that Bertie, who worked there, was so mad at the doctor for charging Brett Morgan that dollar she wouldn't even speak to Eloise because she worked for the doctor. The whole Morgan clan was up in arms about it. There were threats that it would be brought up in a union meeting, and all in all there was a huge huff about it. Needless to say, this shook us up badly. Mr. Ramsey's admonitions the night before took on a sinister relevance. Bonta could hardly eat dinner for stewing, and when he was worried, I was alarmed.

He kept asking why people wouldn't come to him with their grievances rather than spreading and magnifying them behind his back. And all this had to blow up just when we thought things were going really well. Brett was sire of half the mixed Hatfield-Morgan group down Long Branch way, though no one of the clan had been willing to pay for his medical care. We tried to reassure each other, saying by all rights it ought to blow over. After all, paraplegic Jimmy Morgan was totally dependent on Bonta's care and had to call on him every few days. Without Bonta he would probably have to go back to California. Two of the other Morgan men couldn't have forgotten completely the long hours he'd spent so recently delivering their wives.

Things looked a little more comfortable later that afternoon when Eloise took Susan over to the store and found Bertie as nice to Susan as usual. And the postmistress, another clan member, sounded friendly enough to Bonta when he got the mail. He had gone over deliberately to test the waters.

↬ But the next day was highlighted by Bonta's grim talk with Dan Dubois, who was married to a Morgan. Dan walked by the back fence just as we were leaving for the office, and Bonta broached the subject himself, asking, "Did you hear I had a time with Brett Morgan the other day and may have been a little rough on him?"

Bonta had touched a raw nerve. Dan looked up sort of sideways, the way he had to, and said emphatically, "I sure did. I didn't want to bring it up myself, but I'm right glad you did. I been wanting to tell you. There's several cases come to my attention where you was talking smart to folks. And that don't go over so good! It wouldn't surprise me none if the medical grievance committee might want to talk to you about it."

At least Dan had the decency to tell you face-to-face what was on his mind.

Bonta said, "I'm sorry to hear that. Yes, I'm sure sorry some people are dissatisfied. If I've been a little short sometimes lately, you know how dead tired I've been with all these deliveries and no sleep. I can hardly see straight. I just wish people could understand a little. And I'm always ready to talk to anybody who has a problem with what I've done."

"Oh, I know that, but you see, Doc, when folks is sick, you just can't count on them being reasonable. You better be real careful or you'll get yourself into trouble. The minute you start talking smart around here, you better be ready to fight. And I don't mean just with fists. I mean with guns!" Dan brought his fist down on the top rail to underscore the point.

Bonta's concern was written all over his face. "My God, I've only been trying to do my best for them."

Dan may have felt a little sorry for Bonta, as he reflected, "Course, this wouldn't be the first time they was that kind of trouble. They almost run Doc Nichols out the holler, too. He said he wouldn't take care of some woman who hadn't been in to see him before the baby was due. He said he'd send her in to the hospital, but he wasn't about to touch her himself. Well, that raised a rumpus like you never seen. The medical grievance committee was all set to call on him in his office, and they was planning to kick his teeth in. I heared what was up, so I asked Mr. Ramsey to be there, and he finally cooled things off. He stuck by the doc all right, but it took some fancy talking."

Of course, Dan was one about whom Mr. Ramsey had cautioned us. But this sounded like straight information meant for our own good, and we wanted to believe that Dan was talking like a friend.

Bonta showed him the documentation that the dollar charge for an unnecessary house call was perfectly allowable, but Dan said it wasn't so much the dollar as it was the lecture. Bonta had to acknowledge to him that perhaps he shouldn't have told the men he couldn't keep going on wild-goose chases with so many really sick people needing him.

I was sure part of the problem had been Bonta's own fatigue. I began to think maybe we should just get away every weekend the way Mr. Ramsey said. Even Dan told Bonta he ought to get out every other weekend. But Bonta wouldn't desert all those women who were counting on him. I understood his loyalty to them, but I wondered why the women couldn't do something to cool their men down. Vern never used to stay in camp weekends. His absences occasioned a lot of criticism, but it seemed you were criticized whether you were conscientious or not.

I couldn't imagine resorting to fists, let alone guns, as soon as something upsetting occurred. Even though the men had agreed to the dollar charge, it was clear they couldn't accept it because it labeled their fears as unjustified. Even more important, the least suggestion of a reprimand became an intolerable insult, capable of igniting the whole clan.

I felt almost sick wondering what would happen. Would tempers flare and then die down as fast as they had risen? Or would this build up to some unpredictable climax? In retrospect it certainly had been unwise of Bonta to let his frustration show, but he was exhausted and only human. There were moments when washing our hands of the whole place was the only thing I wanted. I was glad we were going to Kingsport the next day. Both sides could use a breathing spell.

Bonta hoped Dan would repeat his comment that he was so exhausted from all those deliveries that he couldn't see straight, that when we got back from the coming weekend away he would be a new man. So I hoped and prayed things would have quieted down by then.

ᔐ   We left for Kingsport after office hours Friday, which meant a late start. We ate our picnic supper across from a massive rock wall along the way. The cars approaching behind us threw huge shadows on the cliff. The last rays of the sun turned their images into elongated gray monsters, coming closer and closer, and finally engulfing us, as the cars whizzed past. Susan clapped her hands at each climactic moment. A child could watch this with delight. To me the shadows were threatening reminders of the turmoil swirling around us back in camp.

On the way we did a lot of soul-searching about developments in the Brett Morgan case. Bonta told me again about that time he was accused of taking sides in the office. That involved part of the Morgan clan, too. That episode had frightened Bonta no little bit.

This whole concept of a clan had been a revelation to me. Of course, I'd heard about Scottish clans, even vaguely about "the Hatfields and McCoys, those restless mountain boys." But now I was faced with the reality of the fierce loyalty that bound the members of such a group together. What affected one affected all. I contrasted it with the distant relationship that existed between me and my numerous first cousins and felt a little envy at the network of support these clans provided their members. They extended well beyond first cousins here. Such a community must give a growing youngster a wonderful feeling of security. But the clan system certainly precluded objectivity when any member was involved in a dispute.

What with recent warnings from both Mr. Ramsey and Dan, from their totally different perspectives, I wondered if it was even safe to stay.

Bonta said bitterly, "You know the guy who brings Jimmy Morgan to the office is so mad about it that he wouldn't even drive him to get his shot this morning. Jimmy got somebody else to bring him. And this, after we stayed in the hollow three weeks, just so I'd be sure to be on hand for his wife's delivery."

Then he paused and said in a different tone, "But you know, before we get too carried away, we have to remember we owe them something for paying in every month—every month they're working, anyway."

Perhaps we were merely a handy target for venting their frustrations about the strike. If that was part of the explanation, it was just our bad luck to be the scapegoat.

"Whatever the reason," Bonta said earnestly, "I hope things will have simmered down by the time we get back. There's not a heck of a lot I can do about it now. Just remember their hypersensitivity in all future dealings and never breathe another word that could be construed as criticism."

In Kingsport Jack was interested in what Bonta had to say about practice in the coalfields. Jack was in general practice and so busy he suggested Bonta might consider joining him. He couldn't have chosen a more opportune moment to approach us if he was serious. It was tempting. He and Phyl drove us around the town, with all its new buildings and well-tended residential areas. It was hard to imagine the convenience of having a hospital right next door instead of forty-five miles away over West Virginia roads, or a well-stocked grocery store, for that matter. We talked over his offer at length on the way home, weighing the pros and cons of accepting that, staying where we were, or pursuing the various residencies we were considering.

The visit proved a revelation to Susan. Jack and Phyl's daughter Beth was half a year younger, and we thought the two children would play happily together. When Beth found her way into Susan's room that first morning, Susan clambered out of bed, saying in awestruck tones, "Baby!" As the day wore on, however, she faced an unexpected challenge. Everything she picked up Beth confiscated. Baffled, Susan ultimately resorted to beating Beth to it, handing over everything Beth might demand—even her own precious blanket! Distressing as it was, it was probably time she learned that the world wasn't all as sheltering as her little haven in Coal Mountain.

The next few days after our return were uneventful. Bonta even had a couple nights of uninterrupted sleep. We wanted to get along with everyone, and there was no real reason why we shouldn't. I kept hoping we had exaggerated the Morgan problem as we mulled over the rumors, that our worries were groundless.

By Wednesday things seemed quite normal again. One of the Kilmer youngsters from the green camp brought down a familiar note. "Send that stuff for nits and lice. All the young ones got them again." That was one family that believed in sharing. I must have sent up a gallon of Kwell lotion already.

As we both waited for the mail, I had a pleasant chat with Mrs. Maynard, the wife of the head of the produce department at the store. I asked how the photography class for the Boy Scouts was progressing.

"Why, the boys must like it fine—they keep coming. But Jim gets mighty upset working with them when they have the itch, and seems like most of them do. Says he sure hopes the hypo kills them bugs."

Knowing someone else shared my feelings, I felt better about my own reservations in the knitting class as I guided needles grasped in those itchy hands.

One woman came to the office, afraid she might be pregnant again. She said she'd waited to come till she knew I'd be there. Just as Mr. Ramsey had surmised, as an outsider I was sometimes more acceptable than Eloise when people were especially concerned about privacy.

As I covered her with a sheet preparatory to the examination, she looked up and said, "You know, some folks say they'd as soon you treat them as the doc."

That was something to ponder! Gratifying but a little scary. "Well, that's very flattering, but I only do what my husband tells me to do when it comes to taking care of people. I do like to help, but he's the one with all the know-how."

Credentials valued elsewhere were meaningless here. After all, people in the area trusted Sadie, and her skills were based entirely on experience, so perhaps this misconception about my abilities wasn't as amazing as I first thought.

On Friday, January 27, the radio announced that John L. was willing to resume negotiations with the operators. Our men lost one shift because some of the younger miners favored joining the wildcatters. Most of the miners in the UMW still wanted to work, but, as before, they wanted the protection of a contract more. If the government invoked an injunction to force them back without one, it could mean troops to enforce it. The turmoil seemed endless. I wondered if the men were reaching their limit, their anger ready to boil over, given the slightest additional heat.

One of Bonta's house calls involved a baby he recently delivered to one of the Morgans. They seemed very friendly and even thanked him, so that was cause for a little hope that the Brett Morgan row had finally blown over, especially since one of the clan asked me in the store why Susan hadn't kissed her lately. Had we been telling her not to?

⚡ The following Monday we waited to see whether our miners would join the ninety-six thousand wildcatters. They didn't. They continued to carry out Lewis's bidding, sticking with the three-day week. The radio said there was only a twenty-five day coal supply aboveground, and some governors and mayors were demanding that Truman do something about it.

As if the strike problems, the Brett Morgan affair, and the rainy late January weather weren't depressing enough, there was another disturbing report on the radio. Legislators were debating whether or not the United States should try to make a super bomb to stay at least one jump ahead of the Russians, now that they had the atom bomb and were presumably working on their own super bomb. That kind of global worry made our own problems look paltry, but the effect was to increase the urgency of our making wise plans for the next step. So again we talked into the wee hours. Bonta's method was to garner all the facts he could, study all the alternative paths that might be open, and decide very rationally on the best course. I tended to jump to conclusions intuitively, but we usually ended up with a common answer. It was the source of lots of conversation anyway.

⚡ The first of February brought only a continuation of the rain. It drummed on the roof all night. All the creeks were flooded. Road Branch was simply impassable, and the road out of camp was threatened by serious erosion.

The next morning the dreary weather matched the gloom engendered by the uncertainties over the negotiations between Lewis and the operators. It looked as though they were reaching a critical stage.

According to the radio, the operators walked out of the conference with Lewis. They said they would agree to a five-day week for seventy days while the president's fact-finding board met, and they would abide by its decisions. Lewis would have to agree to this plan within two days or Truman would be forced to invoke Taft-Hartley. About a quarter of the membership in the UMW were defying Lewis and his three-day workweek order, staying out of the mines. Everyone in camp was tense.

Then Eloise introduced a new complication for us. "I won't be around much longer, 'cause I'm going to Kentucky and marry Tommy."

She didn't sound particularly happy about it, and she looked more determined than joyful. We felt sure this was a decision born of frustration. We'd already expressed our reservations about the wisdom of such a course, so we were reluctant to say much more, especially when it might sound self-serving. Of course, we wanted her to stay. She'd become an integral part of our family, and we all loved her dearly. In the office she had become indispensable. There were no other young people who had finished high school, and we couldn't think of a single other person who would be as capable as she was.

We finally asked if Tommy would be willing to work in the mine if we could persuade Mr. Ramsey to hire him, just so we could keep Eloise.

She thought about that for a minute, twisting her handkerchief nervously as she considered. "Well, I'd like to keep working this way. Sure, I guess if Mr. Ramsey'd give Tommy a job in the mine, he'd like that. And then we could both stay here in Coal Mountain."

I felt obliged to add, "Tommy doesn't seem to be having much luck finding a job outside, but I hope if he comes back here, he won't give up thinking about other opportunities later."

"We'll see what can be done, then," Bonta promised.

After Eloise left, he turned to me. "You know, if Eloise goes, I'd be tempted to say the hell with it and leave, too. I'm not sure I want to stay here if things get any more difficult than they are already. My God, we're still worrying about the Morgan clan and the strike, now Eloise, bombs, whether I'll have to go back in the navy, and where I'm going to get a residency. You'd think a little stability in life wouldn't be too much to expect!"

Next day the radio reported some violence at the Marianna Smokeless Coal plant, not so very far from Coal Mountain—about five men involved in a shooting. Someone told Bonta one had been killed, and another report had it that all five had been killed. Even if the story should prove to be only a rumor, it had already increased the tensions in our own camp.

It looked as though Lewis was going to reject the president's proposal for a study of the situation by a board while the miners resumed regular work for seventy days. Some radio reporters said if Truman imposed an injunction, Lewis would bring suit to have the Taft-Hartley Law declared unconstitutional on grounds of involuntary servitude. He would surely be a hero to labor if he could get the law declared unconstitutional. As it was, the men wouldn't know whether they were to strike or not till Monday morning when they reached the portal. So the whole camp was keyed up, just holding its collective breath and waiting.

Dan Dubois told Bonta the shooting at Marianna must have been carried out by someone outside their own local. Since the men in one local had to live together, they simply reported to a nearby local that so-and-so wasn't toeing the line, and some outsider would come in and take care of the matter. This didn't square with Mr. Ramsey's description of the fight he was involved in much earlier, when apparently some miners shot others in their own union, but perhaps times had changed. In either case it was clearly dangerous to oppose your own organization.

Another miner joined the discussion and said he would be willing to do the same thing if he were asked. Certainly if they struck and the government brought in troops to break it up, he wouldn't mind a fight, and if outsiders came in to "take care of" local recalcitrants, he'd join them in the job! It was hard to reconcile this attitude with my impression of this fellow as friendly and easygoing. On the other hand, it fit with what Mr. Ramsey and Dan had both said about the miners' propensity toward violence, and I just had to face the fact that problems down here were solved differently from the way they were handled back home.

Barney, viewing his work here as a job, not an all-embracing commitment, expressed an opinion closer to our own. He said if troops were called in, he'd like to be long gone. Things could really get hot.

We hoped this was just so much talk. Some real shooting would certainly make our little troubles recede into the background!

✍ On Saturday the radio reported Lewis had indeed refused the president's offer, and Truman had set in motion the machinery for invoking the Taft-Hartley injunction. We hadn't heard any local reaction yet, but we were listening hard. It seemed as though any future strike would now be illegal.

Tim Bailey, the chief electrician, came to the house to continue the discussion he and Bonta had had about the kind of radio we should buy. Since Tim was on call all the time, next to Bonta and Mr. Ramsey he probably led the most unpredictable life. He told us about a big washout in one of the abandoned mines, which brought down enough earth to cover up three coal cars and two trucks. The torrential rains had been the worst in everyone's memory, and our tiny creek was so high it almost lapped at the office foundations. Main roads were eroding badly. On a recent trip Mr. Ramsey could hardly get back to camp because of washouts. In places the macadam road on the way to Logan was just falling down the side of the mountain.

Anyway Tim said he didn't see how the company could stay in business with all the problems it had. For instance, after he and ten others installed a new furnace at the tipple, they discovered an imperfect casting in one part, so it all had to be torn down and reinstalled at terrific cost. The only reimbursement by the furnace company was for the single piece of metal. Now these buried cars and trucks would have to be dug out by hand. Meantime very little coal was being mined. This sort of problem could only make things tougher for Mr. Ramsey. We weren't the only ones with cause for worry.

✍ For a change Monday dawned bright and clear. This was the morning we were waiting for: would or wouldn't the tipple be working? We looked out first thing to find it silent and deserted. The men were staying out, defying the impending injunction. It was little wonder, since the radio quoted Lewis as describing Taft-Hartley as "legal blackjack, leading to involuntary servitude," practically an invitation to defiance. The miners wouldn't even let the foremen go up to the mine to do maintenance work. Instead the foremen spent the time tossing pennies in front of the company garage or squatting by the steps of the store. Each collected his seventeen-dollar paycheck for the day, regardless.

Barney came in to the office for a minute, and for once he wasn't whistling. He was discouraged—disgustipated, as he put it—about the whole situation. He was sure the men wouldn't go back to work without a contract, injunction or no injunction.

"I tell you, I don't like the looks of things. Maybe it's time to haul out of here. Got me a new theme song. They been playing it on the radio, so maybe you know it too—'I Just Want to Go Where the Wild Goose Goes.' Old Coal Mountain ain't what it used to be."

I hurried supper in order to be ready when Mrs. Ramsey came by for knitting class, but as the scheduled time came and went, I finally decided the class must have been called off. I persuaded myself that it really didn't matter; it just gave me more of the evening for sewing.

⤙ Tuesday Eloise reported a most unusual thing. She said a truck had gone through camp early that morning, and a man with a bullhorn told the men to come to a special union meeting at 2:00 P.M. I hadn't heard it—maybe it didn't come up our back road. It seemed as though everybody gathering for the meeting decided to sandwich in a visit to the doctor as well, so afternoon office hours were extremely busy. There was a general air of expectancy everywhere, and we were as excited as everyone else.

I had to go to the company office midafternoon and found a uniformed policeman standing guard outside, a large group of men nearby, and another group clustered in front of the garage—cars all over the place. As best as we could figure out from the rumors floating around, the union fieldman had come in since our local union's last meeting and called this session to select pickets. So it looked as though the showdown was coming.

We finally managed to get a news report on the radio. No wonder there was a lot of excitement. Truman had just appointed that fact-finding board, finally taken the first firm step in invoking Taft-Hartley. One district union official was quoted as defying the injunction that would follow, saying, "You can't mine coal with an injunction, and you can't mine it with bayonets either." Most miners were reported ready to do whatever Lewis directed.

Bonta asked Mr. Ramsey to come to dinner, because we'd learned Mrs. Ramsey had gone to Kentucky (that was why there was no knitting class), but he refused, saying he was expecting trouble. Bonta said he sounded genuinely disturbed. That didn't do anything for our own peace of mind. We were used to thinking of Mr. Ramsey as unflappable, the one person really in control. We suddenly realized that we leaned on him as much as the rest of the camp did.

Shortly after dinner Mr. Ramsey knocked on our door. He was wearing his white miner's hat and a heavy red and black checked lumber jacket over his woolen shirt, and I detected the usual bulge of his whiskey flask in the hip pocket. He said he just felt like talking to someone. We were more than willing listeners.

"Yes, when I talked with you this afternoon I was plenty mad. All those men, running around like a bunch of little boys. All carried away with excitement over the trouble they were cooking up. And never a thought about how this was going to affect everybody down the road. Yes, I was plumb disgusted with them."

It was actually good to know he was human enough to feel some anger over their behavior.

"But I'm getting back some balance—the perspective I have to hang onto just to keep going." He said earnestly, "You know I wouldn't hurt these men for anything. I know what a hard life they have, the struggle they've had to win whatever successes have come their way. I was one of them once. I know they're naive. They behave like children. They're ignorant, and they don't use the sense the good Lord gave them. But somehow I feel a kind of compassion for them, even when they mess everything up.

"Actually, you know, I feel sorry for them when I think about their future. Coal's losing its markets, and this strike's helping put the skids under it. And there are just too many miners. A lot of them are going to be unemployed. And most of them aren't going to fit anywhere else. I don't know what's going to happen, but from where I sit, it ain't going to be good."

Those were the attitudes that made us respect Mr. Ramsey so much. He was big enough to understand the larger scene and big enough to accept his men the way they were. It was obvious he had a lot on his mind, and we felt honored that he trusted us enough to share his thoughts with us.

"Of course, I suppose there's a selfish side to my thinking, too. After all, I represent the company. And whatever hurts the men in the long run hurts the company."

He took another sip of his whiskey and water, while Bonta added some coal to the fire. The room had cooled down as the fire burned low. I knitted while I listened.

"You know, I look at the local union-company relationship as a sort of ritual. It's almost a play. Everybody knows the parts and the lines pretty well ahead of time. When I've got a ticklish situation to deal with, I know certain words and certain tactics will produce a certain effect. Sometimes you have to get downright devious. I may sow a word in one place, and by and by I get it back from some distant spot that was my real target.

"Sometimes I've had good luck with a different strategy. I'm on reasonable terms with the union president, so I tell him to cuss me out roundly in front of the men and swear up and down that he hates the company and is going to fight to the death for everything the union wants. Then I'll do just the opposite and say the union is terrible, it's wrecking everything. Then the men leave, satisfied with the impasse. Then he and I get together privately and work things out sensibly. Truth is we couldn't get along without each other."

Attending school only six years apparently hadn't interfered with his acquiring a lot of wisdom along the way.

"Why, just yesterday the men came in to talk about keeping the foremen and even the emergency maintenance crew from working. I asked them what they'd do if one of their toilets got plugged up and Nick wasn't available to fix it. Well, they allowed as how they'd never thought of it that way. Guessed they'd have to think it over a little longer. I couldn't help being frustrated with them.

"After all their stupidity and shortsightedness Larry Watson—he's the union president, you know—stopped on the way out and asked me, 'You aren't mad at us, are you?'" He shook his head at the recollection. "Can you believe it? But I try to remember they're just children and sort of pathetic at that."

I resolved to try to cultivate more of Mr. Ramsey's philosophy.

"And don't think you can trust the foremen any more than the union men. They may theoretically represent the company, but they'll go right back to the union with everything you tell them. It's all right if they cuss the union up and down, but don't you try it. Most of them were union officers before, and that's where their hearts still are. Why, they've even relayed to the men whatever little maintenance jobs I've had to ask them to do during this three-day stall. They just want to keep the pot boiling. After all, they'd rather not have to work themselves, since the company has to pay them regardless of whether they do or don't. Got to figure out people's motives—only way you can hope to keep on top of it."

Mr. Ramsey didn't need any comments from us; he talked on without any prompting, pausing only for a swallow now and then.

"I'm doing everything I can to keep things going smoothly. But I really think they're sort of egging me on to give them an excuse for making trouble. I almost believe they resent sweet reasonableness because it interferes with their chance to make something big and exciting out of life."

That could explain a number of things, I thought.

"They do know when I'm mad, but the only way I show it is by walking to my office with my eyes straight ahead. If I don't greet each of them as I usually do, they know something's wrong. Take this morning. I went up to the mine with two of the engineers to check on things. We're afraid of flooding in Number Nine. And at the foot of the hill a knot of about fifteen men met us. They were all carrying long knives and whittling away on big sticks. I smiled and they smiled, and we both said, 'Why, we were just out for a little walk.' It all passed very peaceful like, but I knew they could have turned on me with those knives as easy as not. It was scary—and again, kind of pathetic."

Bonta managed to get a question in while Mr. Ramsey pondered this encounter. "Why do you think Lewis has been dragging things out this long with those three-day weeks? He succeeded in cutting the coal supply down a while ago."

"Oh, Lewis knows there's not enough demand for coal to keep all 450,000 or so in the union working five days a week. With a three-day week he can keep most of them getting a little something, and the more he keeps in the union, the bigger his power base. I got a hunch Lewis would like the government to take over the mines and make him boss of the industry.

"How any operator can keep going these days is a mystery. Red Jacket's beginning to hurt bad. They've barely broken even since July, let alone made a profit. The men never stop and think how important it is to them to keep the company from going under. They told me they figure the operators are out to bust their union, and by God they're going to bust everything they can lay their hands on." He shook his head as he reflected on their lack of foresight, then added, "You know there's no way on earth they'll ever make up what they've lost in this struggle."

Bonta asked, "What about the prospects for real violence here? Do you think things could boil over?"

"No, they talk a lot, but I don't expect anything very serious. I stay real close to the men. Not much happens around here I'm not aware of. Mighty few developments come as a surprise to me. And I haven't heard anything yet to lead me to expect anything real bad."

That was reassuring. We knew the turnover rate here was far less than in most camps, and it was clear why that was so.

"But just a parting thought. If anything should happen, you be careful. You do everything in your power to avoid the appearance of taking sides. I couldn't vouch for what might happen if you didn't."

The following Monday, February 13, brought a new blow. Of all times for another problem—this one totally unexpected, from the distant past! Someone had mailed Bertie a clipping of Mary's little article in the *Louisville Times* about Coal Mountain, and Eloise said everyone at the store was mad about it: Alison, Mr. Maynard, even Eva. Alison was about to send a picture of the camp to the paper to prove we didn't have shacks in Coal Mountain. She said next time she went to New York City and people asked her where she came from, everyone would laugh at her because they'd remember what Mary wrote about Coal Mountain. How flattered Mary would be! Alison expected the company to sue Mary for writing such disparaging things about its camp.

On rereading the article—once I screwed up my courage—I supposed I could see why they were upset. Of course, they assumed everyone in the country had analyzed the article and cared as much as they did. It was true it didn't describe the camp itself, which was more attractive than most, and it was datelined Coal Mountain, the implication being that the shacks the miners were repairing were right here.

We let it be known that we weren't responsible for what Mary did. They had spotted her byline in a moment and knew that was the doctor's wife's sister, and if we got run out of camp, that would be why. This new rumpus was all we needed. It probably took their minds off the strike for the moment, but it was really sad that they had so little perspective that this could bother them so much. If the situation hadn't been so worrisome, it might have been amusing.

The radio was full of news reports about the grim miners refusing to go to the pits, but ours didn't look particularly grim. They were all crowding around to get the mail, which was delayed, exchanging the latest news, including, no doubt, outrage at Mary's article, and everybody seemed relaxed enough—except Bonta and me.

❧ Trouble in Coal Mountain

Bonta crossing Cub Creek on a house call. Crude footbridges often provided the only means of crossing the many creeks that ran through the region.

16. The Ax Falls

Three days after the infamous clipping arrived the camp was still buzzing like a hive of angry bees. I remembered Mrs. Ramsey's reaction way back in October, now amplified a thousand times. At the first of this, I was scared, then amused, and now I began to be really angry! We told Eloise it didn't bother us particularly. Coal Mountain was no better or worse for whatever Mary might have said about it, and we certainly didn't feel the need to apologize to anyone for living here. This was all too ridiculous.

Eloise told me that Alison was angry with me because I was supposedly laughing about the whole affair. I would never have guessed. When I went to the store she was friendly as could be, telling me all about some taffeta she had ordered; she showed me the pattern for the dress she was going to make with it.

We decided to check with Mr. Ramsey to see what he had to say about it. As we presumed, he did know about the clipping and added the news that Alison actually had sent a picture of Coal Mountain to the paper. He was no more perturbed about this crisis than most of the others around there. He said he had to save his adrenaline for the more serious things in the wind, like the growing possibility of government seizure of the mines.

Maggie Bannister banged on our front door after supper. She was almost hysterical, screaming that her mother was dying. Mrs. Bannister had apparently fallen out of bed and was incoherent. When he arrived, Bonta found her back in bed and unable to recall falling out.

"Just had a bad spell, Doctor." She turned her face to the wall and burst out crying. "If only I could get better!"

As he tried to calm her, Bonta wracked his brain for a solution. During his last couple of visits, he'd been thinking about giving her some estrogen in light of her hysterectomy and decided this might be the time to start her on it. He left her with a prescription.

❧ Mr. Ramsey was far off the mark when he predicted the miners would soon be back digging coal. Things actually looked bleaker than ever by mid-February, and reports were that the country was now down to a seven-day supply. The men held local union meetings and seemed determined to see this strike through to a contract, in direct defiance of Lewis's order to go back to work. But it made us wonder if they might be doing his secret bidding after all. Strategies could get pretty devious in this business, judging from our own experience that what appeared on the surface wasn't always the reality. We learned later that this interpretation of events was widespread.

Bonta was surprised and pleased when Doug Blake, the young union leader Mr. Ramsey had warned us about, came to the office on Saturday on a nonprofessional visit. He asked if Bonta would be interested in playing chess with him. Bonta wondered how Doug knew chess was a hobby of his and where he had learned the game himself. Certainly the suggestion was more than welcome. Ever since losing his chess partner in the navy, Bonta had wished for a replacement. Besides, Mr. Ramsey had described Doug as highly intelligent, and while he had warned us to be on our guard with him, surely it would be interesting and helpful to know him better. Since he was a power in the union, we might even gain a new perspective about what was going on in camp.

As Doug left, a Mrs. Ratliff came in, looking quite tense about something. After his long talk with her, Bonta told me she had asked him to keep their conversation absolutely confidential, since she was concerned lest her husband might somehow hear about it, and she seemed fearful of his reaction if he did. Bonta didn't tell me and I didn't ask, but privately I wondered if she might be pregnant; I couldn't think of anything else that fit the picture. If that were the case, I could see why she didn't want to have a baby at her age. She was in her mid-forties and had a son, Braden, already in his late teens. Knowing that her husband was much older than she was, I thought it unlikely he'd be pleased to assume the additional responsibility of a new baby.

Mrs. Sam Dean from across the way came over to the house in the evening. She was middle-aged, friendly, and seemed to have a lot of common sense. She had been very helpful on a number of occasions, like the time she watched Susan while I took care of Mrs. Bannister, and said she'd be glad if we called on her any time. We thought she might be one to take Eloise's place if it came to that. She had some encouraging reports about people who approved of the job Bonta was doing. We could use some of those. She herself had noticed that no matter how late it was, Bonta took his own good time examining her father when she brought him in, even after office hours, and that he always had time for those who needed him.

She told us about a friend of hers who had been present at a delivery a few months earlier. While waiting for the baby to come, she and the other women present had debated taking the *New England Journal of Medicine* which Bonta was reading and burning it. I really didn't understand why, but apparently his absorption in it offended them. Since then Bonta happened to talk to this woman about the importance of keeping abreast of the latest medical developments. Mrs. Dean said now her friend was spreading the word that a doctor ought to spend his time studying while waiting for a delivery.

Since Mrs. Dean was interested, we chatted at length about medical care outside the camp, the areas in which medical progress was being made, and the relative advantage of office calls versus home calls here. When she left, we felt she was taking along some ideas that could help explain to others in camp what Bonta was trying to accomplish.

The next evening went to a pessimistic discussion about the prospects for a war soon, what with the latest reports on the huge air force the Russians were supposed to be building. We decided that Bonta would be better off in the service than not and that women would probably be drafted, too. Maybe I could get a research job.

In light of all the uncertainty, having another baby was probably unwise. However, I was beginning to be suspicious that it was too late for second thoughts on that score. I was secretly thrilled beyond words and hoped my pregnancy wasn't just in my imagination.

The next Saturday evening Doug Blake came over as he promised, to challenge Bonta at chess. The game required an hour and a half of silent concentration, marked only by wretched groans and satisfied grunts, till Doug finally shouted, "Check!"

Talk turned inevitably to the strike. Bonta did more listening than talking, wanting to learn Doug's position before he said too much about his own views. Doug was concerned about the long-term consequences of the strike and confessed that he didn't think the coal industry offered him much future. He wanted to get ahead in the world and eventually own his own small business. He was toying with the idea of an auto repair shop or perhaps a gas station. But for the moment he was playing the game hard right here in camp. He was for the union, but he had little use for the union officers. We were impressed by his independent outlook.

At breakfast on the first Friday in March we had a long talk with Eloise about her getting out of Coal Mountain. Like so many young women in search of glamour, she was now thinking about becoming an airline stewardess. She had really been down in the dumps for some time, and Thursday's mail without a letter from Tommy was no help.

When I asked her later how her morning in the office had gone, she flounced into a chair, looking exasperated. "Oh, just like every morning. The only thing keeping me here is Mama, and one of the other girls could take care of her, if I wasn't around. I don't see why it's always got to be me!" Her voice softened a little as she continued, "And course, Tommy. I keep thinking he'll come back." Her tone changed. "But then he don't even write." She was so frustrated she got up and paced, perhaps to hide a tear. "I'm just sick and tired of being around here. Same old thing every day."

If only some intelligent fellow with real ambition and some education would appear on the scene, I thought. I still wasn't convinced

Tommy was the right one, but I had to admit there was a dearth of eligible men around the place.

Just then Bonta came in from a house call after morning office hours. Seeing Eloise looking so unhappy, he said in a bantering tone, "Come now, Eloise. Your problem is solved. That young engineer who's coming in for a physical this afternoon is just the man for you!"

"Pooh, I saw him when he came in to make the appointment. He's so old and so big." She dismissed him out of hand. Clearly no bells had rung.

I perked up. "Well, how interesting. Tell me more."

Bonta looked encouragingly at Eloise as he explained, "His name's Jerry Drummond, and I found out he's single. He got his engineering degree at Morgantown. He's not all that old either—only twenty-five." He looked at me for confirmation that this was worth pursuing and then turned back to Eloise, who was avoiding his eye. "You really ought to check up on him, Eloise."

"Why, that's fascinating," I said. "Why don't you go over this afternoon instead of me, Eloise, so you'll get to meet him—learn a little more about him?"

Eloise turned her back on the discussion. "He don't sound the least bit interesting." She started to walk into the bedroom where Susan was playing.

Bonta suddenly turned serious. "Well, Eloise, we don't like to see you so unhappy. We're sorry you're feeling bad, but it's not very pleasant for everyone else to have you sighing and grumping around all the time. We understand your life isn't a bed of roses, but you know that's true for most people." He was speaking to her back, but she had stopped and was listening. "Now if there is anything at all we can do to help, we're more than anxious to do it. Just tell us. But you know, if nothing can be done to change things, one has to become a bit philosophical. If you'd only try to look on the good side of things instead of the bad, you might even feel better. If you could only pretend to be your usual cheery self, you and everybody else might be a lot happier."

Eloise didn't answer, devoting herself deliberately to fussing with Susan's hair. She must have taken his words to heart, however, because when I returned from afternoon office hours, she flashed a smile. Whether just for show or not, it was a welcome change.

Friday, March 3, was important for more than Jerry Drummond's arrival and our talk with Eloise. The local news that evening reported that the preliminaries were over, and a Taft-Hartley injunction had actually been slapped on the union, making it a federal offense for the miners to strike now. Truman was finally convinced that the coal supply was so low nationally as to constitute a crisis. We heard schools were closed in Chicago for want of heat, though the students were expected to listen by FM radio to five hours of classes a day. Our own coal was down to a few lumps, and we nearly froze the night before under three blankets. Talk was that Congress would authorize Truman to seize the mines, regardless of the outcome of current negotiations.

Sunday, March 5, brought the long-awaited banner headline. The threat of seizure had done its work. The new contract was signed! The long strike was over! Everyone was out shouting and celebrating, hitting each other on the back and congratulating each other on winning the big fight. Mr. Kilmer rushed down the road, almost dancing in his elation, waving his cap and grinning from ear to ear. "We done it, we done it, we did!"

Dan Dubois made his way over to the steps of the store to join the growing crowd of men, peering from side to side, agreeing first with one and then another that, "Dammit, we pulled it off, didn't we?"

Harvey Burgess's crown of sandy hair was conspicuous above the others, as he thumped his comrades on the back and waved a bottle triumphantly above the throng.

The agreement came only hours after the president asked authority to seize the mines. The men were deprived of the clause that required them to work only when willing and able, their memorial periods for those injured in the mines were limited to five days a year, their pay was raised seventy cents a day, and their workday remained eight hours long. The agreement was to run for approximately two years, and the operators estimated it would raise the price of coal by anywhere from fifteen to sixty cents a ton.

The union was acquitted of the charge of violating the preliminary injunction, though Doug Blake remarked to Bonta later over the chessboard that the government sure hadn't looked very hard for evidence that the union winked at the strike, its sanctimonious public pronouncements notwithstanding.

Doug believed in pushing hard for the betterment of the miners, but he was capable of being objective about events. He could understand the long-range consequences of certain actions, and he had reservations about the wisdom of Lewis's strategy. "Sounds good now for the men to be back to five days of work, but I ain't sure how long it can last. From what I read, this strike's hurt coal long run."

But for the moment everyone rejoiced. The end of the uncertainty was a huge relief. The men could start to get back on their feet financially. Now maybe everybody could put aside the bad feelings that had been floating around, and we could all just get on with the show.

Monday the miners flooded back into camp. The store was mobbed, since their full credit had been restored. Eloise kept looking for Tommy, since he'd promised to return once a contract was signed, in hopes of landing a job in the mine. She'd had no recent word from him, but she looked so happy anticipating his arrival that I almost hoped she wouldn't be disappointed.

That evening the new engineer, Jerry Drummond, came over at Bonta's invitation. After the preemployment physical the two men had chatted a bit, and Bonta learned that Jerry enjoyed an occasional game of chess, too. This discovery was mutually pleasing, so that evening the chessboard came out again. Conversation turned out to be at least as important as the game. We learned that Jerry grew up in Beckley, West Virginia, one of three children, and before going to the University at Morgantown he had served in the army. He must have been something of a rebel, however, because he admitted hating regimentation and had no use for the military. In fact, he made a point of staying a buck private after he was drafted, when he clearly had the capacity to become an officer.

He asked if there was anything interesting to do in camp.

Bonta glanced at me as coconspirator, and I saw the glint of the matchmaker in his eye as he answered, "Why, we'd be glad to introduce you to a nice young lady—the girl who works for us—intelligent, attractive."

He was watching Jerry to see whether this information was of interest. Jerry was listening.

"Yes, she's a real gem. I think you'd do yourself a favor if you looked her up."

At least the seed had been planted.

❧ The men started to get the coal out in a hurry in spite of some troubles. A machine breakdown closed one of the mines temporarily, and Joe Horvath told Bonta that some of the men weren't bothering to work. Now that they were assured of a five-day week a few were in no hurry to start the grind. But the coal cars were full of shiny graded coal, and the trains were creaking along all night. We were startled and grateful late one evening when someone filled our coal shed.

Mr. Ramsey showed us a copy of the contract when we stopped by his house on Wednesday. He looked more relaxed than he had for weeks, but he shook his head as he said, "You know, the men think they won, and I guess there's no point telling them they really didn't."

"That's an interesting viewpoint. How do you figure?" Bonta asked.

"Well, you know they lost two things that mattered a lot to them in the past—their willing and able clause and their unlimited memorial days. Those were things the operators really wanted out. Sure, they got a small raise in pay, and they think they got back steady jobs, but we'll wait and see. They didn't get the shorter workday Lewis was after, either. No, sir, the companies really won."

"I guess they're all so glad to be back working that nothing else much matters at the moment," I suggested.

"Sure, that's OK for now. But like I told you before, the market'll be glutted in two months on this five-day workweek, and then they'll be out of luck. I tell you this strike lost them more than they know. The country's turning to oil. Industry can't count on coal anymore with all this on-again, off-again nonsense."

"Hmm. Maybe their idol has done them more of a disservice than they realize," Bonta mused. "He sure has them in the palm of his hand. It's kind of sad to see them suffer for his power play."

❧ We managed to leave camp shortly after lunch on Saturday for a necessary trip to Williamson for supplies. As usual after such a trip, it was midnight before we reached home. The fire was low, the house cold, and stowing the groceries an unwelcome chore. We always prayed at such moments that no one would notice the lights we had to turn on. But no luck this night. Answering a knock at the front door, I found Mrs. Bannister. She shook her head in answer to my inquiring look as she said, "No, I ain't sick this time. I been waiting up to tell you they're turning the power off tomorrow morning at nine to repair something, so you better fix your breakfast before then. Ain't going to turn it back on till one-thirty either."

This act of neighborliness was remarkable. Staying up till midnight was a real sacrifice in a community where most went to bed with the birds.

Within a week just what I hoped wouldn't develop did. With the strike settled, people went back to talking about us! Eloise said a Mrs. Swift had asked Eva when the doctor was leaving, that the union was giving him thirty days to get out because he had been charging a dollar for house calls. That was a wretched new rumor. I told Eloise he'd done it only twice, so far as I knew, but I could show her the contract authorizing such charges.

This development made me feel as though we were living in a mine field (no pun intended); you never knew when you'd step on one as you tried to go about your business. I must say I felt distinctly cool toward Mrs. Swift when I bumped into her one afternoon; it was these things that went on behind our backs that were so disturbing. But we couldn't confront anyone; it would just make a bigger issue of it.

I was sure Eloise would soon cease to be a reliable source of information because the Horvaths were known as such strong supporters of us. At the store Bertie told Eva that she'd heard about this thirty days' notice business, but she wasn't telling her anything because Eva liked the doctor too much.

In spite of everything, the old Brett Morgan affair was still a live issue.

With the men back at work, I was as busy afternoons as Bonta was, giving shots, changing minor dressings, and handing out medicines. Bonta persuaded Eloise to give her mother shots, too, though that took some doing. He told her he simply couldn't be running up to the green camp as often as her mother needed them, more and more frequently as the days went by. If Eloise couldn't do it, Mrs. Horvath would just have to be hospitalized. Poor Eloise! She even hated to take babies' temperatures. And I remembered how hard it was for me to give my first shot. I still wished the task on Bonta when I could. But more credit to Eloise; she screwed up her courage and did it. In the process she proved something to herself, and she expressed her love and loyalty to her mother in a very concrete way.

I found Mrs. Bannister in the waiting room the afternoon of Wednesday, March 15, looking more relaxed and cheerful than I'd seen her in a long time.

"That medicine the doctor give me sure worked wonders, and I come for another prescription. I'd almost forgot how it feels to feel good."

Bonta had found an answer that seemed to work, but he said he'd keep his fingers crossed. He was learning, too. We'd never know whether it was really the estrogen, merely the passage of time, nature itself, or her religion that turned things around. We just hoped the improvement would last.

Brett himself came in "for a shot of penicillin for this arthritis." He couldn't have been friendlier. Bonta spent a good deal of time checking him over and gave him some more medicine for his heart condition. Not one indication was given about any coolness between them. Their talk was all of the strike settlement and how much better things were since.

When Bonta told me about Brett's visit, he said, "My God, I don't know what to think. From all the rumors I'd have expected him to come in with a loaded gun. I feel like asking, 'Will the real Brett Morgan please stand up?' "

☙ Bonta looked up Mr. Ramsey on Friday to ask about that persistent rumor that we were being given thirty days' notice. This time it cropped up because Mrs. Bill James came in to show us her latest paintings before we left. She'd been copying pictures from an art book and spread out on Bonta's desk several attractive watercolors of still life, mostly vases and bowls of fruit.

"I'm real ashamed of them, but I wanted you to see them," she responded to our compliments with modest pride.

We wanted to know the reason behind this latest report. Dollar charges? Talking smart? Or maybe because some time ago Bonta sent the ambulance committee a note saying that it had not been necessary for one of the men to use the ambulance to go to the hospital for a diagnostic X ray. Bonta only wanted to keep the ambulance in camp for emergencies and protect the union's treasury, but this was apparently interpreted as talking smart to the miner in question. Or could it be that he was treading on the private preserve of some of the union men?

Larry Watson, the union president, had come in to discuss this note about the ambulance, and Bonta even offered to write an apology to them when he saw the hornet's nest it had stirred up. Larry remarked that a few men had also complained about overcharges, but nobody was upset enough to make a date with the medical committee to talk it over with them and the doctor. Larry himself wasn't too concerned about the dissatisfactions expressed. Goodness knows, we were concerned. But his playing it all down was encouraging.

This had been Bonta's first meeting with Larry. He was a great big man, broad-shouldered and brawny, with a florid complexion and thinning dark hair. He sounded reasonable enough. Bonta certainly wanted to get along with him as the union president, but he was very cautious. Even though Mr. Ramsey managed to work with him, there were those who accused Larry of being two-faced.

Strangely enough, this rumor about our being given thirty days' notice was one Mr. Ramsey had not yet heard.

"But I don't think I'd let it bother me too much. It's a pretty standard rumor round the coalfields. It's too bad you didn't just dodge the ambulance issue. But I don't think anything'll come of it."

Seeing how concerned Bonta was, he suggested, "Why don't you start some rumors of your own? How so-and-so wasn't all that sick when you chased down to see him?"

Since that was actually the root of the Brett Morgan problem— Bonta's saying that Brett wasn't sick enough to warrant an emergency call—that idea seemed no help at all. Besides Bonta scrupulously kept medical matters confidential, though he did share with Mr. Ramsey his suspicion that a patient he had just seen might have silicosis.* This

---

*Lung damage resulting from inhalation of silica dust, which can lead to serious impairment of respiratory function

of course horrified Mr. Ramsey—just one more worry for a harried superintendent.

✒ March 25th. Ugly rumor became ugly fact! The union actually gave Bonta his thirty days' notice! Larry Watson and three others marched into the office and stood by the desk without saying a word, obviously ill at ease. Then one of them carefully placed the notice on the desk—all very official, union heading and union seal, signed by Larry as president, his brother Danny as vice-president, Freddie Kilmer as secretary, and Elton Jamison as treasurer—stating that after April 30 the contract between the union and the doctor would be considered null and void.

They watched as Bonta read it. He told me he felt his ears redden, he was so angry, but he managed to restrain himself. He put the paper down, leaned back, and asked, "So. What's the story?"

They hesitantly listed several complaints: the ambulance mix-up, several gripes about overcharging. One person had complained that Bonta hadn't done him any good. Of course, there had been no meeting between the grievance committee and the doctor. Nobody had brought a problem to the medical committee either, or if so, we hadn't heard about it. Only two days before, Larry had assured Bonta that all was well, and Kilmer had pooh-poohed any notion of trouble brewing! Then ignoring the fact that the contract had already been broken, they warned Bonta to stay away from Dan Dubois, because he'd been complaining about the doctor to everyone who'd listen and could do him more harm than good!

I learned about all this when I went over to see whether Bonta and Eloise were thinking of quitting for lunch, since it was getting so late for a Saturday morning. They were just coming out the door, and Eloise looked very sober as she shook her head and said, "Bad news!"

Then Bonta thrust this paper in my hands and said, "Read it."

At first I couldn't believe it. Then I had the strange feeling that the day had shifted into some other time frame. The pleasant routine morning suddenly became a thing of the remote past, and my emotions were all in a turmoil: anger, the excitement of meeting a challenge, a feeling that my distrust had been justified, almost a lack of surprise because "I knew it all along," and above all, a sense of our standing together, isolated and embattled in common cause against a hostile world. At least we knew now where we stood.

We headed for Mr. Ramsey's house with the notification as soon as Bonta cooled down a little. We found the Ramseys just finishing their lunch.

"Come on in. Have a cup of coffee with us," Mr. Ramsey urged cordially.

"No, thanks," Bonta said grimly. But we went in and sat down at the table. "I brought something to show you." He handed Mr. Ramsey the paper.

Mr. Ramsey finished reading it, flushed red in his turn, and said, "My God, I never thought it would come to this. Those fools! What do they think they're doing? Believe me, they won't get away with this. The company'll back you all the way!"

Bonta put both elbows on the table and leaned forward, hunching his shoulders. "Well, what do we do now?"

Mr. Ramsey leaned back in his chair and quietly considered for a few moments. His expression gradually changed from one of anger to one of disappointment. "You know, when I think about it, they're more to be pitied than condemned for being so shortsighted. You realize what they've done to themselves? They think they hired you, but of course you and I know the company did. Now they think they're rid of you. But if they try to bring in somebody else, the company'll refuse to provide a house or an office for any new doctor. Oh, if the men demanded it, we'd have to withhold their three dollars a month for him. But there'd be no inducement for anybody else to come in. Can you imagine how some other fellow would feel, knowing how they treated you, and with the company against him?"

His expression brightened a bit as he grasped for something positive in the situation. "Of course, things aren't hopeless. It's possible you can get that union contract back if we work on it right."

Those thoughts were worth pondering for a few minutes. Then Mr. Ramsey said with sudden decision, "Well, we've got to go to Williamson and see Dr. Meade right away. I'll call him and let him know we're coming."

Bonta suggested that Susan and I could come along for the ride and stay with Mrs. Meade while the men talked strategy.

"Poor Mr. Ramsey," I said on the way home, "this is all he needs—one more mess. He's had a bad enough time for months with the strike, and now we have to dump our problems on his shoulders."

"You're so right," Bonta agreed. "But as far as we're concerned, I feel better facing the reality than living in the fog of all those rumors. It was like floundering in quicksand." He added thoughtfully, "Maybe Providence is giving us a kick in the right direction. Maybe this is the time to get out and go after that residency."

"That's all very well and good, but residencies don't start till July, and this is only the latter part of March." I started putting on Susan's coat. "I guess what bothers me so much is that you've knocked yourself out to give them the best care you know how to give. You've upgraded the office. You've stayed in camp weekends. You haven't even taken the vacation your contract specifies."

"Anyway," Bonta said as he checked to see that the fire was under control, "my conscience is clear, and that's what matters most to me."

I commented bitterly, "It's not going to be easy getting through the next thirty days with everybody watching to see how we're taking it and saying heaven knows what behind our backs!"

"What do you think they've been doing for weeks already?" Bonta shook his head. "You know, part of the problem is I've tried to talk to them as though they could understand a rational approach to things. Mr. Ramsey has told me over and over that you can't reason with most of them. He says you've got to sugarcoat any unpleasantness they have to accept and never come straight out with the facts." He shrugged. "Well, it's water over the dam now. Guess I've learned some things in the process, but it's sure been the hard way. At least we'll soon know who our friends are—if we have any!"

During the trip Mr. Ramsey reiterated what he'd already told Bonta at his house. "You can easily get everything back if you're willing to fight for it. You can just stay on in private practice, and they'll come to you because there's nobody else to go to. Or you can make up your own private list of men who sign up with you and pay in as they have before. Whichever way, the company'll help with the mechanics. Why, I wouldn't even be surprised if the union asked you to make a new contract. I wouldn't put it past them to blow things apart like this and then think they could just turn around and expect things to go right back the way they were. But if they ask for the old contract back, I'd turn them down. No, don't settle for the old one. Hold out for more favorable terms."

Reflecting on the situation, Mr. Ramsey stared vacantly at the trees and hills whizzing by. He summed up his conclusions. "Why, you've really got lots of options. Yup, it's up to you to make the next move."

In Williamson the three men conferred for a long time in Dr. Meade's office.

On the way back Bonta and Mr. Ramsey rehashed their discussion. Dr. Meade had been as taken aback as Mr. Ramsey had been, and he had had no more helpful suggestions to offer either. He agreed with Mr. Ramsey that the withholding should be raised to $3.50, if negotiations were in order. That was what the company withheld for the doctors in Red Jacket's other mines. He was sorry it had come to that and blamed the strike situation for what he described as the miners' unusually short tempers. Now it was a waiting game.

There were thirty days to get through before the contract became void, and a lot could happen before then.

On the return trip Mr. Ramsey shared some of his own problems with us. Some of the higher-ups in the company had complained about the quality of the coal coming out of Number Nine mine, and there was even talk of finding him some other job in the company, much as his past services were appreciated.

He spoke of this possible demotion without rancor. "It might be best if they do bring in someone new, someone younger. It's really very rare for a superintendent to stay as long as I have after opening up a mine." He said philosophically, "I've changed jobs before, and I reckon I can manage again if it comes to that."

He kept going back to his favorite topic, the men. "I've tried to do right by them. Tried to keep them from hurting themselves. Like I said, they're just children. They're brought up from the cradle to believe the company is out to do them in, and they learn union loyalty along with their mother's milk. I don't see as there's any way to get them to see the big picture—to get them to recognize that they need the company as much as the company needs them."

I thought a lot about what Mr. Ramsey said. I just wondered if we all suffer from some fatal flaw that works against our own best interests.

"Don't you think more and better education would help?" Bonta asked.

"Education's not going to change them now. Maybe the next generation, or the next one after that, but I doubt it. It all starts too early."

I thought of our feeble attempts at education about preventing the spread of worms and was tempted to agree. Still, Bonta and I felt that education offered the only hope of informing people's attitudes, whatever the situation.

Mr. Ramsey continued, "You know, I stand at the portal every morning, waving in salute to each of the cars loaded with the men entering the mine. And they all wave back. It just gives me that grand feeling that I'm doing what's important for us all. Oh, I'm not stupid enough to think they all mean those friendly grins. But I swear, I think it's more important for me to do that than to do a lot of the paperwork the company seems to think I should spend my time at. I tell you, if the men think I care, and God knows I do, they'll dig a lot more coal for the corporation in the long run."

Mr. Ramsey said, almost talking to himself, "Oh, I know you could befriend some of them all their lives, and the minute they thought you crossed them up, they'd as soon knife you in the back as not. But that's the way they're brought up—they can't help it."

He turned to Bonta who was still fuming silently over the injustice of their attack on him. "I wouldn't want to feel the way you do, not for the world. No point in being mad at them. Won't do any good. Just makes you miserable yourself."

He suddenly brought his thoughts back to practical realities. "But that reminds me." He was emphatic. "Whatever you do in the weeks ahead, don't let any one man feel he's in the doghouse so bad he feels persecuted. Larry Watson can be pretty belligerent, especially when he's drunk. And that's more often than not. He's not above using a gun. Always fight your own battle, but always use soft words."

17. Looking for the Pieces

The next day, Sunday, was crammed with talk, rumors, and conferences. Mrs. Dean and Sam, her husband, were gratifyingly sorry that the contract had been broken. Mrs. Dean said Bonta and Vern were the only decent doctors they'd ever had here, and she didn't think people truly wanted Bonta to leave. She was relieved to hear that he was considering staying on in private practice. Sam came over to the house just to let Bonta know that he hadn't had anything to do with it.

"Hell, Doc, I was working when they had that meeting, and I didn't even know what they was up to. Can't tell me most of the men really wanted this to happen."

When Bonta explained that he might start a private list of men who wanted to sign up with him, Sam volunteered, "I'd sure be proud to take that there list around for you. I know some other men who'd be glad to do the same. You know what I think? I think it's all on account of the ambulance. Some of them figure you was butting into their private business, interfering with their own plans for the ambulance, when I knowed you was just trying to keep it in camp for emergencies."

Bonta asked how important he thought the complaints about high fees were. "Shucks, I don't think many of them are mad about that. I only heared a few talking about that."

Needless to say, such support was very comforting.

Eloise came down and said her father had missed a whole shift just so he could be at the meeting. He'd tried to speak up in the doctor's defense, but nobody would listen at all. He was completely ignored when he asked if anyone had gone to the doctor to straighten it out. Eloise said it was all the work of Rick Addison, the chief ambulance driver, Dan Dubois, and Freddie Kilmer. Dubois didn't say anything at the meeting, but according to the Horvaths he'd done his dirty work earlier.

Eloise said, "Oh, he'll come around and talk real sweet to your face. Be real sorry about everything. But don't you believe him for one minute. You can't trust him nohow."

Of course, that meshed with Mr. Ramsey's warning that Dan bore watching and with Larry Watson's admonition to stay away from him. We didn't know what to think. Dan had always seemed friendly enough.

Harvey Burgess and his wife Amber, who lived near the Horvaths, were already crowing over Eloise's impending loss of prestige in camp. Eloise reported that Amber had said, "Just too bad you won't be able to make all them new clothes anymore! What a shame, your ma'll just have to lie there and suffer without any more of them free shots!"

Let somebody appear to be down on their luck, and all the venom seemed to pour out. Eloise was a real spitfire in our defense, and when Amber taunted her by saying she bet there wasn't anything she wouldn't do for the doctor, Eloise's eyes must have flashed as she retorted there certainly wasn't and she was proud of it. We hastened to tell her that we'd be around a while yet, and while we were here, she'd be working for us as long as she wanted to. Needless to say, we'd continue to help her mother in every way we could.

No sooner had Eloise returned home than her little brother Pete came down, reporting, "Mama's just took a real bad spell and needs the doctor right away."

Apparently Mrs. Horvath had become overexcited, first worrying that Bonta would be leaving and then finding out from Eloise that he would be staying a while yet.

After Bonta finished talking with her, he told me he sauntered into the living room and said, "Joe, hear there was a bit of excitement in the union meeting yesterday."

Mr. Horvath launched into a tirade. "The cows! Just cows! They all sat there, just dumb. Nobody ain't said a thing till they called for the vote. And then only a couple said yes to giving the doc his notice. The rest just kind of whispered around it weren't up to them. I tried to tell them how bad sick folks like my wife here needs the doctor in camp, but there weren't no talking to them. I got so mad when they wouldn't listen to me, I almost cried!"

In his broken English it must have been quite the story. The more excited he became, the stronger the Hungarian accent. He reported the ringleaders had packed the meeting with a lot of Long Branchers who hadn't been to a union meeting in six months. Very few from Coal Mountain itself were there, and there were only about fifty at the most. He was sure there were a dozen men in the green camp who would sign up with Bonta immediately.

Later Dan Dubois came over to the house on a transparent pretext, and Bonta invited him to come in. Dan introduced the conversation by asking, "Hey Doc, I guess you've heard the bad news?"

As if we might not have heard it!

"Well, it was just bound to happen, and there wasn't a thing I could do to stop them. Oh, I tried all right. I sure tried. Why, I told Joe to explain how important it was to keep a doctor in camp for sick folks like his wife. But it wasn't no use. Why, them Long Branchers just ganged up against all reason."

The two men sat at the kitchen table. When Bonta asked why he thought it had happened, Dan cocked his head so he could look Bonta in the eye. "You know what the story is. Larry Watson and his brother Danny, they want to bring in a chiropractor from over Welch way. He's a friend of theirs, and there might even be some money passed between them. Who knows? Anyways, they want to get you out so there's room for him."

"That's the first I've heard of that," Bonta said. "You don't think it had anything to do with the ambulance?"

"No, that wasn't no problem. Overcharges? Well, I heard some of the men complaining about them extra charges being held out against them."

Bonta explained, "You realize those extra charges have been piling up, some of them from slips the men signed as far back as last June.

The company didn't hold them out till the men started earning regular pay. I've been taking care of people for months for little or nothing. I guess I can see how they'd be upset if they don't realize that."

Dan's indignation escalated to outrage as he talked. "Well, they should have talked to you about it. They should have gone to the medical committee before they kicked you out. I tell you, it puts me in mind of the way Judas turned in Christ Himself."

This outburst was amazing. Was Dan playing games? It was hard to believe.

Bonta pursued the opportunity to make another point. "They may think they can bring somebody else in, but they'd have a hard time finding anyone who'd come after this blowup. You better believe I'd never have come if they'd broken their contract with Nichols this way."

Then Bonta described his plan to develop a private list which the miners could sign. "You understand, Dan, I'll continue to give the people here the best care I know how to give, but it will just cost them more as private patients, now that the contract is broken. Soon as the thirty days are up each visit will cost what it used to cost for a whole month's care. Of course, if they want to sign up with me individually, I might consider that."

Dan responded as Bonta had hoped he would, saying earnestly, "Well, Doc, if you got a list we can sign up on, just count me in. Yes, sir, I'll tell them how it's going to be now." With that Dan got up awkwardly from the chair, made his way down the porch steps, and started down the road, left hand behind his back as usual, filled with new insider information he was anxious to share with any who would listen.

Mr. Ramsey was more than a little nervous about the possibility that the fracas could precipitate another strike. Obviously his job was to keep things running smoothly in the interests of maximum coal production, and keeping a doctor in camp was just part of the balancing act. The union leaders had really put one over on him with this move, but he seemed confident that things would straighten out, all in good time. Bonta told him, however, that we were interested in staying only so long as it furthered our goal of saving for a residency, and we didn't have indefinite amounts of time to clear things up. Residencies would start in July, so a decision to stay another year or leave at the end of this first year had to be made soon. A lot of the better residencies were undoubtedly filled already.

Mr. Ramsey said he approved of all Bonta had done so far and begged him not to goad the men into a strike. He again warned that it was a good idea to have Dan on our side because he could be a dangerous adversary.

My own reaction to this really surprised me. I felt so detached from it all. Mr. Ramsey asked Bonta how I was taking it all, and Bonta told him I was feeling just about the same way he felt: anxious to have things smoothed out, ready to change course if need be, distressed at the double-talk we kept hearing, pressed to choose among alternatives for the coming year, and above all, still groping in the dark for the real reason behind the blowup. We just didn't feel we deserved this. At least we could be a little more objective about it now than we could be when we were shadowboxing with vague whisperings.

I was reluctant to tell our families about this latest development. Father would say it confirmed all his opinions about unions, and Mother might be nervous about coming down for her planned visit, with things so unsettled and evidently hostile. It had taken a lot of persuasion to get her to agree to come in the first place. Bonta's parents had already been campaigning for us to leave, and this would certainly add fuel to that fire.

The thing that bothered me most was that the people who stuck by us were the ones who might absorb some of the hostility directed toward us and would suffer from the increased cost. We were both sure that no one would consent to pay fee-for-service charges anyway, so as soon as they needed care, they'd sign up on the private list Bonta was going to start. If we raised the withholding cost on that to match the going rate elsewhere, as Mr. Ramsey and Dr. Meade had recommended, that would hurt the very people willing to return.

〆 Problems never come singly. Early the next day Bonta was called to see Mr. Ramsey. "He's had a queer spell!" was the message Randall sent from the office. Mr. Ramsey had apparently collapsed at his desk, and the men had managed to get him home.

Worrying about a possible heart attack or a stroke, Bonta hurried over but couldn't reach any firm diagnosis. He was anxious about Mr. Ramsey's condition and went back several times during the day to check on him. Not only were we distressed because of our great affection and respect for him, but to have him knocked out at this particular moment could be disastrous for us, too. Poor Mr. Ramsey! I just hoped our problems hadn't precipitated this. He had had so many worries already.

A miner came to the office that afternoon demanding his records so he could switch to another doctor outside of camp. He said this other doctor had been taking care of a particular patient Bonta considered neurotic and had found totally uncooperative. "Why, she's coming along like a queen!"

This direct assault sent me flying to Bonta's defense. My objectivity evaporated. I found myself taking criticism of him more to heart than he did himself. Anyway my impulse was to say let's pitch it all. In a more reasonable frame of mind, Bonta figured if he could make a go of it without the likes of this discontented fellow and that unreasonable patient things could be more comfortable than before. But he was depressed, much more pessimistic than he had been, mostly because of Mr. Ramsey's sudden illness.

From the crowd in the office in the afternoon, one would never have guessed that the doctor had been invited to leave. They really didn't understand what a hole they'd dug for themselves. Bonta could refuse to treat them, could even deny them hospital slips. The hospital had told us they wouldn't admit anyone without a physician's referral. And of course the company had promised to make it hard for anyone else to come here. Bonta never even considered retaliation, but the options were there. He was pretty sure this had been engineered by relatively few malcontents, and he would never turn away someone who needed help. Of course, for a month things were to go on superficially as before.

Dan came to the office begging for a few minutes of Bonta's time, all upset because he had heard he was being accused of running the doctor out. "Yes, they're all saying it's my fault. Tell me, Doc, did the men who handed you that there notice say I done it?"

Bonta considered a moment just how much he could share of what the delegation had actually said. He didn't want to inflame passions any more than he could help, but he did want to be honest. "Well, they at least implied that you weren't a good friend of mine."

Dan's eyes flashed, and he would have straightened up if he could have. In a suddenly resolute tone he said, "Hah! so that's it. I tell you, we ought to call another meeting then to reconsider. Yes, sir. Why, there was hardly anybody there at the last one. Couldn't have been more than thirty men." He shook his head. "Course you only need ten to make a quorum, so I suppose it was legal-like even so."

As Dan set off on a new mission, Bonta concealed his amazement at the size of the quorum for an organization of four hundred men.

Several patients came in full of sympathy, saying Long Branch was one of the worst districts in the state and that people just didn't know how much medicines and medical care cost outside. One interesting hypothesis offered was that the men didn't like Bonta because he was such a good labor doctor, and they didn't want so many babies!

The school principal came to pick up some more medicine for his migraine headaches. No one had made the right diagnosis until Bonta saw him and put him on Caffergot. This had done the trick. Mr. Woods was grateful and sympathized with Bonta's situation.

"I've had my own run-ins, but I've got a school board behind me. When things get rough, I just tell them to go to the board and ask them to get rid of me. No, this camp's a rough one to handle. Sometimes I'd like to leave, but this area's where I grew up, and a job's a job."

We heard that some people were getting angry with the Horvaths for blaming Dan, who, they said, was really falling apart because of these accusations. If true, that was a most unfortunate development.

The day was noteworthy also for its strange weather. The wind blew in huge gusts all day long, though the temperature remained unusually balmy for the end of March. One blast sent my sheets flying off the line after having dried them in record time. The office was suffocatingly hot because we couldn't turn off the radiator, so the windows were open to the gale. By the time we left, I felt like a sparrow after a good dust bath. No wonder Bonta had complained about the wind the previous summer, and he warned me this was only the beginning.

ॐ Tuesday, Mr. Ramsey had another dizzy spell, which alarmed Bonta further. He planned to take him to the hospital to be thoroughly tested as soon as it could be arranged. Mr. Ramsey was rather drowsy but did say he thought something might be done to help Dan.

It was kind of touchy, to say the least, to suggest that the Horvaths stop being so vocal against Dan and for us. Bonta did tell Eloise that this was her home and she shouldn't let her position in the office alienate her from the community, much as we appreciated her loyalty. We didn't want her to get hurt. After all, she'd undoubtedly still be here long after we left, whenever that might be.

⁊ The company president, James Collins, and vice-president, Arthur Taylor, came to the house at noon on Wednesday to inquire about Mr. Ramsey's health and the ticklish situation here with the union. They were greatly disturbed by both developments. Obviously our problem had an impact on Mr. Ramsey's already precarious future. He hadn't been aware of the growing dissatisfaction with Bonta's work and failed to defuse it. Now the tensions might even precipitate another strike. Meantime it looked as though Mr. Ramsey might be unable to function at all. The company had been through so much turmoil that any new threat to stability was cause for alarm. Bonta reassured them as honestly as possible, trying to protect Mr. Ramsey, but of course everything was uncertain.

Susan's speech had improved to the point of being embarrassing on occasion. She pulled on my skirt and kept telling me that Mr. Taylor had a hole in his pants and that he should stop playing with his keys. I was relieved that his attention was elsewhere and managed to shush her.

Luckily the men didn't stay long, because Bonta was anxious to get to the hospital with Mr. Ramsey.

Unfortunately, after reviewing his records and checking him over, no one there had any helpful ideas about his problem either. They were as baffled as Bonta was.

Since Bonta was away, the office stayed closed in the afternoon. I was actually relieved because I found myself tiring easily after lunch these days. There was no longer any doubt about my being pregnant. I was losing more meals than I could hang onto. There should be an easier way to do it!

Eloise and I had a chance to chat and forget all our problems while we baked cookies together. I hoped to get her interested in some good reading. Apparently in high school a system of exchanging book reports ensured that almost no one actually had to read a book. She told me she hated movies and presumably books that didn't turn out "right." Killing the hero was strictly poor policy. As her only reading at present was an occasional *True Romance*, I was determined to tempt her with something more worthwhile but still palatable. It had been gratifying to see her grow the past months. She had assumed so much new responsibility at the office and at home; she had learned a lot about dealing with people. Most of all, she had become a treasured friend.

We talked at some length about her mother. As she spooned batter onto the cookie sheets, she said, "I just hate to give her them old shots. I swear she don't mind them half as much as I do." She paused to put a batch into the oven. "You know them Holinesses are a big old nuisance. They come up wanting to put some old healing rag on her stomach and telling her it'll make her all better. This healing rag come from some preacher over in Kentucky. They tell her all she got to do is pray, but she don't want none of it."

Her description was full of scorn, but her tone abruptly changed as she looked hopefully at me and added, "You think it'd do any good?"

I yearned to comfort her, but honesty made that difficult. "Well, Eloise, there are some problems that a healing rag might help if the person believed in it hard enough."

She interrupted, saying regretfully, "That's just the trouble. She don't believe in it, not one bit. And I don't know how to make her. Them Holinesses, they jump around and yell, and that just makes her worse."

I had to tell her, "I'm afraid your mother's sick with something no faith healing can cure. I guess God could work a miracle if He wanted to, but I don't expect one here. None of the doctors at Welch know how to make her better either. The best anybody can do is to try to make her as comfortable as possible. And that's where you come in, Eloise. Those shots you hate to give do take away the pain for a while. I know how you feel about them, but they're the best gift you can give her. You have a right to feel very proud that you're taking that responsibility."

✻ On Thursday morning I met Mrs. Bannister at the company store. She obviously had something important on her mind. "I'm so glad to see you. You remember you told me once about how you taught biology somewheres, and I been wanting to ask if you'd be willing to tutor Maggie in biology this summer. She failed it last year and couldn't take it this year. She's got to make it up and pass a test, and she don't want to go to summer school way over at Welch."

I said I'd certainly be glad to consider it if she could give me some more information about what was needed. That might be very gratifying. I added, "If we're still here."

Mrs. Bannister commented bitterly that people didn't appreciate what they had. "Besides, if it's money that's the problem, they ain't got no idea how lucky they are right here. And Doctor here, he's done me more good than all them doctors at Welch and Bluefield."

Each day brought a significant fresh development in our situation. Mrs. Ramsey came to the office that afternoon. When Bonta realized she was in the waiting room, he invited her in immediately. She accepted the chair we offered, as he asked, "How is Mr. Ramsey? Any change in his condition?"

"No, and that's not what I come to talk about." She seemed to look at her lap for courage, then faced Bonta with a look of resignation. "No, what I come to tell you is that he's resigning. Come May 1 he'll be through here."

Bonta received this news without too much surprise, in light of what Mr. Ramsey had told us on the way back from Williamson. But it was very sad to contemplate the downfall of a strong and vital man who had accomplished so much.

"To tell you the truth, he's really retiring before they fire him. The company's told him he's got to get out five thousand tons a day, and the best he can get the men to do is more like three thousand. Things have been so messed up. Mr. Collins admits he don't expect anybody else can do any better, but he says the stockholders are making a lot of noise. Seems they got to have a scapegoat."

Bonta said, "I'm awfully sorry things are turning out like that. I just hope our problem with the union wasn't the last straw that brought on his illness."

Mrs. Ramsey was displaying a dignity and candor beyond our expectation. "Who knows? It's true Mr. Collins was surprised John hadn't known the trouble about you was brewing so as he could head it off. They're mighty scared this could make the men strike again. But there's a limit to what one man can know and do. He's had more trouble this past year than anybody should have to bear in a lifetime. Maybe his getting sick like this is a blessing in disguise. Gives him a graceful way out. Nobody'll be surprised at his leaving so long as he's sick."

She continued with some bitterness, "That company's never appreciated him like he deserves. He's worked his heart out for them, and they never give him a good house, never paid him what he was worth to them. They figured they could get away with it because we're stuck up in this hole away from everything else. And everybody says this local is one of the worst ones around to deal with."

She half smiled to herself as she said in an altered tone, "Course, everything has a good side and a bad side. The good side is that we been a lot closer since he took sick. When you need each other bad, you do appreciate each other more."

I knew just what she meant by that last remark. Probably no other circumstances could have led us to value each other in quite the way that this isolation from family and other support systems had done.

Bonta reflected on Mr. Ramsey's resignation later. "It's ironic, isn't it, that the very men he's devoted his life to have chewed him up in the end. First the production problems, then the strike, and finally our ouster. And he's been so kind to them. I'll wager he isn't blaming them even now. Remember how he said he felt compassion for them even when they fouled things up."

As we prepared to leave the office, he said, "Mr. Ramsey's going is unfortunate enough to make me lean toward leaving ourselves. When the company brings in a new man, he'll be swamped by all kinds of demands, especially the need to get out more coal. We'll just be small pawns in the big picture. After all, all he'll know about us is that we're the center of a dispute that's merely an added headache for him. He won't have any idea about the merits of the case." He added decisively,

"I think we ought to make another trip to Columbus this weekend to check on that residency again."

Sam Dean stopped us by the gate, calling out, "Hey, Doc." When he caught up with us, he reported, full of pride at what he'd accomplished, "I been talking to maybe a dozen men, and they're all fired up and ready to sign up with you on a private list. Why, I bet we can get most of the union to go along."

That was encouraging news. After Bonta thanked him for his help, he asked what he thought had caused the cancellation of the contract. "Well, I don't know for sure, but I heard some of the union big shots want to bring in their own man."

That was Dan's story, too.

We kept trying to put the bits and pieces of information together, whatever the source, in an attempt to get a picture of what was really going on. A major problem was never knowing which pieces were counterfeit.

In any event, we decided to go to Columbus the next day.

Meantime Eloise was struggling with her own battles. She desperately wanted to go to Kentucky to join Tommy. According to indirect reports he had found a job, but she didn't know what sort of work it was. She felt trapped. Whenever she mentioned leaving, she was accused of callousness toward her mother. "How can you think of such a thing right now?" I sympathized with her rebellion against deferring her own life for the sake of her family but felt helpless, knowing how badly her family did need her.

She was as staunch a supporter for Bonta as ever. She told us someone had asked her if she'd work for the next doctor, and she'd answered hotly, "Never!" I told her she needn't feel at all disloyal if such an opportunity arose and she wanted to accept it. We heard from several people that she and Eva were both so outspoken in our defense that they might actually be antagonizing others against us. We were sorry they'd been drawn into a dispute not of their making and earnestly hoped they wouldn't suffer on our account.

≫ Bonta's conversation with Mr. Ramsey Monday after our return from Columbus left him distinctly depressed. There was to be a meeting on Wednesday, April 5, among the four men who signed the voiding of our contract, the two top company men from Williamson, and Bonta. Mr. Ramsey said he was not going to be present, and we couldn't help feeling that was sort of deserting us in our hour of need. We were still leaning on him, even though we should have known better under the circumstances.

He also said some of the Long Branch faction were so irate about what they called overcharges that they had asked the company office to stop payment on their back bills. That was the ultimate frustration. We could document every single charge from our own books, and we had never sent in a slip that the patient didn't understand at the time, authorize, and sign, or mark with his own X. It had to be because the charges had accumulated since before the strike, and people's memories were so short. As soon as they felt better, they forgot how grateful they were at the time. Of course, I have learned since that people are the same everywhere.

We spent a lot of time talking about alternatives for the future. Even though the residency at Columbus wouldn't be available for another year, others, though less prestigious, could certainly be found. We looked over jobs listed in *JAMA* and the *New England Journal of Medicine* and planned to do some scouting for openings in other coal camps in the area. The troubling fact was that we really thought this was the most attractive camp around, and of course we'd just decided to spend another whole year in Coal Mountain when everything fell apart.

My pregnancy added one more complication. I was ready to have the baby down here, but Bonta was in favor of sending me home to deliver. I wasn't willing even to think about that, remembering how I'd felt the summer before, waiting to come to Coal Mountain.

18. Bottoming Out

꙳꙳꙳ Uptight about the impending meeting, I told Bonta if they wanted to call him a money grabber, it would serve them right if he just left. And I was sick and tired of their saying one thing to our faces and another thing behind our backs. I'm afraid I was so upset I wasn't much help to him. He was amazingly calm. Perhaps trying to soothe me actually helped him.

He reminded me, "The worst they can do has already been done, and there's just a chance this confrontation in the presence of the company officers can straighten things out." He stood up to leave. "Most important, I know I've never cheated anybody. I've got nothing to hide. We'll just have to let it play itself out."

So, with a reassuring kiss he set off for the company office, promising to report verbatim all that transpired.

Mr. Collins, the company president, Mr. Taylor, the vice-president, and Dr. Meade were already in Mr. Ramsey's office, looking over the maps of the mines that covered the walls, while they waited for the four union men to come down from work.

Mr. Collins expressed the company viewpoint. "Oh, this will all blow over. It's just a tempest in a teapot! The usual kind of thing that goes on in the coalfields."

Bonta wasn't so sure.

The four miners, Larry and Danny Watson, Elton Jamison, and Freddie Kilmer, tramped in, black with coal dust, proudly wearing their black miners' hats, swaggering in the knowledge that the big boss had summoned them from the mine. Their pants were tucked into their heavy work boots, now grayed by dust. The quartet were a study in contrasts. Larry was stocky and big all over, and his brother was just a thinner version. Both men were of medium height, with similar broad features above firm jutting jaws. Elton, by contrast, was tall and thin, his receding hair elongating his face. Freddie played Mutt to his Jeff, small and usually bouncy but now sober and awed by the importance of his position. The curly hair sticking out from under his hat gave him a puckish look in spite of himself. It was in keeping with his personality that he confined his participation in the conference to emphatically nodding or shaking his head, as the words of his comrades required.

Bonta told me afterward they could have posed for a poster: "Labor on the March!" They were fired up.

There was barely room for everyone in the small room, and Randall had to bring in some extra folding chairs.

Mr. Collins appropriately opened the meeting with a brief description of the problem as he saw it and turned to Larry as the top union official for his comments.

Larry sat up straight, feeling both puffed up by his importance as president and nervous at presenting his case to the company's top officials. Once he started speaking, however, all hesitancy left him. "Well, you see, it's like this. Doc here," glancing toward Bonta and quickly returning his gaze to Mr. Collins to avoid eye contact, "Doc made a call on Brett Morgan. You all know Brett's head of the Morgans around here. Well, Doc said the men should have brought Brett in to the office instead of getting him down there, and he talked right smart to them men, and he charged Brett a dollar for what he said was a unnecessary house call." By then he was clearly relishing his role. "And we don't let things like that go by without doing something about it."

This was actually the first time Bonta had heard Larry mention the Brett Morgan problem. He'd always talked about overcharges.

Danny, the vice-president, backed up his brother's statement, saying, "Yes, sir, that was a irregular and unwarranted charge." Danny liked to use legal-sounding phrases.

Elton Jamison, the treasurer, unexpectedly enough said, "No, if you look at the contract careful, it says the doc can charge a dollar like that."

Bonta was pleasantly surprised by this evidence of fairness. The two brothers professed astonishment, looking at each other to see how to respond. There was no question in anyone's mind but that they knew well enough what the contract said. Larry collected his wits first and said, "Well, of course, in that case," here he sounded heartily concil-iatory in light of this supposed revelation, "Well, that sure do make a difference! That sure puts a new shine on it."

A moment's pause, however, provided him with a new strategy. "But that there contract was never ratified by the body of men. No, sir, it never was." He was convincing himself as he embellished the story. "Why, the wrong men signed it in the first place, and it ain't never been read out in three union meetings, like it was supposed to." He ended on a triumphant note. "No sir, it ain't no valid contract!"

Next came the matter of the ambulance, and Bonta asked Larry if he had told the men that he'd offered to send a written apology for his criticism of what he had considered an inappropriate use of the ambu-lance. Larry muttered that he hadn't but immediately changed the sub-ject. "You know, course, where all this trouble's coming from—Dan Dubois. He's been going around cussing the doctor up and down."

While Joe Horvath and Larry were light-years apart on the breaking of the contract, they did agree on Dan's role in fomenting the discon-tent. It certainly was bewildering. Dan sounded so sincere when he protested such accusations.

Larry must have realized they were just plowing old issues and getting nowhere, because in a sudden fit of honesty, about his own feelings at least, he exploded, "Well, the trouble is the men just don't like the doctor!"

At this Mr. Collins and Mr. Taylor just leaned back and laughed out loud. Bonta laughed about it when he told me later, but at the moment his vanity was stung, and he asked how many men had been at the critical meeting.

In the face of all reports to the contrary, Larry blustered, "Oh, I'd say 150." Nobody there disagreed.

Bonta said if the majority really didn't want him around, he cer-tainly didn't want to stay.

At that point Mr. Collins decided it was time to intervene on behalf of harmony and started talking about Bonta's qualifications and the company's satisfaction with his work. "It's not exactly surprising that problems have come up, if the doctor's been trying to live up to the terms of a contract the union doesn't even know exists."

Bonta suggested that if a new contract were to be negotiated, it might be good if a certain percentage of the men signed it. This would reassure everyone that it was what the majority wanted.

Larry insisted this would make it into a private list, and after two more explanations he still didn't understand the point. "But if that's what the body of men want, I'd be first to sign to pay in, no matter what."

Bonta wasn't sure he'd heard correctly.

Larry continued, "Now we'll just get this all figured out. With that there contract being no good, I'll just take the whole thing up with the body of men. We'll call a special meeting Saturday week." He spoke expansively, as though no one need be disturbed further about the matter, now that he was handling it.

Mr. Collins seemed to feel it was a good idea to go along with Larry's offer and said if the next meeting brought no resolution to the problem it would be time to work on a private list of those who wanted to sign with the doctor.

Giving Bonta a broad wink, Elton sidled over to him as the others filed out. "Look, Doc, if you stay, you just come around and see me. I'll keep you out of trouble. If I'd knowed all this was cooking, I'd have called it off, but I just never heared about it till it was too damned late."

Bonta managed to swallow any comments he felt like making. Elton was thick as could be with the Watsons.

It looked as though the only thing we could do was hope enough of our friends showed up at the next meeting. It was discouraging to realize that a number of them were at the previous meeting and either never spoke up or were never heard.

Eloise came back to the house as Bonta was finishing this report. She started talking about the way the men signed slips against their paychecks, not only for the doctor, but for the store and for gas.

"You know," she said, "they don't seem to know that when they sign a slip it means they're going to lose money from their pay. A lot of them can't read, course, or if they can, they don't even know what ought to have been held out against them or how much they was supposed to get."

"That puts them completely at the mercy of the company, doesn't it?" Bonta asked.

Nodding, Eloise continued, "You know, Carl next door, he can't even count, and his wife's always snitching a few dollars before he can hide his money, and he don't never know the difference."

Bonta took advantage of this opening to stress the importance of getting an education. "Don't let your brothers quit school, will you? And you know, you really ought to think about Tommy's prospects without a high school diploma."

Eloise professed to be thoroughly disgusted with Tommy at this point. "Humph—Tommy! He never come back to the mine like he said he would. And I ain't heard from him in ages. If he figures I'm going to set home and wait for him any longer, well, I ain't!"

It would take more than words to convince me, but I hoped she meant it.

Bonta went over to see Mr. Ramsey. He took his chessboard along, so I hoped they'd have a pleasant time in addition to talking over the morning's meeting. Bonta knew from speaking with Mr. Collins that morning that Mr. Ramsey had asked for a month's vacation and apparently had completely sloughed all responsibility. Mr. Ramsey had said that a curtain fell between himself and anyone who started talking about mining business. He was through caring about it.

What a pity! It was sad to see someone go from such strength and total involvement to such complete withdrawal. But as Bonta said, "I guess we can all take just so much pressure before we reach our breaking point."

I mused, "If we stay on ourselves, it'll sure be strange and lonesome without him."

⚘   Eloise was noticeably brighter when she arrived for work the next day. She was as good as her word and had accepted a former beau's offer to go out to a movie the night before. She said she'd had a good time. She told him, though, they'd never hit it off, because each one was so acutely aware of the other's intervening romantic attachments, but if he wanted to come up and watch her color Easter eggs the next Saturday night, he could.

Mr. Ramsey was puttering in his yard when Bonta finished an early morning house call next door. The two men met by the fence, and Mr. Ramsey told Bonta that he was feeling relieved because he'd just had word that Mr. Collins was sending someone in to the camp next day to take over the business of running things.

"Yes, it's good they've found somebody else. Things have changed so much since I started here. I've been at it too long already. High time somebody else with some new ideas and lots of energy took over. Yes, I'm done with it all. Too many things just piled up, more than I can take."

He looked around to make sure that his wife was not within earshot and lowered his voice as he continued. "Sure, the strike and all the rest had something to do with it, but I think a lot of it has to do with family problems. Alma and I get into some real battles over our grown children. She often doesn't see things my way. And would you believe it—she's been jealous about every move I make. And at my age, too! Oh, she's been wonderful since I got sick, so I don't want to say too much about it."

I was surprised when Bonta later mentioned Mrs. Ramsey's jealousy. I never would have guessed that that entered into their relationship. However, I was not too surprised to learn of the existence of friction between them. Mrs. Ramsey tended to make judgmental statements, and I'd seen a less attractive side of her personality at the knitting class. I'd surmised that this might be indicative of what could go on at home.

The remarkable thing was not that Mr. Ramsey's strength was not limitless but that he had withstood so many and such varied assaults for so long. Bonta had urged him to get away for a while. A change of scenery might help him develop a fresh outlook. We did hope he'd find fulfillment in other ways. He would always be on our list of most admired people.

✄ There were a few repercussions from the meeting the day before. Dan stopped us by the gate and said things looked a little better "for our cause," but in answer to Bonta's question as to whether he thought most of the men really disliked him, Dan answered he really couldn't say. That was a depressing sort of reply. Then he told Bonta about some irate young father.

"He come in for some medicine. His young one was running off."

Bonta had given him something for the boy's diarrhea and also explained that it would be helpful to cut down on the child's food intake as well till his gut quieted down. Apparently this additional suggestion was ill-advised, because the fellow left in a huff (though Bonta hadn't realized it), threw the medicine in the creek, and drove forty miles to see another doctor! It looked as though the more you explained, the less they believed you. If that was why they didn't like us, there wasn't much we could do to improve relations.

That was bad enough, but worse followed. Dan said, "There's some talk about slapping a fine on anybody who comes to you if you stay. That makes me mad. I'll fight that one if they try to put it across. Ain't nobody going to tell me who I'm going to see."

Somebody must really hate us. That could get pretty scary.

Bonta was down in the dumps. He said, "I should have done long ago what Meade suggested. I should have ordered three colors of aspirin, and if one didn't work, promised them the next would. Put a little hocus-pocus into it all. Well, live and learn the hard way, I guess."

The uncertainty made things feel awfully temporary. Bonta had slacked off on his medical reading. He didn't even seem to care about keeping up the business routines at the office. At least I could keep those going. But I confess that afternoon when I went over to the post office and noticed that the incinerator by the back door had tipped over, I just gave it a kick. It might as well stay that way—let the next guy straighten it up!

When Bonta gave paraplegic Jimmy Morgan his shot, he told him he'd better start looking up another doctor, because we might be leaving if things didn't straighten out in a hurry. Jimmy had been relying on Bonta's staying on in private practice and looked worried. He knew he'd have to go back to the California sanatorium if there were no doctor in camp, because going outside twice a week for shots was almost impossible in his condition. I hoped he'd let a few people hear about his problem.

Mrs. Horvath was unfortunately starting to swell up with ascites again; fluid from the tumor was accumulating in her abdomen. Though it had been a while since she'd had to go to the hospital for a tap, it wasn't a good sign. In spite of her poor condition, she sent down with Eloise an adorable yellow dress for Susan. She had combed the catalogs for something cute for her for Easter. I couldn't believe her generosity when it came to both money and caring. Eloise still took Susan up to visit Mrs. Horvath frequently, because it seemed to be one diversion her mother really enjoyed. Of course, Susan liked nothing better.

Mrs. Doug Blake came to the office to see if there were any births to report in the *Red Jacket News.* Her job as reporter for the company gave her an inside track on community affairs. She stayed to chat about the gas station a few miles from camp that she and Doug had recently bought. We promised to fill up our car at their pump when we went out. It sounded as though Doug had started on that independent business he told us he wanted to develop so he could quit the mine.

✀   The following Monday Barney came over to visit while I was hanging out the clothes. He set down an armful of old boxes he planned to burn by the edge of the creek. He wasn't one for politicking, he said, but he did hope our problems would be solved to our liking.

"Me, I been fixing up my yard. Yup, cleaned out all the dog mess from winter. Most made me sick doing it. But it's better now, and I'm going to put wire fencing all around inside them boards. Can't stand them critters and what they do.

"Hey, you heard the latest news?" When I shook my head, wondering what next, Barney continued with a hint of scorn in his voice. "You remember our talk about them snakes? Well, a couple days ago two fellows was bit by rattlers down Long Branch way—handling them in the churchhouse. One already died, and I guess the other one's touch and go."

So they really did handle rattlesnakes. I was thankful these tests of faith weren't going on in camp.

"And when I told you to check the yard, I wasn't fooling. A dog got bit by a copperhead this morning just up the road here a little ways. No sirree, you can't be too careful."

That inspired me to clean up our yard. I threw out some old boards by the coal shed to make the place safer for Susan. She still spent hours just "walking around" or standing on the rail, lecturing everyone who came down the road.

Barney kindly added my trash to his pile, and a little crowd gathered to admire the resulting big bonfire.

When a couple of little girls came by with a doll, on a sudden whim I suggested that the doll looked pretty sick and offered to give it a shot. They thought that was a great game and went off for reinforcements. They returned shortly with the doll in an "ambulance," and the little boys pulling the wagon said the patient had developed measles. It was all great fun until they brought the youngest Kilmer boy down, claiming he was a drunk. The children's acceptance of drunkenness as an illness interested me, and I thought it a shame that it was so familiar to them. Since the boy wasn't very happy about this, I prescribed a good rest in his own bed and sent them all back up the hollow.

During the past few days several people had confirmed the rumor about fining those who came to Bonta for care, by telling us how dreadful they thought that was. They were all on our side and voluntarily suggested they'd spread the story they'd heard that some other doctor was paying Larry and his brother to oust Bonta.

Doug Blake, coming by to share the news about his gas station, told Bonta he wanted to let the men stew in their own juice a while, but he thought it would all work out. His advice was the same as Dr. Meade's: "Get different colors of aspirin, sound real firm when you talk to them. And give them rituals they got to follow."

He'd heard that one man came away from the office in disgust. "Doc told me to come back if these pills don't work. If they don't work! Don't he know nothing at all?" So poor Bonta was painfully picking up pointers for future use.

Mr. Kilmer called him to chat by the back fence. He always acted as though he were pulling all the strings, when most of the time he was the one being pulled. Of course, he'd been silent at the meeting with the company men. "Well, sure, I did sign the notice we give you. But there weren't nothing I could do about it. It was all the body of men at the meeting."

Bonta said his meeching manner disappeared as he declared, "But things is different now. You ain't got no cause to worry now. You'll see, things'll work out just the way I want them to."

That wasn't much reassurance!

While these conversations were going on, I visited with Eloise and made an angel cake with one of the two goose eggs that Mrs. Clay Morgan had brought to the office. I was as impressed by its size as Susan was. Mrs. Morgan had invited us to come to her home to show Susan the geese and those chickens that had to be caught with a net.

Eloise reported on another movie she saw with the same young man, though she'd insisted on walking out behind him so nobody would suspect they had come together.

On Thursday Mr. Taylor, the company vice-president, came back to the house to try to settle the previous week's mess. He explained to Bonta, "I've talked to Larry Watson. I told him how much the company is counting on him to put this new unionwide contract across, emphasizing the influence he has with the men as union president. So be forewarned. Larry'll be coming to see you pretty soon with big plans and his usual bluster."

Sure enough, along came Larry to the office that afternoon, where he helped himself to the chair by Bonta's desk. Crossing his legs ostentatiously, he began by complaining about people who "messed" behind his back and "pinned things" on him, when it wasn't his fault because he just had to do what the body of men wanted!

"Why, if I couldn't come up and talk it out man to man, if there was anything wrong between me and Doc here, why I'd as soon just go on down the holler! The big trouble was this old contract just weren't legal. That's what the problem was all about. It weren't never drawn up proper by the right people."

At this Bonta extracted from his desk drawer the scrawled note on which Mr. Kilmer had written the names of the union committee charged with negotiating the contract and handed it to Larry.

Clearly flustered by this evidence of his own error, Larry admitted grudgingly, "Well, yes, now I can see that the committee was authorized all right."

He spent a moment figuring a way out of this spot. "But they never read it to the men three times like they're supposed to." He ended on a note of great conviction. "No, sir, it still weren't legal and binding."

Bonta had no rebuttal to that, so Larry continued, full of false modesty, "Now I hadn't figured on going to this next meeting, but it looks like the company's counting on me to straighten things out. Yes, sir, ain't no better company nowheres than Red Jacket. So, long as they need me, they can count me in." He positively swelled with importance. "And if the body of men need to talk something over with you, Doc, I'll send for you."

He stood up and concluded this interview in his most pompously gracious manner. "If they don't, you can count on me letting you know how the vote went. Right away, soon's we get it all settled. You know I ain't a man to go back on my word, no matter what!"

Bearing a copy of Vern's contract which Bonta gave him to study, he left like a circus ringmaster retiring after the final bow.

    Saturday, April 15, was the day of the big meeting that was supposed to get us a new contract. Luckily Bonta was so busy with patients he didn't have time to wonder what was going on up in the churchhouse where the union met. Nobody came to get him as Larry had said they might, and around noon we saw the cars and trucks dispersing, so we knew the session must be over. Sam Dean stopped in for a minute to say that our side had won, though there were three men against Bonta—Larry Watson, his brother Danny, and Elton Jamison.

It was at least an hour later, after Bonta had given up waiting and come home, when the Watsons came to the back porch.

Larry announced, "Well, Doc, the men have studied on it, and they decided they want you to stay." He conferred this ultimate favor like royalty granting a pardon. "We wouldn't have had none of this trouble if only people would all been willing to settle things man to man. I always say that's the only way to do business."

Bonta nodded, so Larry continued, "Now this time the men had things explained to them right. It's just that nobody spoke about it the right way the other time." He added magnanimously, "After all, Doc has a side in this, too!" As if his outraged sense of justice cried out at the previous hastiness.

Danny, Larry's faithful echo and local sheriff as well as union vice-president, had the gall to warn Bonta that you couldn't trust these men—they'd be friendly to your face and stick you behind your back!

Elton Jamison was on hand, too. "Doc, don't you have no truck with nobody but the officers of the union. You just can't trust nobody else."

The upshot was that the men had finally decided to have lists that each would sign if he wished to pay in after the thirty days were up, and Larry, of all people, would take them around, soliciting signatures! Meantime Bonta was to operate under Vern's contract, which actually was more favorable than our own old one. They'd get these lists circulating in a couple of weeks.

By then a group had gathered by the back fence to watch the proceedings on our little porch. Old Preacher Harrington, still wearing that shapeless hat, had pushed his way onto the bottom step, his gray curls bobbing as he nodded earnestly, not understanding a word. He apparently wanted Bonta to do something for him and was bewildered by the confusion. Eloise did her best to catch the drift from the living room, and kept exchanging glances with me as I tried to work inconspicuously around the kitchen, listening for all I was worth.

Piecing the story together later as reported by Sam Dean and Joe Horvath, I decided the proceedings must have gone something like this. The most vocal against Bonta was, of course, Larry, the president himself, but Elton Jamison contributed his share of criticism. Danny Watson was a little quieter than on earlier occasions, waiting to see which way the wind was blowing. When Larry proposed fining anyone who went to Bonta if he stayed in private practice, Sam Dean got up so hopping mad that he cussed him out. "By God, ain't nobody going to tell me how to spend my money or take care of my family. No sir, by God!"

He was fined for profanity!

Doug Blake talked a lot on Bonta's behalf. Bless those evenings of playing chess and sharing ideas. He and Larry came close to a fight when Larry insisted the original contract was illegal. Doug apparently blew up. "If that ain't legal, I'll kiss your ass at sunrise!"

So he was fined, too.

And Danny, Larry's brother, went so far as to threaten to put both Larry and Doug in jail! Sam said Danny hadn't dared to threaten only Doug, or the whole place would have exploded. Sam said majority opinion clearly gave that round to Doug.

Sam told everyone at the meeting that his grandmother had been near death. Another doctor had said she was so far gone there wasn't any use giving her any more medicine. And now she was up and looking after her own house, all because Bonta took care of her. Bonta said privately it was providential the flu had nearly run its course about the time he saw her. On such chance does fortune hinge! Then Sam introduced a motion that the men who wanted to continue to pay in their three dollars a month to the doctor could sign as individuals on a list Bonta would keep. Apparently there wasn't much hope of persuading the Long Branch contingent to go along with a unionwide contract again. Sam was elated that it was his motion which finally passed.

All the talk about Dan Dubois's responsibility for the mess culminated in a motion by the officers, Larry and company, to have him thrown off the ambulance committee. The men voted Dan right back on the committee. Apparently the majority thought he deserved to keep that responsibility. Though the Watsons accused him of trying to get Bonta ousted, this exchange showed that at least Dan was not identified with their Long Branch coterie.

In any event, Larry's image as leader had been tarnished by this defeat, and he might suffer in the next union election as a result. Glad as I was his balloon had been punctured, it was downright scary to know that he was going to bear a grudge against Bonta as the cause of his difficulties.

We spent a long time sorting out the various versions of what happened. Actually not one thing had changed. At first I'd been sort of euphoric, with all this talk of "our side won." But in fact, the union had graciously consented to let Bonta keep his office and house, which the company had promised him anyway. And they'd allowed him to try out an alternative that had always been available to him if they refused to sign a unionwide contract. After all, the foremen already signed up as individuals, so just extending the same arrangement to the miners themselves was no big deal. So we were still in a muddle.

Until and unless the miners signed up on those lists, Bonta would be in private practice. This meant a change in his relationship with his patients. Now he would have to establish a fee schedule for each service rendered. No longer could patients expect to receive care with no thought for the cost. He also had to decide on the terms of the contract which individuals could make with him if they chose. Should he keep the $3.00 monthly charge, or should he follow Mr. Ramsey's and Dr. Meade's advice and raise it to $3.50? There were so many decisions to be made. We ended the evening perusing medical journals for alternative jobs and residencies.

19. What Now?

On Sunday Bonta was limp after all the tension of the day before, so it was touch and go as to whether he'd make the effort to go to a medical meeting he'd planned to attend in Mullens forty miles away. Susan and I had expected to stay home if he went, but it was such a heavenly day that when he worked up enough ambition by noon to go we decided to go along for the ride, too.

While he went to the hotel, Susan and I window-shopped, admired babies out for an airing, got excited about a school bus, and had ice cream cones, before going back to read in the car till the meeting ended.

Clearly fired up, Bonta returned to report a conversation he'd had with a doctor who was about to quit at Dun Eden in four or six weeks and was looking for a replacement. He planned to go into partnership with a doctor in Welch. Dun Eden was a much bigger operation than Coal Mountain, with over twice as many men on the payroll, and the pay-in was $3.50. Of course, it was a killing pace for one man, but we might be able to find another man, maybe even persuade Bonta's brother-in-law, who was about to start a residency, to come down and work it with Bonta. The company provided an eight-room office and a large steam-heated house, both rent free. Blissful thought! This doctor said it was a large, stable company. In fact, we'd heard Mr. Ramsey say the same himself, and the mine was within hailing distance of Beckley, which would be a big plus. The doctor didn't actually offer Bonta the job—that would be up to the company—but he seemed as enthusiastic as Bonta was.

We'd certainly want to take a look at the place. But my reaction was that it was only one more confusing alternative to throw into our pot. If we felt swamped by the work in Coal Mountain, I couldn't imagine tackling more than twice as much, and what was to say we'd be any more successful at finding another doctor to help than this fellow had been after months of looking? Or that their union would be any easier to deal with than ours?

We stopped on the way back to get gas and look over Doug Blake's new gas station. Bonta chatted with him by the pump.

If I'd had premonitions after the meeting Saturday about the hazards of alienating Larry, Doug confirmed them when he warned Bonta to carry a gun whenever he went down Long Branch way. "You never know!"

✍ Pondering Doug's recent admonition made me wish Bonta would take the advice his father sent him in an airmail special delivery letter (waiting at the post office on Tuesday): "Get out of that hole and come back to civilization!" He told us Bonta's brother-in-law was sure Bonta could get a surgical residency at the hospital where he was in training in New Jersey. What could be more tempting?

Bonta said going to New Jersey would be something of a compromise, since it wasn't as high-powered a program as the one he'd looked forward to at Columbus, so, for the moment at least, I counted that out. Besides, Bonta insisted he didn't want to run away from a fight. By now his depression had disappeared, his normal optimism had returned, and he was demonstrating that he was bigger than the situation.

We were reflecting on that when someone knocked at the back door. Who should it be but Larry! I eavesdropped from Susan's bedroom.

You'd have thought Larry was Bonta's best friend! He was planning to take cards around for the men to sign for this private list. He swore seventy-five percent of them would sign.

"Course you just can't trust everybody. Some of these people will talk nice to you and stab you behind your back." He shook his head at the thought of such insincerity.

"Oh sure, Doug Blake's a good boy, just a hot-tempered young chap. He was actually spoiling for a fight at the first of it when I told the men about how the contract weren't legal, but just soon as I explained it all, he quieted right down. Course I wouldn't respect a man who wouldn't stand up for his rights anyway. Why sure, me and Doug's good buddies."

He finally got around to his reason for coming, which was to get some help for a minor infection. Bonta took him over to the office.

I couldn't resist telling Doug's wife about this little chat later. I simply couldn't believe anyone could lie so glibly. Mrs. Blake was much entertained. Only she gave me the warning that was becoming all too familiar: Bonta should go well armed to Long Branch. Larry sober would probably be all right, but beware of Larry drunk.

While on a house call, Bonta heard some spontaneously proffered stories about the troubles the company'd had ever since it opened Number Nine mine. It seemed there were three fellows continually causing problems. One of them would go over to the lamphouse and say, "Well, boys, let's not work today!" And they'd all dump out their pails and go home. Who but Larry and Danny Watson and Elton Jamison! And Bonta had never so much as breathed a word about their connection with his own difficulties.

After supper we set out for a look at the big mine at Dun Eden, the place Bonta was all excited about. We went by a side road so he could check on a patient on the way. It was some trek. We'd stupidly forgotten our flashlight. We never even thought of bringing the gun; I could hardly picture us with a gun anyway. But we remembered Doug's recent advice as we neared Long Branch.

The road up the side hollow was wicked. We found the house, looking as though no one was home, and Bonta couldn't get to it anyway, what with fences, mud, and cows. Luckily the patient's brother-in-law happened by and reported that she was all right. He promised to tell her the doctor had stopped to check on her.

The roundabout route took forever, and the road was so deserted that it reminded Bonta of his earliest days in camp. He told me once again about how depressed he was when he first arrived, almost to the point of tears: the terrible responsibility, the overwhelming loneliness of it all, and the unnerving isolation. He recalled that twist of fate that had sent the car back in the direction of the camp when he'd been ready to leave or stay, depending on which way he could rock the car out of the muck. I wished there were some way to cheer him up now.

We finally hit the hardtop, vowing never to go that way again, and eventually found Dun Eden. It was a tremendous camp. It looked like a veritable city in the dark. I felt immediately cut down to size by it all and quite inadequate to the challenge. We inquired for the doctor's home and found it was a gorgeous brick mansion high up on a hill.

Luckily the doctor was in. He turned out to be something of a blarney artist, bent on selling the place to Bonta. He showed us his well-equipped office, which was awe inspiring compared with our pitiful setup. But he kept no patient records beyond the reports the hospital sent. He saw over a hundred patients a day and generally worked himself to death. That pace didn't allow much time for the kind of individual attention Bonta felt was important. And with that many people to care for, and hardly any records at all, his encounters with patients must have been pretty impersonal and, I would guess, superficial as well. Maybe his equipment was better, but I sort of swelled up inside with pride because I was sure our people had a better deal.

Suddenly the doctor switched tactics and proposed that if Bonta would join him there he might stay on himself. Two would certainly make the job better for both of them. If only his personality had been a little more congenial and his medical practice standards a little different, it might have been tempting. But to me it just looked like too much confusion. Ours in Coal Mountain was bad enough. It reminded me of that story about the beggar who asked everybody to hang his problem on a line so each could choose the one he wanted to live with, and everyone ended up choosing his own!

Mr. Ramsey's troubles brought him and his wife closer; ours did the same, close as we were to begin with. I wished I could help Bonta make this big decision about the future, but in the last analysis it was up to him. Actually, of course, talking it over, as we seemed to be doing most of the time, was a help in itself. I believe sometimes you're not quite sure of what you think till you put it into words. I was proud of the way Bonta continued about his business, without letting his own problems interfere with getting the job done. He still kidded patients along, still enjoyed Susan's comical conversations, and bore the uncertainties with patience.

Though I objected to the prevailing attitude that women didn't count for much, for the moment it made it easier for me. While Bonta was the focus of all the turmoil, I could easily stay in the background.

My problem was actually very different: finding the energy to keep going. I felt continually queasy and dragged out. This pregnancy was no fun.

Mrs. Ratliff, the patient who had wanted her problem kept confidential, had recently come to the office, and this time I'd stood by while Bonta confirmed that she was indeed pregnant. She told us, "I was sure hoping it was just a false alarm. I don't want this young one— not at my age. And my man's all shook up, too." She looked ready to cry. "You're sure about it?"

Unfortunately, Bonta was sure.

In fact, she and I had essentially the same due date, but she had been experiencing no nausea. Well, I preferred my physical problems and happiness about the pregnancy to her physical well-being and unhappiness. I felt very sorry for her. She even timidly asked if Bonta couldn't do something to terminate the pregnancy and looked utterly despondent when he assured her that that was impossible, sympathetic as he might be.

Larry Watson one day, Elton Jamison the next. He woke us up to ask Bonta to send his father to the hospital. In the kitchen they had another of those incredible conversations, as Elton brought up the matter of the ruptured contract.

"Don't know what them fellows was thinking about. Can't nobody tell me you ain't a good doc. Why, you even been in the navy! If these folks don't know when they're well off, well, that's their tough luck. I know, I do."

He warmed to his subject, waving his long arms about as he put on a show of comradely reminiscence. "Oh, we've had some dillies up here. Why, we had one doctor who was so drunk every evening he couldn't hardly stand up. No, sirree, folks won't find a doc's good as this one again."

Bonta listened to all this in his pajamas and robe, hardly able to keep a straight face, as he got out a slip for the hospital.

Elton bent over the table, squinting at the form Bonta was filling out. "Yes, siree. All this talk about changes. Why, you and me know what medicine costs, by gee, and if the others don't, that's just too bad."

He departed, clutching the piece of paper and nodding self-righteously. If I hadn't heard him with my own ears, I wouldn't have believed it.

❧   Eloise and Eva were doing their best to keep the more dedicated Holinesses away from their mother. These Holinesses kept coming in to pray over her with much stamping of feet, shouting, and wailing and planned to bring the healing rag any day. They talked about people they'd known who had knots in their throat just like the one Mrs. Horvath had in her stomach, and as soon as they were saved, they were good as new.

One of them asked Nan why the family said their visits disturbed their mother. "Why, we've never so much as hinted about what truly ails her!"

Poor Mrs. Horvath required more narcotic every day. You'd think they'd have left her in the peace she wanted and deserved.

Eloise confided to me that the young man she'd gone out with a couple of times only made her more lonesome for Tommy. She finally admitted that she'd actually written Tommy to come get her so they could be married.

I was disappointed. Tommy hadn't done anything I was aware of lately to press his suit, and now she had taken the initiative. As far as I knew, he might not even have a job. I felt sure this was an act born of frustration at being kept here by her mother's illness, simply a way out rather than any mature commitment. Well, the letter had gone, and there was nothing we could do now but wait and see whether Tommy showed up and, if he did, what happened then. Obviously the situation had some worrisome implications for us. Losing Eloise would push us closer toward leaving.

20. Starting Anew

My mother was due to arrive in Williamson on Monday, April 24. Being true to form, I started the day by losing my breakfast. I had every reason to expect that this phase would be a thing of the past in a few weeks. Bonta insisted that I take a short nap after lunch, knowing how much I needed it. It was becoming increasingly difficult to resist Eloise's offer to go to the office in my place. However, so far I had managed to keep my promise to myself to stick with it, no matter what.

Luckily I felt better by midmorning, buoyed by the thought of Mother's arrival shortly after noon. So I set off with Susan to meet the train and even felt fairly comfortable about taking the car. It was a glorious spring morning, and I actually enjoyed the trip in spite of a number of stops for Susan: for something to keep the sun out of her eyes, for a drink of milk, for fixing the car bed which kept falling apart, etc. I even had time to do a little needed shopping at the A & P before the train arrived.

Heartfelt hugs and kisses over, Mother and I began a marathon exchange of news. The sixty-mile trip back over twisting roads seemed to take no time at all, though I detected some apprehension on Mother's part, as she tried to help me brake on the curves. She enjoyed Susan's jabbering even if she didn't understand much of it; eight months had wrought a lot of change in her only grandchild.

The signs of spring enchanted us at every turn, the delicate green of new leaves like a gauzy veil on the mountains, the redbud and the dogwood like bright exclamation points. Mother was especially appreciative because spring was so much more advanced here than it was in New York. All my concerns about the future slipped away in the enjoyment of the moment.

I waited with news of my pregnancy till Bonta could share in the telling. Mother was happy for us, but just as I had anticipated, she began to talk about the advisability of my coming home to have the baby. It was not like Mother to try to interfere in the decisions of her children, but I think she was jolted by the ride down here and the isolation of the place. I still had no intention of leaving Coal Mountain to have the baby. I'd seen plenty of babies born right here with no big fuss, and I didn't see why our baby had to be any different.

Mother was interested in Bonta's report to us both on his meeting that morning with company and union officials to discuss setting up those individual contracts between the men and the doctor. Bonta and Randall explained to the union officers that with individual contracts in place the union as such would have nothing to do with the matter any longer; their medical and grievance committees would be irrelevant.

It took them an eternity to catch onto the fact that it wasn't possible to deal individually and as a group at the same time. I guess Bonta clinched it when he said the union wasn't involved when a particular miner owed Sears a bill. Anyway the light gradually dawned on Elton Jamison, and then one by one they began to comprehend. They were so horrified to think they would no longer have a finger in the pie that they decided the whole matter had better be reconsidered. Would we get a unionwide contract after all? They planned to call another meeting to digest this new insight.

We showed Mother around the camp: the office, the road up to the mine and the tipple, the lumber camp, and the strip mine road, which was by now so undermined by cave-ins we could hardly drive on it at all. We told her she'd seen all the things Mary had seen, and we were very glad she had no plans to write an article about the place.

She was never one to stay long away from Father, and sure enough, in spite of the distance she'd come to get here, she insisted on heading back home on the early afternoon train Wednesday, barely forty-eight hours after she arrived. So Susan and I took her to Williamson and saw her safely on her way, but not before she had quite a lot to say about how we "ought to leave that rugged, godforsaken spot, and the sooner the better."

Bonta and I spent the evening discussing strategies for the future, spurred in part by Mother's injunctions to leave and more by speculation on how things might work out at the next union meeting. Before going to bed, we wrote for an application for that surgical residency in New Jersey, available in July, which Bonta's father had urged us to explore. At least it might give us the option of leaving if we decided we wanted to.

❧ Saturday brought yet another momentous union meeting to decide our fate. We were a little cocky about the likelihood of their asking for a new unionwide contract, a little too cocky, as it turned out.

After lunch Mr. Kilmer came in to see whether Bonta would inspect everyone for crabs in the bathhouse and informed him that everything had gone just as he, Kilmer, had said it would—smooth as could be. They'd voted to continue individual contracts. Mr. Kilmer reported this as though he had been responsible for seeing that exactly what the doctor wanted had been done. I decided he honestly didn't understand the difference between a unionwide contract and individual agreements. He seemed to think they'd instituted a dramatic new policy.

Doug Blake later told Bonta that there were too many Long Branchers there again, and to avoid further trouble, Bonta's supporters had let things stand. He said the Watson crew had packed the meeting again, and I guess our friends had been a little too complacent.

With that disappointing news, a change of scenery seemed in order, so we set out for Pineville. There we bumped into a carful of Coal Mountain neighbors, Barney among them. He confided that he was getting out, going to look for another job far away from West Virginia.

He said glumly, "I'm plumb fed up with everything. Mr. Ramsey's out of the picture, and you and I know he was our best friend. Me, I'm on the wrong side of the fence in the union." He ended with utter disgust. "Anyway, I hate Coal Mountain!"

That triggered Bonta's urge to wash his hands of it all, too, and he said to me impulsively, "Let's just drive over to Dun Eden to see what it's really like—you couldn't be sure from our look at it in the dark."

By daylight the camp was most depressing, crowded, frighteningly big, and full of dingy houses. Luckily we found the doctor. He was no longer so sure of leaving, and we learned that before we could come the company would have to build a house for us. As far as I was concerned, that ended consideration of Dun Eden.

❧   What a queer new feeling—we were in private practice all of a sudden! I had to admit it changed my attitude toward the people waiting outside the office Monday morning. All at once we were anxious for patients. The transition made me vividly aware of the difference in incentives in private versus prepaid medical practice. Before this Bonta had been able to concentrate on his patients without any thought of money. Patients' problems, not what to charge them, were the whole focus. Now suddenly patients and income had become synonymous— no patients, no income. The shift made us realize how ephemeral was the security we thought we'd had under the union contract. It had seemed such a comfortable financial situation.

We had to explain to each one who came in that the union contract no longer covered their care so we had to charge private patient fees; a single office visit now cost more than their former monthly withholding charge. Of course, if they'd rather, they could make an individual agreement with the doctor, under the same provisions that were in the old union contract. The company office was keeping a list of those who wanted to continue the monthly withholding.

To no one's surprise all who came in immediately decided to visit the company office to sign up before asking Bonta to see them. The problem was that there were certain families who continually needed care, and we could afford to give it to them only if those families we never saw also paid in their three dollars. That's how insurance works. But those who never needed help were hardly likely to drop in to sign up.

Eloise brought us up-to-date on her romances when she came in after lunch. She sat down at the kitchen table, rested her chin in both hands, and began, "You know that engineer you talked to me about? Well, he asked me for a date a couple days ago."

My hopes soared, only to be dashed as she continued, "Course I told him no, I'm engaged."

Why hadn't he asked her before she wrote to Tommy to come get her?

"But then I bumped into him at the beer joint last night, and he asked me again. I been thinking about it, and I told him maybe."

"Well, good," I said encouragingly. "It can't hurt to get to know him a little."

"Maybe not. Anyways, I wrote Tommy and told him not to come right now. I don't feel like getting married this weekend after all. I don't know why really, but I just think it'd be too soon."

That was a relief, but this casual way of planning and canceling a wedding left me almost speechless.

"You know, I'm scared of Jerry. He's so old and so big." She thought a minute and added dreamily, "But he sure does have the most beautiful brown eyes."

She looked at me out of the corner of her eye, and I couldn't tell whether she was teasing, saying this for my benefit, or whether she meant it. Only time would tell, but at least now there was a little time.

I showed Eloise my latest project. I'd found a lovely little backwater with great masses of frogs' eggs and brought home a cluster of them in a bowl. I'd been having fun showing Susan how they develop.

I always took my embryology classes to nearby marshes on egg-collecting expeditions. To me nothing symbolizes spring so much as spring peepers calling to each other, and in spite of being (having been?) a scientist, or perhaps because of it, I never cease to wonder at the way a frog's egg develops into a frog. Who would ever have thought to stick a tadpole stage in between! And what a miracle that two eggs that look alike, a frog's and a toad's, know enough to turn out differently!

I wanted to pass along a little of that excitement, that sense of mystery, to Susan, and the sooner the better. Of course, I was really doing this as much for me as for her. Anyway the tadpoles grew fat and leggy on the stuff I scavenged, and Susan was enchanted. I felt sure the neighbors would think it all very peculiar. Eloise was tolerantly amused.

When Susan and I went up to the tipple to take pictures, we found seven or eight different kinds of flowers right by the roadside—gold, pink, pale yellow—each one a prize. The sun was shining, the air was fresh and fragrant with the smells of spring, and nearby a phoebe was plaintively calling its name over and over. Film could capture only the smallest part of this tranquillity, but I did my best to preserve it. I let Susan pick a few of the blossoms. She clutched them tightly as we headed for the office so Daddy could smell them, too.

Tuesday's mail brought Eloise a letter from Tommy saying he would arrive on Friday afternoon. He hadn't yet received hers, telling him not to come. Things couldn't have been more confusing, and Eloise was frantic, shifting emotionally from one scenario to another. I hoped she wouldn't do anything irrevocable before she figured out what she wanted!

A few men came to the office in the afternoon just to tell Bonta they wanted to sign up, which was encouraging. Intriguingly enough, Larry showed up, having already signed in the company office.

He told Bonta, "You just can't figure out what these men do want."

And Mrs. Abe Lincoln Davis appeared, too, to settle an old bill of fourteen dollars, incurred because the Davises were private patients. "Well, you never know when the Lord might take you, and I just like to have things straightened out. We sold a cow the other day, and I said to Abe, I said, 'I believe I'll just get this off my mind.'"

I was incredulous when I learned she and Abe had actually walked all the way from Road Branch into camp. Abe's condition must have improved considerably since our last encounter. I wouldn't have tried that myself.

Bonta settled the bill for half the amount, and Mrs. Davis left with a fervent, "God bless you!"

A letter from Bonta's mother came in the afternoon mail, pleading with us to take the residency in New Jersey. We seemed to be the only ones who thought it might still be worthwhile to stay. Bonta was weighing all the alternatives. Should he hold out for a topflight residency, take the less prestigious one, find another coal camp job, stay here in private practice, stay here with a list of miners paying in independently, or stay, counting on a unionwide contract. I certainly wished he could set his priorities in order. As soon as I adjusted to one alternative, I'd find that another one had just come into favor.

On Wednesday it finally happened. Eloise had a date with Jerry. "He ain't as scary as I thought."

"How nice you finally agreed to go out with him," I said.

"Oh, I didn't agree. I got tricked into it. Nan had a date with Hank to go to the movies, and they asked me to come along. Then they stopped the car at the clubhouse to pick up Jerry. I was so mad. I told them to drive on, but they said they couldn't just leave him standing there. So I said I'd go sit in the back where the car was all dirty from the miners so Jerry wouldn't get his good clothes all dirty. And then he piled in back, too.

"We stopped at the beer joint for a coke, and Jerry said he wanted to go on to the drive-in. Then Hank was afraid his car wouldn't go that far, so if he didn't drive us back and get Jerry's car. And then he and Nan decided they didn't want to go to a movie after all, so Jerry and me ended up going alone.

"I'm scared to death somebody'll tell Tommy I was out with him. I tried to hide my face so nobody'd see me, but it didn't do no good. Jerry asked me who I was hiding from, and I said nobody—my head just hurt."

"But you did have a good time, once things settled down?"

"Oh, it could have been worse," was the best I could get from her.

We decided our occasional but calculated comments to Jerry about Eloise's virtues must have fallen on fertile ground. At least he was persisting in spite of the lack of encouragement.

After the first day of explaining the private fees and the alternative of signing up, we got tired of going through it all, so we posted a sign outside the office, briefly outlining the situation. We watched people come to the office door, stop and look over the sign, and then make a beeline for the company office before returning to the waiting room. We smiled every time it happened. It didn't take long for them to realize how much better off they'd been before.

The company finally made an effort to solicit signatures, too. Randall went over to the lamphouse to get the men back on the list. In all, about half of them signed up. That helped.

But we were thinking about that New Jersey residency a little more positively, perhaps swayed by both our families pleading with us to "come home!" And certainly by my advancing pregnancy. I had a few disturbing contractions reminiscent of the problems that sent me to bed for two months when I was pregnant with Susan.

Bonta, too, finally gave up on Dun Eden when Jerry told him it was a rough place where tempers flared at the slightest provocation and knifings were an everyday occurrence. He said it was a dangerous mine—that men working there were frequently injured.

The pit committee* called on Bonta once again to make arrangements for him to check the men for crabs. He explained that now that he was in private practice his obligation was to those who had signed up to be his patients, not to the union, and while he would be glad to accommodate them, they'd have to pay for it. This set them back a bit, but there wasn't much they could do but agree.

Just before going to bed Thursday night we looked out the back door to check on the sudden storm, high winds, heavy rain, and violent thunder and lightning. As if that weren't exciting enough, we discovered dark smoke billowing from the lamphouse, with angry red sparks shooting up from below, tinting the clouds crimson. Bonta thought it looked like an electrical fire of some sort. We grabbed an umbrella and a flashlight and ran over to investigate.

The roar of the blaze was frightening, and a crowd of onlookers quickly gathered. Several of the men still wearing their miners' lamps tilted their heads to direct the beams up at the roof of the building. Then someone turned off the current from the mine. The sparks subsided, the roar ceased—Bonta was right. The excitement was suddenly over. Tim, the electrician, was on hand to oversee the situation. He reported that the two men in the shower might have been electrocuted, had they touched the metal wall. No one was hurt, however, and the crowd gradually dispersed in the lessening rain.

We heard later that the doctor had been called to revive half a dozen men.

꙰ The weekend came and went without Tommy, giving Eloise a little time to sort out her feelings.

Somehow the whole atmosphere around the camp gradually

*A union committee to oversee working conditions

changed. People began to take it for granted that we were still around, still taking care of them. We no longer heard those disconcerting rumors about what might happen, because the worst had happened. The odd thing was that nothing had really changed, except that we felt better about our situation. With our dignity intact, we had survived the worst the Watsons could do and hadn't given in to any unreasonable demands. Bonta felt he was now independent, not beholden to anyone, and free to do what his own best judgment dictated. Those who came to the office came because they wanted to, not because the union said they must. So we enjoyed a real sense of emancipation. Free enterprise was rather neat after all. As to staying or leaving, at least we had the satisfaction of making our own choice.

Afternoons were always busy. On Tuesday Bert Teller came in from the clubhouse. He called me by name, an event so unheard of that it deserves mentioning. His urinary bleeding had been attended to properly at the hospital to which Bonta had referred him, but now he had a bad case of cellulitis* in his hand. He had no idea where he picked up the nasty infection. Bonta soaked his hand in hot water, and the heat and the moisture made it open up and drain, which was what Bonta wanted. It looked ghastly. Bert himself didn't look much better. After Bonta cleaned his hand, bandaged it, and gave him a shot of penicillin, he asked Bert if there were anything else he could do for him.

Bert said forlornly, "If this don't get better soon, you can read the last words over me, Doc."

That evening Doug Blake came by to challenge Bonta again at chess. Even though he had to open his gas station early the next morning, the conversation went on till nearly midnight. He told us in some detail about an invention he hoped would pay off in the mines, and it did sound promising.

✎ Thursday, May 11, was a beautiful spring day. While I hung out the laundry some youngsters came up the road with their arms full of gorgeous golden azaleas. They stopped to give Susan a branch. When I asked where they'd found them, they said they grew up on

*An infection causing inflammation to spread through the tissues beneath the skin

the slope just above the railroad tracks and insisted on my keeping half of them.

The day brought some very personal excitement—the baby quickened! It certainly made the little guy or gal seem much more real. And it made me feel even more of an obligation to take the best possible care of it.

That development precipitated another discussion about alternatives, which ended with our mailing an application for that New Jersey residency, though neither one of us was wholly pleased with the prospect. By then the company had signed up most of the men, and there was even a rumor going the rounds that there would be a big blowup at the next union meeting to replace the present slate of officers. If it ever came to pass, it could mean renegotiating our whole relationship.

There had been few deliveries lately, so Bonta had had a chance to relax a bit, read journals, and play those chess games with either Doug or Jerry of an evening.

Eloise and I managed to do quite a bit of sewing together. While we were cutting out a dress for Susan after office hours, Mrs. Bannister came over just for a visit. Before she left, she asked if she could borrow the pattern when we were through.

"Been wanting to crochet Susan a little dress for the longest time. I got some light blue yarn would look real pretty on her."

It was gratifying to realize that she had continued in reasonably good health. Bonta hadn't been called up the road to see her for weeks.

% The following Monday I saw Jerry heading up the back way toward the green camp and wondered whether he had a date with Eloise. Tommy never even wrote after receiving Eloise's letter telling him not to come after all. I thought if he really cared he'd have rushed back to see why she'd changed her mind. I hoped she'd stop pinning her hopes on him.

I couldn't visualize her in some little house up a hollow, even as sparkling clean as she'd make it, bringing up a raft of kids with easy-going Tommy sitting around doing nothing much. He didn't act as though he even appreciated her adequately.

Of course, we had no guarantee that Jerry was the right man for her either, but he certainly offered more of a future than Tommy did. He had that degree in engineering from Morgantown. Bonta had found him good company when they shared those long conversations and exciting chess matches. He was tall, well built, and the only possible flaw in his appearance that Eloise could point out was his thinning hair, hardly a significant deficiency. Granted, he was five years older, but his maturity could be a real plus for her.

We only hoped we'd be around for the end of the story. We wanted whichever outcome would make her happy in the long run.

A week later we were stricken by Luke Hutchinson's disastrous accident. The office had been crowded all that steamy, hot day, and the interruptions were incessant. At five o'clock Bonta was about to close the door and start on house calls when one of the men came tearing in all out of breath. "Doc, you got to come up to the tipple quick—looks as though Luke's cut his feet." I heard them end the sentence with "off," but apparently Bonta didn't and was hardly prepared for what he found. He left for the tipple right away, but I was amazed to hear him say with some annoyance as he walked out, "There are times when I could cry!" If ever there was a real emergency, this sounded like one to me.

At least he got there promptly. Luke was still up on the tracks, with both feet horribly mangled, one stripped from the ankle down with the whole anterior half hanging by a few tendons. Bonta finished the amputation with his jackknife! The other foot was half missing, twisted over to one side and crushed.

The men had been told never to jump on the front end of a moving car—always the rear end. But Luke took a chance, slipped, and fell. One foot was crushed under a wheel, and in trying to kick that one loose, the other one was caught under the oncoming wheel. I had no desire to see the result.

Bonta gave Luke a huge dose of Demerol, sent back for gauze dressings, put on tourniquets, and sent him off to the hospital with Barney. The ambulance had left earlier with another patient. Luke's brother went with them. I could tell when they left, because a mob, both children and grown-ups, came streaming back from that direction and up the back road. A carnival couldn't have attracted more onlookers. Bonta went down the hollow to talk to Luke's mother about his condition.

Barney told us later that he made the forty-five miles in something like forty-seven minutes, curves and all! It was a miracle they weren't all three killed. By then the bleeding had nearly stopped, and, still numb from shock, Luke was not in as much pain as one might expect. The doctors there talked over the situation with him and persuaded him that amputation of both feet at the ankle would be the best thing to do in preparation for prostheses. They promised him he'd soon be walking on new feet!

Barney said, "My own feet been hurting ever since. And I'll never eat hamburger again long as I live."

The whole camp was subdued by the tragedy.

     Harry, Luke's brother, told Bonta a couple of days later that Luke's morale was really good, and the family was feeling more hopeful about his future than they thought possible at the time of the accident. Good prostheses could accomplish a near miracle for him.

Eloise reported that Jerry had come up the night before while they were doing some repainting, and she had closeted herself in the back room with a paintbrush. He barged in bravely and sat around quite a while while she tried to work. "You know, you can't do a thing when somebody's watching!"

She claimed to be quite annoyed by it all, but I didn't really believe her. I kidded her about how lucky it was I'd had her do all that cooking. "Yes, it'll be good for Tommy or Jerry, one—aw, shoot!" she added, wallowing in indecision. ("Aw, shoot" had spontaneously replaced "Aw, shit" quite some time ago.)

I could hardly understand such a problem, but of course the two men did represent two very different futures, and the one with Jerry was the less familiar. She suggested we leave all our household furnishings if we left so then she and either Tommy or Jerry could move right in.

Bonta had a long talk with her about the relative prospects of the two, urging her to think very carefully before she did anything she couldn't undo. They even talked about the possibility of her going to college. Jerry, too, had encouraged her to consider that. More power to him. Well, we'd probably butted our noses in too much already in our role as Pygmalion.

That night Susan gave the scraps from her dinner plate to Friendly Doggie again, a ritual that had become something of a habit. This friendly pup had become an institution a month earlier when he wandered in the back gate and we offered him a bone. Needless to say, he became even more friendly. Now he'd caught on to her going out the front door and walking around the house, to avoid being knocked over as she opened the back door. So, much to her astonishment, this time he met her on the front porch before she took a step.

21. Harmony at Last

The office was busy all through May, and the few men who hadn't yet signed up immediately did so, once they needed Bonta's help. Bonta was a little smug about the fact that one miner who had loudly declared he'd never sign up finally needed his services. Then he couldn't wait to sign. This miner, Charlie, came in sporting two black eyes and several lacerations and claimed he was beaten up in bed while he slept.

Jerry gave us a fuller version of the incident. The fellow had gone down to the beer joint after it closed, but the woman who ran it invited him in anyway to have a cup of coffee with her. Her husband came home a little later and found him there. He was so mad he fired a couple shots as the guy started to leave. Charlie leaped out the nearest window, and the husband chased him all the way home and gave him a beating he wouldn't forget right away.

Eloise told us that he'd been so battered he spent the next two days in bed. It sounded as though she had the correct story, though, when she added, "Oh, he been in bed all right when he got beat up, only it wasn't his bed!"

Her sisters and some of the neighbors teased Eloise, she said, about going out with Jerry. Eloise scoffed, "Oh Poo, you're just jealous," but their remarks about being seen with someone "so old" obviously did undermine Jerry's cause. However, she didn't cancel another date, so perhaps all was not yet lost.

One day while checking insurance claims I found one which so intrigued me that I showed it to Bonta. It was a report one of the miners had brought in for the Compensation Commission. It spelled out in a neat but labored hand, "Caught finger in conveyer belt. Bursted end of left forefinger. Nail and meat come off."

On Thursday, May 25, Mrs. Doug Blake brought us a message from the company office directing us to call the New Jersey hospital. We went over feeling both excited and anxious, knowing it must mean at least some progress toward acceptance and wondering every step of the way whether that was what we really wanted or not. I myself would have been just as happy if it fell through, now that things seemed to be on an even keel again.

As leaving became more probable, I began to appreciate more and more all that Coal Mountain offered me: the satisfactions of our working partnership, our friendship with Eloise and her family, the mountains, flowers, brooks, even the frogs to enjoy and share with Bonta and Susan. It's ironic that only as we are about to lose something do we start truly valuing it as we should have valued it all along.

Of course, I reminded myself that there were times when I hated the place with a passion, when patients pursued Bonta so relentlessly he was exhausted, when the union gave us grief, when the roads were muddy and dangerous, when the coal exploded! But somehow right then, with things so pleasant, the days so beautiful, I wasn't sure we should change anything.

I began to think about life as a resident's wife; that would be no unalloyed bliss either. Bonta would be home only every other night at best, no doubt just as exhausted as he had been so often in Coal Mountain. And we'd be living in separate worlds again. Being together for the birth of the baby was the one big advantage. And Bonta would feel better about the medical care I'd have, not that I wanted to take any foolish chances with the baby's welfare myself. More fundamental still, this would be the first step toward that specialty he wanted, for which the whole year had been preparation. I determined to work up some enthusiasm if the move really came to pass.

The phone call was a request for a personal interview. Bonta said that would be impossible because of the distance and his lack of time. This probably also reflected his own ambivalence about the appointment. He still yearned for the residency at Columbus and still debated the advantage of a second year in the coal camp to make that possible. When the director indicated he could make his decision without an interview, I felt he'd probably offer it to Bonta, and we'd be leaving.

✎ We played matchmaker Friday night. Eloise had offered to give me a much-needed permanent, and we'd agreed that Friday would be a good time. Then Jerry asked her for a date that evening. She told him she couldn't go because she had to fix my hair, even though she knew very well that any other time would have been equally accept-able to me. That was just an excuse. Then Jerry asked her if he could come over and watch. It didn't occur to either of them that I might be a reluctant subject, and the two of them agreed that he could show up at our house about the time she was expected.

Sure enough, I'd just rinsed my hair when Eloise came in the back door and Jerry knocked at the front.

Eloise acted as though she hadn't noticed his arrival. She established herself in the kitchen with me, while Bonta entertained Jerry in the living room.

Eloise wound my hair on curlers, chattering on about camp gossip. "Alison's got herself a good new job in the company office. She thinks she's so smart. She's acting real stuck-up."

She told me about the excitement two houses down from theirs in the green camp. "They shot two copperheads yesterday evening. Fred Blankenship saw one of them while he was working in his garden. Six feet long, he said! Him and Harvey Burgess went out after it with their guns. They was turning over rocks everywheres looking for it. They figure they found the nest, 'cause they was two of them in it. The other one was eight feet long!" She shuddered. "They shot them both."

Meantime Bonta and Jerry had started another of their chess battles. Jerry gamely pretended it didn't matter that Eloise was in the kitchen ignoring him. This evening the talk turned to music. Jerry told Bonta he tolerated Tchaikovsky, loved Bach and Mozart, and listened to records every weekend at home.

"Can't find anything worth hearing on the radio—that's for sure," he complained.

When I paraded through the living room to get some conditioner from the bathroom, Jerry couldn't hide his amusement at my appearance. I didn't blame him. I wrapped a towel over the curlers and sat on the arm of Bonta's chair for a few minutes to see how the game was going and to make it easy for Eloise to join the group. Jerry looked expectantly toward the kitchen now and again, but she never emerged. She apparently busied herself straightening things up out there, humming to herself as though perfectly content.

I gave up waiting for her and returned to continue with the permanent. Eloise informed me that I was the talk of Coal Mountain. "They're real surprised to see you in that shape."

Weren't doctors supposed to have children?

"Mrs. Staton, she asked me if it was true, and I told her it was. She said she knowed it all along, 'cause way back when the doctor caught her baby he said he'd have to order one for himself."

Imagine Mrs. Staton taking that joking remark seriously and remembering it all this time. It was made a good two months before we decided another baby would be welcome. You never knew which words would take root.

"Alison told me like it was big news that Mrs. Ratliff's pregnant, too. I didn't tell her course I've knowed it for weeks. Now her boy Braden's so mad he can't hardly stand it. She'll make him look after the baby just like he was a girl. And Pete Ratliff sure ain't happy about it neither."

On a more serious note, Eloise told me she had to give her mother ever more frequent hypos to keep her comfortable. She was still badly torn between feeling sad and frightened by her mother's worsening state and resentment at the claim it made on her.

Bonta and Jerry fought it out over the chessboard, and I guess Bonta finally won about the time I went in to report that the permanent was finished.

Jerry strode into the kitchen and gallantly thanked Eloise for the date. She tossed her head, muttering "Humph!," but she did let him put her sweater around her shoulders, and they did walk out together.

Bonta and I looked at each other, shook our heads, and burst out laughing. "Well, that was a big fizzle!" Bonta said. "We may have corralled them under one roof, but it didn't advance our project very much. I wondered if Eloise was ever going to speak to him. Jerry has the patience of a saint. But I guess he'll need it if he's going to take on that woman!"

On Sunday Bonta made time after lunch to accept Mrs. Clay Morgan's long-standing invitation to come down and show Susan their baby chicks and the geese that had laid the eggs she'd sent us. The three youngest girls were running around the yard in nothing but panties. It was so hot I was tempted to let Susan do likewise. Mrs. Morgan was pregnant again, just a little further along than I was, in fact. That diaphragm never did come out of the bureau drawer in time to do its job. This would make her ninth, and for her sake, I did hope it would be the boy her husband wanted so badly.

She sent one of the older girls "to bring the geese up from the bottom," but finally had to go herself. She caught a couple goslings and then had no trouble persuading the geese to follow her back, vigorously hissing their objection to the kidnapping. The adults were formidable, but we fended them off while Susan held one of the fluffy goslings, awestruck by the responsibility. I was relieved when we returned them to their parents, who hastened back toward "the bottom," mollified.

We adjourned to the chicken yard where a little procession of ducklings trailed behind a large and anxious hen. Clearly the adoption was mutually agreeable. In their hatchery the Morgans had about a hundred two-week-old chicks, and the children transfixed Susan by picking them up and letting them flutter down over and over.

Luckily we had brought the camera. Bonta took pictures not only of the children and livestock but of both of us pregnant women. Mrs. Morgan and I compared notes on due dates and wished each other luck.

Later in the afternoon Eloise came by for more medicine for her mother. She said she figured it was safe to knock because I hadn't hung out the flag we'd agreed would signal a disastrous outcome to the permanent. On the contrary, the results were most gratifying.

She reported on the rest of her date with Jerry. "Oh, I had a pretty good time. When I'm with him, it's never as bad as I expect it's going to be. We drove around in his car. Uh huh, we was out until after twelve." She smiled a private smile.

As she turned to leave, she added, "You know them snakes. They wasn't that big. When they measured them, they was more like a foot and a half, maybe two."

I guess they were just as poisonous, whatever their yardage.

✌︎ It was a good thing we both had a good night's sleep that Sunday night, because it would be the last for some time. Eloise came to the office Monday afternoon with a specimen carefully wrapped in a tissue. Placing it on Bonta's desk, she asked, "Could this be a bedbug?"

As neither of us had ever seen one, we didn't know.

"Well, it come off your bed!"

A frantic search of Bonta's parasitology book revealed the awful truth: yes, it was a bedbug! I prayed it was a lonely visitor and dashed home to investigate. As I tore the bed apart and checked the frame and springs, I discovered to my horror that these were not casual invaders but well-entrenched members of the household, and heaven only knows how long they'd been there without our knowledge. Distressing, humiliating, embarrassing!

While I continued to work on the bed, Eloise went to the store for some Black Flag. She lied gallantly to the clerk, "They got some ants over to the doctor's house."

When Bonta came home, he brought the parasitology book, but we found our best information on the creature's habits in the plain ordinary dictionary. We saturated the place with Black Flag, alternately laughing at ourselves and feeling embarrassed.

Eloise kindly insisted they lived in all these old walls and many of the houses were riddled, which was patently absurd. After all, the camp was built only seven years earlier, and bedbugs lived on blood, not wood! Obviously Bonta picked them up somewhere when he was trying to catch forty winks waiting for some woman to deliver, but I should have found them before this. It was too plebeian to have an infestation of bedbugs. Cockroaches would even have been more forgivable. I rather thought Eloise secretly enjoyed our discomfiture. At least she thought it was funny. She told me quietly it took them about three or four days once to get rid of them, but when Bonta asked her a few minutes later how long, she casually changed this to three or four weeks and clearly enjoyed his crestfallen look without offering to alter her statement.

ᴥ How right I was about sleep. Inspection had revealed heretofore unnoticed little red spots on our shoulders where we'd been bitten. There was very little rest as we tossed and turned, wondering what might still be sleeping with us. I lay there imagining bedbugs all over the place, and in the morning I found a baby bug on my side of the bed, bloody, too, when squashed! Morning brought a frantic session of washing clothes, blankets, sheets, and stripping Susan's bed and vacuuming that, too. Luckily no more showed up.

We received a letter from Bonta's parents, saying they were planning to come down for a quick visit. I trusted the bugs would be long gone by then. I could imagine few things worse than admitting to my fastidious mother-in-law that we'd had bedbugs! If she knew, she'd never come.

On Thursday, June 1, the afternoon mail brought confirmation of Bonta's appointment to that residency. I felt a little like flotsam being swept first in and then out by the waves on the beach. I was honestly a bit numb about it all. And Bonta was certainly not enthusiastic. In fact, he said he'd take a day or two to think it over before he signed the contract.

That evening proved distinctly unpleasant for Bonta. We were just about to sit down to a fried chicken dinner which Eloise had fixed when a burly, rough-looking character showed up at the back door. In a peremptory tone he demanded to see the doctor, and when I asked what the problem was, he growled, "He got to come down to my house."

From his enigmatic remarks Bonta finally figured out that his wife was in pain but never could get any information about why. The fellow was exasperated at Bonta's stupidity in having to ask where he lived. "Way down beyond Long Branch, at Reedy and across the creek from Ronnie Witt." Muttering a surly, "And hurry up," he turned on his heel and left.

Bonta was none too happy at the prospect of spending the night in the same house with this character, since he assumed that the woman must be in labor. But he had no choice. He did take time to gulp down some dinner before leaving.

While he ate, he stewed about whether or not he should take that gun along as he'd been advised to do when going near Long Branch. Alien gesture though it might be, it was nevertheless a nerve-tingling prospect.

"What do you think? This fellow sounds mighty unpleasant, so maybe it's only sensible to take it." He started on his pie. "Of course, the idea was protection against Larry, not against anybody else."

He vacillated all through the meal. But as he finally set his empty coffee cup down, he stood up, threw his shoulders back decisively, and said, "Well, damn it anyway," and slipped the gun into his hip pocket. "It can't do any harm, and who knows? It might do some good."

As he left, I didn't know whether to be glad he'd taken it or alarmed because of the implications. I knew I'd be uneasy till he returned.

He startled me out of a light sleep at 2:00 A.M. by coming in with the emphatic announcement, "My God, that was one uncomfortable evening! Almost makes me ready to sign that New Jersey contract."

As he undressed he explained. "That guy really made me apprehensive. He spent the whole night just rocking on the front porch. Looked really belligerent. You know how he sounded when he came to get me. He only stopped rocking when he had to get another pack of cigarettes. Then, cussing to himself, he'd come into the house, glare at me, and stomp past his rifle which stood right there by the door."

"Whatever was he so mad about?"

"Why, I guess they both thought I ought to fix things up so she could have this baby without working at it—no effort—no pain. But when I'd try to help her out with a shot, she'd whine and push the needle away. Talk about a crybaby!"

"Sounds miserable. And you were all alone with her?"

He finished buttoning his pajamas and went into the bathroom, calling out, "No, luckily a neighbor lady was there—had been there most of the day, I gathered. She was a big help. It was one of those places with no light but a kerosene lamp. Lucky my flashlight batteries were fresh."

I thought of the time I'd held the flashlight for him for Tildie.

"At one point I asked the guy to help me out by blowing up the Kelly's pad for me, but he just grunted and shook his head. I was really disgusted. Needless to say, after it was all over, the neighbor lady and I cleaned things up alone. And he never even got out of his chair to say good-bye. We left together. She said she'd never go through another experience like that as long as she lived. And I can tell you, I felt the same way."

"Well, it must have been kind of reassuring to have that gun in your pocket," I suggested.

He came back to the bedroom shaking his head. "No, surprisingly enough, it didn't feel right at all. Guns and delivering babies just don't mix. No, I'm not built to use a gun—except for target practice. And I'm not going to carry it again." He sounded so worked up that I wondered if he'd ever get to sleep. "Sure, the guy was mean and scary, but guns aren't my style and don't fit my business."

As he fell into bed, he added, "Oh, I have to admit to feeling a certain sense of power. But you know, I felt as though I were acting in a grade B movie. I'd feel that hard lump in my pocket and think I ought to be swaggering through the swinging doors of some saloon!" He switched off the light. "But that's not me. No, you can say all you want, but even if I needed to use it, I just couldn't."

We spent Friday evening soul-searching about the best thing to do with the contract for the residency. We had been able to save what seemed to us like a fairly large sum of money, and this residency would pay at least something to stretch our nest egg. That disturbing delivery was a reminder that, in spite of our recent pleasure in the place, Coal Mountain did have a dark side that couldn't be ignored. Things were comfortable enough at the moment, but who knew when the next crisis would blow up?

After one last look at all the options and all the pros and cons, we finally decided to accept the offer. That meant we'd have to let Dr. Meade know our intentions right away. The time was already too short.

So in spite of a full waiting room Saturday morning, we managed to leave for Williamson by noon to tell Dr. Meade we were going.

It was a rather silent trip. Bonta was still stewing. I was still thinking about how beautiful this country was, how I hated to leave just yet. I never expected to drive those twelve miles of dirt road wishing it wouldn't be so soon before I'd be going over them for the last time! Of course, Bonta hadn't signed the contract nor sent a telegram of acceptance yet. He reminded me that the residency program was such that we'd probably have to shift to a different one in a year or two.

We stopped on the way for a picnic at our favorite spot where we were surrounded by the mountains. We had come to love them in all their moods. Mist-enshrouded they tantalized us with their secrets; festive with spring finery, their green slopes bedecked with flowering trees, they lifted our spirits; wrathful in a summer thunderstorm they filled us with awe. That afternoon they were serene under a few fluffy white clouds lazing above their peaks, deepening the blue of the sky. The birds sang all around us, while the wind toyed with the leaves of the tree overhead. I thought regretfully of exchanging all this for a crowded city in New Jersey, acres of concrete, thousands of strange faces, and no access to open spaces.

Dr. Meade thought we were crazy to be leaving. "You ought to stay at least another year, preferably five. Then you could leave with a real grubstake."

He didn't seem too upset, since he happened to know a young doctor who might be interested. It was finally agreed that unless Bonta called him to the contrary he could talk to this young man the following week about taking over.

The trip home provided a nostalgic moment. Along a certain stretch of the road, the night air was redolent with honeysuckle, reminding us of summer nights on Cape Cod. Maybe we'd be back there sooner than we had expected.

Monday, June 5, was the fateful day when Bonta actually took the irrevocable step. He went to the company office with the contract, asked Randall to notarize his signature and keep the impending move confidential, and sent it off in the afternoon mail. I wasn't sure that he wouldn't have squirmed out of it even then, except that he felt he was too far committed. Anyway it was done.

Sort of symbolically, Susan and I took all the tadpoles and five completely metamorphosed little frogs back to their natural habitat. I gave up on what to feed the frogs and was a little tired of feeding the tadpoles anyway. I felt sure they were happy to return to their own kin. Maybe I'd feel the same way when we finally went north!

≈ I cleaned the house and baked in preparation for the visit from Bonta's parents. We expected them late Saturday morning, but they never drove in till suppertime. They said that in spite of our descriptions they'd not realized what the roads hereabouts were like when they set their itinerary.

We talked all evening until late, and they were shocked to find how reluctant we were to leave. But Dad's advice was wise: "Once you've taken the step, don't waste time and energy looking back."

The next few days were busy. Patients filled the office as usual, and Dad went on all the house calls with Bonta. He was entertained by Bonta's pride as he pointed out where all "his babies" had been delivered. Dad inspired us to start taking pictures. We wanted to remember so many things, and somehow we'd not taken nearly as many as we should have. Of course, we couldn't have done it at all much earlier, because people would have thought we were invading their privacy. But by now we were a part of the scenery ourselves, and they didn't mind our documenting our time here.

Mother and I talked over plans for moving; luckily we'd found someone to take our belongings north.

Mom and Dad were pleased to learn about the coming baby and expressed concern about how Susan would take the competition. There was no doubt at all that it would be traumatic for her, but I explained that forcing Susan to share the limelight was one big reason for deciding to have another. They agreed the pregnancy was all the more reason for leaving.

While they were with us, we received a letter from Dr. Meade saying the doctor he'd been recruiting would indeed come. He and his wife would arrive July 3. We hoped they'd be interested in buying some of our kitchen equipment as well as the office supplies. It was sad to think of parting with my lovely refrigerator and that beautiful automatic washing machine.

Before Mom and Dad left, they'd seen enough of the camp and its environs to be more certain than ever that we were doing the right

Bonta on a house call, accompanied by his father. Bonta's parents visited
a few weeks before we left Coal Mountain for New Jersey.

thing to leave. They were typical New Englanders who believed that civilization stopped at the Boston city limits. They'd gathered that this was rugged and isolated, but the reality far exceeded any ideas they'd been able to muster. They were frankly appalled. I was so glad they'd come before we left, because otherwise they'd never have understood what it was like.

🕊   Randall told us that all but four miners had signed individual agreements with Bonta. Things were essentially back to normal. I still felt rocky every morning and tired ridiculously easily, but otherwise I was enjoying the beautiful warm days. The people who came into the office seemed more like friends than patients. We'd all relaxed into more comfortable relationships.

We did miss Mr. Ramsey. He and Mrs. Ramsey had gone on a trip but were due back soon. Meantime the new man Red Jacket had sent in to replace him, a Mr. Hutton, had been managing the place. He stayed at the boarding house and devoted himself to getting the coal out for the company. Bonta had spoken to him once or twice, but that was all. He was rather invisible around the camp, sticking strictly to business, either at the office or up at the mine. It certainly wasn't like the old days when Mr. Ramsey had such a personal relationship with everyone in camp.

Sunday, June 18, proved to be a rather strange day. Bonta was routed out of bed at six-thirty by an emergency call to a delivery in Long Branch. The woman proved to be Larry Watson's sister, about to have her ninth child! I hastily fixed him a hearty breakfast, knowing he'd be gone a while.

Her relationship to Larry caused Bonta to debate all over again whether to carry that gun. Would Larry be favorably disposed toward the doctor because it was his sister so that precautions were silly? Or was it all the more important to carry that automatic, against the possibility that things could turn out badly all around?

I reminded him of his decision after the delivery when he had taken the gun, not that he needed reminding. "If you could never bring yourself to use it, why have it?"

"Do you think Larry knows we're leaving?" he asked me. "Because if he does, he might even figure he's won the contest and pushed me out. Course, he'd be way off base. But in that case, he'd be pretty relaxed about anything I did. I wouldn't be a factor in his scheming anymore."

"I can't imagine any way he'd know. The only three people who know for sure are Eloise, Mr. Ramsey, and Randall, who knows only because he notarized your signature on the contract. And they're all trustworthy and promised to keep it quiet till you're ready to announce it." I buttered a slice of toast for him. "Of course, there are always leaks—somebody in the office who overheard the conversation with Randall and put two and two together. But we haven't heard any rumors about our going. I doubt if he knows."

"If that's the case, the old warnings would still have some weight. The whole thing's so complicated by its being his sister." He snapped his OB bag shut. "Well, I doubt he'd be drunk yet on a Sunday morning. More likely suffering from a hangover from the night before." Bonta wrestled with the decision a few moments longer. "To hell with it! I'll just go, do my job, and hope for the best. That's what I said before, and that's what I'll stick with."

As I stood on the back porch watching him drive off, I wondered why on earth this had to happen almost at the last minute? Suppose something were to go wrong at this late date. I'd been able to put that whole mess pretty much behind me, but now Larry's sister!

It seemed as though Bonta was gone forever, though it really was only a little after noon when, to my immense relief, he pulled the car up to the back fence. He greeted me with a kiss as usual and could hardly wait to tell me about it.

"You can relax! It all went off OK. Soon as I got there, I gave her a big shot of Demerol. They swore up and down she'd been having terrific pains awfully close together. So of course she slowed way down— about stopped. But eventually she crashed through. No problems. After all it was her ninth. Wow, were they all happy because it was a boy!"

As he continued to describe his morning, I started to get out some lunch for him. He stopped me short. "You won't believe this, but I'm stuffed! Seems the Watson clan was having a big reunion down there at Larry's house. Some of them wandered over to see how his sister was doing, and they brought me a whole platter of food: chicken, pork, salad, tomatoes, coffee, a whole loaf of bread. I nearly fell over. What with the reunion and the new baby, things were unbelievably cordial."

"Amazing! Did you see Larry himself?"

"No, he didn't show up, but if he had, I'm sure he'd have been his usual patronizingly friendly self. He's never been nasty to my face. His specialty is stabbing a guy behind his back. I doubt he's changed. I'm just glad I won't have to worry about him, come July." He handed me the soiled gloves from the OB bag he was straightening out. "Yes, no matter how friendly things seem on the surface here, you can never be sure how they are underneath. The minute someone feels injured that old hostility can erupt. No warning either. Half the time I still feel as though my foot's on a banana peel around here."

Much planning and packing occupied the remaining days. We received confirmation that the apartment we wanted was waiting for us, and that helped. In fact, I began to be a bit excited about this next step. It would be good to be nearer our families, especially when the baby came.

Once we let it be known that we were leaving, a gratifying number of people told us how sorry they'd be to lose us. Old Sarah Davis, still hauling well water against all advice, was almost in tears at the thought. She was certain she'd die now. And her daughter Marthy had some kind things to say about me, "Being so pretty and sweet and neighborlike. Just never seen any of the other doctors' wives."

Mrs. Bill James came to the office just to say good-bye. "I sure hate to lose the doctor. And I hate to lose you almost as much. Makes me feel like leaving, too."

Eloise went out a few more times with Jerry, and when she was with him, she had a good time; it was making up her mind to accept a date with him that seemed to be the difficulty. But she still talked about Tommy, too. Unfortunately we wouldn't find out her decision before we left.

On Saturday, July 1, we said good-bye to Barney and Alison. Barney was on the move again. They were finally off, having decided on South Bend, Indiana. Barney grinned as he whistled his theme song, the one about following the wild geese. Their house looked very bare.

He remarked cheerily to Bonta, "I feel as though I was leaving Alcatraz after being in for ten years. I been fed up with this place for months. Glad you're getting out, too. Things around here just ain't what they was."

We certainly hoped this move would be the right one for Barney. He hadn't liked that first Kentucky mine. Neither Detroit nor Coal Mountain had worked out for him. He was sort of a restless soul. I only wished I could be a mouse in the corner to see Alison's reaction to the big world. I'd never forget her response to Mary's article. This change would not be an easy one for her.

After some dickering over price, Randall finally bought our Chevy. Bonta and I both felt like traitors handing over the keys to our very first car, which we considered almost a member of the family.

A couple of days later Dr. Meade brought Dr. Hanshaw and his wife into camp. They stayed in the clubhouse, planning to move into our house as soon as we left. Next day we celebrated the Fourth with a picnic in a pretty spot down by the big river, with the Hanshaws and the Ramseys. The Ramseys were preparing to leave, too. Such sad good-byes. It was just as well we were going, since if we stayed everything would be so different without the Ramseys, without Barney next door, with Mrs. Horvath slipping away.

I kept thinking about Mr. Ramsey and all he'd meant to us both. He'd been a tower of strength right up to this recent problem. Somehow all that proved was that he was vulnerable like the rest of us. He was under such stress—impossible demands from the company, unreasonable behavior on the part of the union, even the domestic friction he'd hinted at to Bonta. And then, of course, our problem. He was so fearful it would lead to another strike. No wonder it got to him. His capacity for leadership demonstrated how little book learning means when one learns from experience. He was unforgettable.

On the way back we saw Dan Dubois. I was glad he'd still be there keeping track of things in his busybody fashion. I felt we'd never quite gotten close to Dan, in spite of all the visits by the back fence. He was still an enigma and a contradiction. We were aware of his concern for Mrs. Bannister and her salvation, knew firsthand his work teaching the youngsters photography and his leadership on Christmas Eve. He was a friendly neighbor over the back fence. But we'd heard rumors of his unkindness to his wife's son and possible harshness to his wife. Certainly there were unanswered questions about his role in our own difficulties. Mr. Ramsey long ago warned us about him, and as unlike sources as Joe Horvath and Larry Watson both claimed he'd laid the groundwork for the breaking of Bonta's contract. All the while with greatest apparent sincerity he professed to be our friend. Clearly there were two sides to his nature.

We'd never know the whole story. What we did know was that he was a survivor, having overcome severe injuries to his body and accusations by his peers. Though bent, he was not broken. In spite of his handicap he walked with dignity. In a way he symbolized to me all the miners of Coal Mountain, persevering, in spite of their educational and economic handicaps, in the work they knew, coping with adversity and problems as they saw them.

Dan peered up at Bonta. "Been some good things and some bad things happen since you come. Guess that's life for you. I sure am sorry to see you leaving, now that you and me, we got this whole mess straightened out."

Having been confused by his darker side in the past, I wondered but was glad to give him the benefit of the doubt.

The two men shook hands.

⚘   Bonta spent the whole day Saturday showing young Dr. Hanshaw around the place, introducing him to the patients who came in and trying to ease him into the job a little more gently than he'd been plunged into it himself.

I spent quite a while talking to Mrs. Hanshaw. She and her husband were both most pleasant, and I felt sure they'd do a great job. She wasn't planning to follow the pattern I'd set by working in the office, but she'd have no trouble coping with whatever happened here, after surviving the Russian occupation of Hungary at the end of the war, staining her face with walnut juice and hiding in the basement of her occupied home.

⚘   On Sunday, July 6, after the moving van departed, we said our painful good-byes to the Horvaths. It was our last evening in Coal Mountain. Dear Mama Horvath gave Susan a plate with a large picture of President Roosevelt in the center and scenes from his life around the edge. I planned to keep it carefully for her until she could appreciate the love it symbolized. Joe didn't say much but wrung Bonta's hand hard. As we hugged Eloise good-bye, she promised tearfully to come see us on her honeymoon, if one should materialize. And the other children stood around solemnly, waving as long as the car was in sight.

They were a remarkably united family, perhaps partly because they were a bit disadvantaged by the community's perception of them as an immigrant family, even though all the children had been born here. We were pleased to have played a small part in improving their social status by our regard for them all, and for Eloise in particular. Joe was a good provider who believed in the value of education and wanted his children to get ahead in the world. He stood by his wife in that tragic time. Eloise once told me Mrs. Horvath had told him to go find another woman since she was so ill, but he wouldn't even listen to such talk.

And how can I describe our feelings toward Eloise? She'd been the bright spot through everything. Her loyalty, her hard work, her humor, her romances, her growing up, even her moods, how could we have done without her?

Monday morning early we turned the car toward the hardtop for the last time. We waved good-bye to Mrs. Jennings as we rounded the corner by the clubhouse. We'd stayed there the night before and thanked her for all she'd done for us. I looked for a last glimpse of the Ramseys as we passed their house, but they were nowhere to be seen. We felt a pang as we drove past our black Chevrolet parked in front of Randall's house. Then out past the lumber camp. The pile of sawdust was still smoldering. Just a few days before, we'd taken a picture of the week-old twins Bonta delivered in one of those houses. On past the schoolhouse. Past Leatherwood where we'd forded the creek. And to no one's surprise the new bridge was now barricaded as unsafe.

I thought of the day I arrived and the way Bonta had pointed out those important spots. How much had happened since then. I felt like a different person. I'd fulfilled my resolve to be useful there. It had been a priceless experience. Working in the office, I'd learned about both human vulnerability and human toughness. I'd developed a different set of priorities in a place where those in the academic world

I'd known counted for nothing. Coal Mountain had taught me the meaning of small-town living, small-town gossip, small-town intimacy. Some of it had been good, and some of it had been hard to take. I'd even learned a little about evangelical religion and looked forward to a return to our own church, though some of those old hymns would always set my foot atapping.

Susan kept jumping from one side of the backseat to the other, as she shouted excited greetings to the animals along the way—a horse, several cows, Jake Blankenship's pigs, one of the two old donkeys that wandered around, and the geese by the Clay Morgan house. Little did she know just how much her life was about to change. She'd reigned like a little monarch from her post on the back fence, assuming that everyone coming down the road was paying her court, as many of them good-naturedly did. The whole Horvath family made her the center of attention; she considered Eloise almost her personal property; Eva spoiled her at the store, and Mama Horvath showered her with love and new dresses from Sears. No longer would she be free to walk around her little domain as she loved to do (of course, she'd no longer slip in cowpies either). Not only would she be leaving all that, but she would shortly have to share with the new baby.

Bonta was silent as he drove, though I noticed his eyes were taking in all the old familiar places. I thought I knew what he was thinking. He was looking toward the next step with mingled anticipation and anxiety. It was almost what he wanted but not quite. It would be good to get back to a hospital with all the resources he'd missed down here. Good to get back into a scrub suit and the operating room again. But how would it be to take orders from the next one up in the hierarchy, now that he'd been his own boss for so long? And how about sticking to a rigid schedule after he'd been such a free spirit. True, he'd been at everyone else's disposal in camp and could never count on peace and quiet. There had been unending nights away on deliveries, but there had been slack moments, too, and chess games with Jerry Drummond and Doug Blake and time to hang over the back fence sharing the latest gossip and settling the day's problems with Dan Dubois and Barney.

Yes, he was looking back, too. Pride in having given the people his very best effort medically, pride in having weathered a difficult situation. He'd learned how to take being put down without falling apart, and he'd figured out how to win back what he appeared to have lost. Though not unaware of his own limitations, he had come through it all. Surely he must recall with some amusement his terror over that first home delivery. He had gained a healthy respect for what nature can do on its own, a respect that would affect the way he practiced medicine in the future. And he'd had many demonstrations of the fact that we are not always in control of events—the union problem, Mrs. Horvath's illness, Mr. Ramsey's downfall. One rapidly acquired humility in this business of living.

I wondered if he were thinking at all about how this would affect me and us. We'd be going back to traditional roles. The arrival of the new baby would push me in that direction anyway. He or she would be good for Susan, too. There were so many unknowns ahead, so many uncertainties. When I thought about the way the uncertainties a year ago had resolved themselves for the best, I was tempted to think maybe there was a plan for us. And who doesn't face uncertainties?

I thought of the Ramseys facing an unknown future. Mr. Ramsey had no doubt reached his peak at Coal Mountain, and I believed a great writer could make his life story into a tale of real triumph and tragedy. We'd witnessed both.

And there was Eloise with her yearnings and her discontent. I had a feeling we'd see Eloise again. I hoped so.

I thought of Luke Hutchinson who'd lost his feet in that dreadful accident. And then I started thinking about some of the others who had made a lasting impression on us.

There was Freddie Kilmer, strutting down the road as if he owned it but usually ending up as someone else's pawn. At least he meant well. And Barney with his cheerful whistle and carefree ways.

Mrs. Bannister, patient and friendly neighbor. The little blue crocheted dress was safely packed.

Of course, Dan Dubois.

The Abe Lincoln Davises, old Abe stewing about the cane wasting on the hillside and Lanny walking all those miles to pay her bill.

Mrs. Dacie Ransom, reading her Bible at midnight by the light of the kerosene lamp and that cherry red stove.

Pretty Laurel Hatfield, sitting up in bed with her dress on, looking so proud of that little baby that was destined to die two months later.

And old Fred Blankenship, my Tweedledee. One of the last things I did was take a picture of Fred on the Fourth of July, holding a great big watermelon from the truckload behind the company store. His grin was about as broad as the melon.

The parade was endless.

As we approached the cutoff and that magnificent scene unrolled itself for the last time down below us, the river steel gray in the early morning light, winding off between the mountains, I had to dig in my purse for a handkerchief. It wasn't the dust that blurred the view. The tears that had been contained so far finally spilled over. The tears were for the end of a unique chapter in our lives. Coal Mountain lay behind us.

The constriction in my throat kept me wordless, but Bonta leaned over and put his hand on my knee. "There, there, honey. We'll make it. Don't you feel bad. This is just the beginning of our next adventure together."

Epilogue

Bonta and I had agreed in Coal Mountain that one reason for that second baby was to keep Susan from being forever spoiled. The competition turned out to be even more effective than planned when I delivered twin girls three months after we left. With the arrival of a fourth girl less than two years later, Susan had a small troop to manage, and manage it she did. Interestingly enough, Mrs. Clay Morgan also had twins (girls!) about the same time I did, though neither she nor I suspected as much that day we watched the geese and the goslings with the children.

Our daughters are grown women now. Susan's career has combined nursing and teaching, part-time now so that she can spend time with her two little boys.

Once all our girls were in school, I returned to teaching at Michigan State University. When the subject of home births came up in one of the science courses I taught, I sometimes told my students about those deliveries in Coal Mountain. My memory of them is still vivid.

Bonta completed his residencies—the year in New Jersey, four years at the Albany, New York, Veterans Administration Hospital, and two at the Rutland, Massachusetts, Veterans Administration Hospital— and was certified by the American Board of Surgery, in part thanks to the money we saved in Coal Mountain. He practiced general and thoracic surgery in Lansing, Michigan, for more than twenty years. In 1979 Bonta decided to join the vanguard of change in medicine and become director of medical affairs for a young HMO in town. It grew to more than sixty thousand members before he left it. He smiles when he recalls his first prepaid practice in the coalfields. He was also the associate dean for clinical services in the College of Human Medicine at Michigan State University until his recent retirement.

When he looked over this record, he winced at some of the outmoded medical practices that of necessity were acceptable back then in Coal Mountain. He agreed, however, that nothing should be changed in the telling. Time has taught us that many of the challenges we thought unique to Coal Mountain are part of life everywhere. We just met them there first. People aren't so different beneath their particular veneers after all.

Through their many letters Eloise and Eva have kept us posted about changes there. As we anticipated, their mother did not suffer for long after we left. As time went by, we heard less of Tommy and more of Jerry. Sure enough, Eloise was true to her promise. She and Jerry did stop and see us en route to Niagara Falls on their honeymoon. They left Coal Mountain and moved to Florida, where Jerry turned his engineering talents to building airports. When their own little girl was born, they named her Susan.

Eloise, Eva, and we are all grandparents now.

We hear that Doug Blake's ambitions were realized. He now owns a prosperous furnace business, his wife still works, and their son is in college.

We have been told that the Ramseys, Dan Dubois, Harvey Burgess, and the Watson brothers are all dead. The warnings about Larry Watson's propensity to violence foreshadowed the end fate had in store for him. Apparently in a fit of rage he killed his wife and then committed suicide.

We have returned to Coal Mountain twice in the intervening years. The first time, twenty-five years ago, the camp looked disappointingly run-down, but the changes a visit in 1986 revealed were a pleasant surprise. The poor cabins along the main road that so shocked me once were gone, replaced by neat mobile homes. The dirt road into camp was paved, and the Guyandotte had been dammed to make a fairly large lake in the vicinity. The old tipple and the clubhouse burned down some time ago.

By some strange coincidence, the only two original houses left were the two the Horvaths and we lived in. Old and drab, they stood in sharp contrast to all the new homes, freshly painted and brightened here and there by flowers.

A deep mine was in operation, and there were plans for another and for a new strip mine up beyond the green camp.

On our first visit Mr. Maynard, who still worked at the company store, told us that Dr. Hanshaw was the last doctor to live and practice there. He said the combination of fewer people and better roads to the outside made it no longer feasible to keep a doctor in camp.

On our second visit we found the company store functioning as a depot from which food was distributed to those in the area who needed it, and the doctor's office had become a dilapidated storeroom.

By far our greatest pleasure was visiting Eva and her husband in their attractive, well-cared-for home up a remote but beautiful hollow and talking with their son and his family, who live just across the creek. The years fell away as we reminisced and shared family pictures. But I was abruptly brought back to the present and forcefully reminded of how much time has flown when Eva told me her son was now managing the deep mine.

Bonta and I often remind each other of the enormous debt we owe the people of Coal Mountain for the lessons our experiences that year taught us. It was truly a year to grow and a worthy preparation for all that followed.